SK

THE STORIES OF KLEIST

THE STORIES OF KLEIST
a critical study

Denys Dyer

Holmes & Meier Publishers
New York

First published in the United States of America 1977 by
Holmes & Meier Publishers, Inc.
101 Fifth Avenue
New York, New York 10003

© Denys Dyer 1977

ALL RIGHTS RESERVED

Library of Congress Cataloging in Publication Data

Dyer, Denys.
 The stories of Kleist: A Critical Study

 Bibliography: p.
 Includes index.
 1. Kleist, Heinrich von, 1777-1811 – Criticism and
interpretation. I. Title.
PT2379.Z5D95   1977   833'.6   76-58356
ISBN 0-8419-0303-4

PRINTED IN GREAT BRITAIN

Contents

	Preface	vii
1.	Kleist's Life and Works	1
2.	*Das Erdbeben in Chili*	13
3.	*Die Verlobung in St. Domingo*	31
4.	*Der Findling*	48
5.	*Die Marquise von O.*	60
6.	Paradox and the Irrational	
	(i) *Das Bettelweib von Locarno*	80
	(ii) The Anecdotes	87
	(iii) *Die heilige Cäcilie oder Die Gewalt der Musik*	92
7.	*Michael Kohlhaas*	107
8.	Themes and Style	151
9.	*Der Zweikampf*	170
	Bibliography	195
	Index	203

For Eric

Preface

This book on Kleist's stories is intended to help those who study his works at universities and to interest readers with little knowledge of German literature in stories that are commonly regarded as masterpieces of prose fiction. I have chosen to treat these stories one by one, rather than attempt to write a synthetic evaluation of them. This means that each chapter is a self-contained interpretation of an individual story, though each does, it is hoped, contribute to a total impression of Kleist as a writer of *Erzählungen*. One story, *Michael Kohlhaas*, I have treated in greater detail than the others. This is because it is a much longer story; and because it is abundantly clear to me, from having taught it, that students experience considerable difficulty with it and require a clear presentation of its many complexities.

I have throughout been concerned to present as objective an interpretation of the stories as possible and to indicate their atmosphere and quality. I have tried to avoid over-simplified conclusions and pre-conceived notions of what Kleist is all about and have been at pains not to fit the stories into the straitjacket of a simplistic view of Kleist's world, believing, with a distinguished German critic,[1] that this has for too long been the bugbear of Kleist criticism. Kleist is a master of ambiguity, and he has a teasing habit of leaving fundamental issues open.[2] As a result critics have exercised their ingenuity

[1] W. Müller-Seidel, *Versehen und Erkennen*, p.3: 'With regard to the literature on Kleist we have to forget a lot of what we have read', and p.5: 'We may venture to use the language of Kleist criticism as little as possible when talking about Kleist.'

[2] Cf. the very valuable article by Klaus Müller-Salget, 'Das Prinzip der Doppeldeutigkeit in Kleists Erzählungen', *Zeitschrift für deutsche Philologie*, 92, 1973.

in providing answers and suggesting solutions not always warranted by a close and honest analysis of the text. I have endeavoured, perhaps not always successfully, to avoid this pitfall.

I have not rounded off this study with a formal Conclusion, since I felt this would only mean that I would repeat points already made in Chapters 1 and 9. I preferred instead to conclude the work with an interpretation of one of the stories, thus letting Kleist as far as possible have the last word. I have tried to keep footnotes to a minimum and to avoid clogging them with scholarly references. I have translated the German quotations in the text and also in the footnotes, where this seemed necessary. I have deliberately translated as literally as possible, so as to convey an impression of Kleist's unique style. Reasons of space have precluded more than a passing reference to the plays for which Kleist is principally known. I have included a detailed bibliography of the stories for those who may wish to study them in greater detail.

I am grateful to the many colleagues and friends who have freely given me advice and encouragement, and also to my pupils, whose loyal support has helped me to complete this book.

1
Kleist's Life and Works

Diese wunderbare Verknüpfung eines Geistes mit einem Konvolut von Gedärmen und Eingeweiden.[1]

Bernd Heinrich Wilhelm von Kleist was born in Frankfurt-an-der-Oder on 18 October 1777. He died in Berlin on the afternoon of 21 November 1811, when, as the result of a suicide pact formed with a lady of his acquaintance, Henriette Vogel, he shot first the lady and then himself.[2]

Kleist's life and works can only properly be understood against the background of the times in which he lived.[3] This is true of any author, however much he may apparently be divorced from the world around him, and it is equally true of Kleist, isolated and erratic genius though he may be. His family background is important. He was the fifth child and the eldest son of an army officer, born into a family that had for long provided the Prussian monarchy with a regular supply of officers, a family whose outlook, though occasionally garnished with a touch of poetry,[4] was steeped in the traditions of Potsdam. Kleist too entered the Guards regiment at Potsdam when not yet fifteen; but to the scandal of his family he broke with tradition and resigned his commission in 1799 to study at the university of his home town. Such a step

---

[1] 'This wonderful linking of mind to a convolution of intestines and entrails.' Letter to Altenstein, 13 Nov. 1805.
[2] Cf. relevant sections in Sembdner, *Heinrich von Kleists Lebensspuren*, 1957, and Sembdner, *Heinrich von Kleists Nachruhm*, 1967. For a brief English introduction to Kleist's life and works see Richard March, *Heinrich von Kleist*, 1954.
[3] Cf. the essay on Kleist by Georg Lukács in *Deutsche Realisten des 19. Jahrhunderts*, 1956; Hans Mayer, *Heinrich von Kleist. Der geschichtliche Augenblick*, 1962; (ed.) Walter Müller-Seidel, *Kleist und die Gesellschaft*, Jahrbuch der Heinrich von Kleist Gesellschaft, 1964.
[4] Notably by the poet Ewald von Kleist (1715-1759) – but he died a soldier's death on the battlefield of Kunersdorf.

was unprecedented and marked him for the odd man out in the family that he was. His military and aristocratic background on the one hand, and his readiness to cut adrift from family tradition to better himself intellectually on the other, are two aspects of the man who found early on that he could not reconcile the roles of 'Offizier' and 'Mensch', of 'officer' and 'human being'.[5] The family's lack of comprehension found ultimate expression in the final confrontation in Frankfurt-an-der-Oder on 18 September 1811, when, during the course of a traumatic meal-time, Kleist found himself treated as a useless and worthless member of society[6] and was doubtless thereby encouraged to pursue his plan of suicide. The family background is important, for Kleist rebelled against it, was drawn by ties of affection and upbringing towards it, and was obliged because of his chronic lack of money to resort to it for help.

The historical background is of crucial importance. Kleist's adult life was spent against the background of the rise of Napoleon and the Napoleonic wars. His native Prussia was put to shame in 1806 by the defeat of Jena, and he died at a time when Prussia was to all intents and purposes an occupied country and the wars of liberation but a distant mirage. During the whole of his creative life France dominated Europe. His plans were for ever thwarted by French influence on the course of events, examples being his intention to settle down in Switzerland in 1802; his journey from Königsberg to Dresden in 1807, abruptly cut short when Kleist was arrested by the French as a spy; the end of his happy stay in Dresden in 1809 with the resumption of hostilities between France and Austria; or the curb on his publishing activities in Berlin in 1811 following brushes with a Prussian government keenly sensitive to French criticism and censorship. During the last two years of his life Kleist, deeply distressed by the course of events in his native Prussia, developed a fanatical hatred of and opposition to Napoleon. The situation in Germany at the time and the issues posed by the relationship between the individual and the state are mirrored in his last two plays, *Die*

---

[5] As he explains in his letter to C.M. Martini, 18/19 March 1799.
[6] 'Als ein ganz nichtsnutziges Glied der menschlichen Gesellschaft' – letter to Marie von Kleist, 10 Nov. 1811.

Hermannsschlacht and, pre-eminently, *Prinz Friedrich von Homburg*. As a writer Kleist is very much involved in his times and concerned with the role of the individual in the society of which he is a part. Whether his stories are set in the past (e.g. *Das Erdbeben*) or have a contemporary setting (*Die Marquise, Die Verlobung*), they are, as will be seen,[7] relevant to the age in which he lived.

The third important factor in Kleist's development is the cultural background. He wrote at a time when German literature had reached a new and undreamt-of peak of achievement and established itself as a leading force in Europe.[8] Within a short space of time the literary movements of Aufklärung (Enlightenment), Sturm und Drang, Classicism and Romanticism succeeded and overlapped one another and threw up not only the literary giants Lessing, Goethe and Schiller, but also a host of other important writers. Kleist was influenced as a young man by the Aufklärung ideals current in Berlin; he steeped himself in the plays of Goethe and Schiller; during his stay in Dresden from 1807 to 1809 and to some extent during the last two years in Berlin he was receptive to Romantic ideas. He was caught up in the philosophical ferment at the turn of the century, and was influenced successively by the ideas of the Aufklärung thinkers, by Kant, possibly by Fichte, and by the more romantically tinged writings of G.H. Schubert and Adam Müller. Like other writers and thinkers of his age Kleist thought deeply about the riddle of the human situation, initially seeing human development along the familiar triadic lines of a past golden age, of a present state of imperfection, and of a future bright with the promise of perfectibility, moving over then to a tragic awareness to some extent anticipating the nihilism latent in the works of the later Romantics, before finally hammering out a set of human values as his defence against despair. In all this Kleist emerges as a man with a consuming ambition to be a great writer, eager to vie with the giants of his time, to some extent an outsider amidst all the contemporary intellectual and cultural development, stimulated by it, but developing his

---

[7] Cf. p.153.
[8] Very well summarised by T.J. Reed, 'The *Goethezeit* and its aftermath' in *Germany: A Companion to German Studies*, ed. M. Pasley, 1972.

own quite personal and original talent independent of any particular literary movement or creed.

Kleist was a lonely man, living, for all his contacts, in a state of almost Kafkaesque isolation;[9] withdrawn even in company; bottling up his thoughts and emotions; his pent-up energy, superficially reflected in a nervous stammer and a tendency to talk aloud to himself, finding release in nervous breakdowns accompanied by a compulsive urge to travel. His moments of poetic elation, when his creative ambitions seemed on the point of being realised, were balanced by moods of suicidal depression, when he would cast around for a companion with whom to quit the world. He made immense demands on the trust and loyalty of his friends, had an intense craving for love and affection, but found it difficult to offer the same selfless love in return. He was intensely earnest, early working out an ambitious 'Lebensplan'[10] along which to direct his energies, and working with complete dedication at his calling as a poet, filing with almost inhuman methodicalness his ideas and inspirations in a card-index 'Ideenmagazin',[11] which he would draw on repeatedly and repetitiously. He was a mixture of the Prussian officer, with a keen sense of logic and order, and the nonconforming individualist, prepared to break with family and caste traditions; a Potsdam guard and a rootless genius; a Prussian civil servant and an erratic writer, now planning to till the soil as a small-holder in Switzerland, now seeking death in the English Channel as a member of Napoleon's invasion forces, hoping for the final overthrow of the French armies as he wandered over the battlefield of Aspern, and searching pathetically for paid employment in the Berlin ministries of the Prussian government in the final year of his existence. He was dogged for most of his creative life by lack of money, and his publishing ventures, not all of them as impracticable and starry-eyed as has been suggested, foundered and landed him deeper in debt. He was at times incredibly unlucky – a popular insurrection accelerated the

---

[9] Very apparent in his letter to Ulrike von Kleist, 12 Nov. 1799.
[10] Cf. letter to Ulrike, May 1799, where he talks about his 'life-plan'.
[11] Helmut Sembdner (ed.), *Heinrich von Kleist. Geschichte meiner Seele. Ideenmagazin*, 1959, has tried to reconstruct it. Note too Ch.5 of the book by Walter Silz, *Heinrich von Kleist*, 1961.

breakdown of a creative period in Switzerland; the fruitful patronage of Wieland was brought to an end by the ill chance that Wieland's daughter fell in love with him; the prospect of fame at Weimar was ruined by Goethe's well-meant but disastrous production of *Der zerbrochne Krug* on 2 March 1808; hopes of patronage at court, encouraged when on 10 March 1810 he ceremonially presented a sonnet on the occasion of Queen Luise's birthday, were dashed by the unexpected death of the queen on 19 July of that year; the daring and successful launching of a Berlin daily paper was irretrievably harmed by the ill-advised publication of an article by his collaborator and evil genius Adam Müller.[12] Circumstances certainly seemed to conspire against Kleist. The unsettled times, with Europe in a state of upheaval and the Prussian government discredited; the lack of understanding on the part of contemporaries for his work, due partly no doubt to its very originality; Kleist's rejection by his family; his own sense of isolation and pride, and the ill luck that attended his projects and incidentally reduced him to a complete state of poverty – all this combined to bring him to despair and made him turn to suicide.

The suicide itself[13] illustrates the paradox that is Kleist. He made a pact with a married woman suffering from terminal cancer of the uterus, a person of no significance but a welcome companion for Kleist. The double suicide occasioned great scandal all over Europe,[14] and received the righteous condemnation of right-thinking people. The partners seemed grotesquely unequal: Kleist, the man of genius sensing that there was no help left for him in this world and putting an end to the most tormented existence man had ever led,[15] and Henriette Vogel, a poor creature with a fatal illness, a doggerel-writing acolyte assisting Kleist as he carried out the final frightful auto-da-fé of his manuscripts. This scandalous affair was then planned by Kleist with true military precision; and in its execution it was a model of what a suicide could be, an artistic masterpiece.

[12] So described by Richard Samuel in the introduction to his excellent edition of *Prinz Friedrich von Homburg*, 1962, p.23.
[13] Cf. ch.10 of Walter Silz, op.cit.
[14] It was reported in the London *Times*, 28 Dec. 1811.
[15] 'Mein Leben, das allerqualvollste, das je ein Mensch geführt hat', final letter to Marie von Kleist, (?) 21 Nov. 1811.

Three incidents in Kleist's life may be singled out to help trace his emergence as a creative writer. The first is the journey to Würzburg he undertook in the late summer of 1800 in the company of a close friend, Ludwig von Brockes. The reasons for this journey, the result of a sudden decision on Kleist's part, are unknown, and speculation on them is futile. Kleist maintained his usual secretiveness on this point, and even his sorely-tried fiancée, Wilhelmine von Zenge, had to be content with assurances that he was undertaking a course of action crucial to her happiness. What is important about the journey to Würzburg is the string of letters Kleist wrote as he travelled via Leipzig and Dresden and then during his stay in Würzburg. They are the letters of an emerging poet testing himself out, now exposed to a whole new range of experiences involving not only an awareness of nature, vastly more beautiful than that of his native Brandenburg, but also the confrontation in Würzburg with a different way of life and different human experiences mirrored for example in letters describing the Catholic churches, the lending library, and the local lunatic asylum. Some of the pedant in Kleist remains as he makes grave observations to Wilhelmine and tots up the letters he has sent to and received from her. But one is very much aware of a poetic force taking shape as Kleist revels in the release from the earnest pursuit of knowledge at the university of Frankfurt-an-der-Oder and the protocol of Berlin social routine. Here Kleist starts to realise those 'seltenere Fähigkeiten', the 'rarer talents' he mentions in a letter to Wilhelmine of 13 November 1800.

A second incident is the letter he wrote to Wilhelmine on November 16/18, 1800, together with an addendum in December 1800. It is an interesting and highly revealing letter. The raw materials – and they are still raw – of the poet Kleist can be discerned in it. There is the pedant Kleist, seeking to educate his fiancée in his own image, a touching and unconsciously heartless schoolmastering of his 'liebes Mädchen' on the basis of examples from Wunsch's *Kosmologische Unterhaltungen* (Leipzig, 1791/94), with a string of either/or postulates combining profundity and banality in an extraordinary fashion. But there is also the poet Kleist groping after images that are to be central to his work, the image of the arch, of the tree in the storm, the contrasting of light and shade, night and day, the references to water, to music, to the mirror image, to fire, the mixture of allusions to the world of physics and the world of nature, some intellectual, some emotional, all noted down in his 'Ideenmagazin'. The raw materials are there for the student of Kleist to discover, but they are not yet refined and fused together.

A third highly important episode is the so-called 'Kant crisis' of March 1801. Kleist had worked out for himself a rigid and rigorous 'Lebensplan', the goal of which was knowledge and happiness, to be achieved through the pursuit of virtue and the dedicated application of reason and will-power. Now a study of Kant revealed to him that absolute knowledge was unattainable by the conscious application of reason and that the knowledge obtained by such means was at the best relative and transitory, conditioned by standpoint and subjectivity. At one stroke Kleist saw his ideals and ambitions in ruins and the purpose of his existence shattered. With the benefit of hindsight it is easy to see that such a crisis was bound to come, whether sparked off by Kant or Fichte,[16] and the fact that he was only receptive to Kant's limitations of the powers of human reason and neglected to note the other avenues towards a higher awareness of the essence of things, suggested by Kant, underlines the point that Kleist was heading for a crisis and read in Kant what he unconsciously wanted to read. A 'life-plan' designed to achieve absolutes of truth and happiness, erected with such hope in the future and pursued with such dogged and unremitting earnestness, was bound sooner or later to founder when faced with reality. Kleist came close to despair, and characteristically set off on another journey. But paradoxically the ruin of his extravagant hopes in conscious rational endeavour confirmed the emergence of the poet in him.[17] It finalised the break with the Aufklärung ideals of his youth; liberated his mind and made it receptive to the impressions thrown up by his journey via Dresden, Göttingen and Frankfurt-am-Main to Paris; and made possible the varied treatment of the problem of knowledge,

[16] Cf. D.F.S. Scott, 'Heinrich von Kleist's Kant crisis', *Modern Language Review*, 42, pp.474ff.
[17] Cf. E.L. Stahl, *The Dramas of Heinrich von Kleist*, 1948, p.6.

truth and appearances that occurs with increasing subtlety in all his works, from the early tragic beginnings to the tentatively suggested solutions of his final works. The Kant crisis is not a tragedy in Kleist's life. It should not be romanticised, any more than should other episodes in his life, and used as evidence to show that he was pre-ordained to lead an existence too glibly described as 'tragic'. It is a necessary stage in his development as a poet.

During the nine to ten years of his creative life Kleist wrote seven plays, left one play uncompleted, wrote eight stories that were published in the two volumes of the *Erzählungen*, several short anecdotes published in the *Berliner Abendblätter*, various essays on art and literature which, though short, are extremely profound and stimulating, articles of a journalistic nature on day-to-day events, and some occasional verse; he also kept up a busy correspondence, in particular with his step-sister Ulrike and with Wilhelmine von Zenge. He was co-editor of an ambitious periodical *Phöbus*, twelve issues of which appeared from January 1808 to February 1809, and much of which he wrote himself. From 1 October 1810 to 30 March 1811 he edited and wrote a great deal of a daily paper, the *Berliner Abendblätter*. There are grounds for believing that he wrote a two-volume novel, which has vanished without trace, and an autobiographical work, which he destroyed when he burnt it along with other manuscripts just before committing suicide. All in all a remarkable achievement, particularly when it is remembered that almost everything which survived him is of a high quality and was written more often than not under adverse conditions.

Of his plays two, *Die Familie Schroffenstein* and *Penthesilea* are tragedies; *Robert Guiskard*, which remains a magnificent fragment, was planned as a tragedy; *Amphitryon* has both comic and tragic elements and ends on a note of ironic ambiguity; and the other plays, *Der zerbrochne Krug, Das Käthchen von Heilbronn, Die Hermannsschlacht* and *Prinz Friedrich von Homburg*, are comedies, or rather plays that have conciliatory endings. This somewhat cavalier classification of his plays serves to make the point that it is wrong to regard Kleist as predominantly a writer of tragic plays. The basic issues in them are dealt with in a variety of ways, tragic and non-tragic, and his dialectical approach is evidenced in his tendency to produce plays in pairs tackling similar themes from opposing angles. So it is that *Der zerbrochne Krug* and *Amphitryon* approach the themes of love and trust from opposite directions; that *Penthesilea* and *Das Käthchen von Heilbronn* offer contrasting solutions to common problems; and *Die Hermannsschlacht* and *Prinz Friedrich von Homburg* deal with the contemporary issues of patriotic duty and individual rights and inclinations in two different ways. Furthermore, after the publication of *Penthesilea* in 1808 practically all of Kleist's works offer non-tragic solutions to human problems.

The first volume of the *Erzählungen*, containing *Michael Kohlhaas*, *Die Marquise von O.* and *Das Erdbeben in Chili*, appeared in September, 1810. The second volume, containing *Die Verlobung in St. Domingo*, *Das Bettelweib von Locarno*, *Der Findling*, *Die heilige Cäcilie* and *Der Zweikampf*, was published in August, 1811. Some of the stories had appeared earlier. *Das Erdbeben in Chili* was first published, under a different title, in 1807; *Die Marquise von O.* was finished in 1807 and published in 1808; the first quarter of *Michael Kohlhaas* was published in 1808; and although *Die Verlobung in St. Domingo* and *Der Findling* first appeared in 1811 it is possible that they were conceived and started some years earlier, though this is pure conjecture. The other stories, *Das Bettelweib*, *Die heilige Cäcilie* and *Der Zweikampf*, were all written towards the end of Kleist's life and were used to fill up the second volume of the *Erzählungen*. It is hardly profitable to speculate more closely on the dates of composition of the stories or on when they were first thought of.[18] Some appear to have particularly close affinities with individual plays, for example, *Das Erdbeben* with *Die Familie Schroffenstein*, *Die Marquise von O.* with *Amphitryon* and *Der Zweikampf* with *Prinz Friedrich von Homburg*. Interesting, however, though it may be to note correspondences between some of the stories and some of the plays, and to track down themes and motifs common to both, such detective work will at best only underline what is obvious to the reader of Kleist's works, namely, the coherent and

---

[18] Cf. Kurt Gassen, *Die Chronologie der Novellen Heinrich von Kleists*, 1920.

consistent way in which, in all of them, metaphysical issues and problems of human relationships are dealt with from a variety of angles.

Kleist called his stories *Erzählungen*, and intended originally to call them *Moralische Erzählungen*, 'Moral Tales', just as Cervantes called his stories *Novelas exemplares*. He did not call them *Novellen*, and there is no reason why he should have done so, although they are now treated as such and viewed as an important contribution to the development of the Novelle in nineteenth-century German literature. The Novelle has been variously defined,[19] and these definitions are of some use so long as they are not applied too literally and too dogmatically. The point about a Novelle is that it deals with some central issue in human relationships mirrored in a situation, the unusual, piquant or paradoxical nature of which lifts it out of the ordinary and guarantees the close attention of the reader. This situation is not then exploited just for its surprise or intriguing effects, as might well be the case with a short story, but, though self-contained in itself, it opens up perspectives and mirrors issues concerning human existence that go far beyond the particular context of the story and trigger off reflection and speculation in the mind of the reader. The Novelle is a highly compressed form of narration, not discursive like the novel, suggesting in its employment of symbol and leitmotif much more than is contained on the printed page. Its focal situations, with their dramatic and frequently ironic reversal of fortune, contain in a nutshell the paradigms of human existence. The particular, initially perhaps innocuous and limited, opening situation of the Novelle turns out to contain, as it were, a depth charge. It operates on the plane of the real world, within a recognised social framework, although the premises of this society may be challenged. It is a highly conscious and highly artistic genre, its effects nicely calculated and its several parts cleverly fused together in a work which, when successful, is a product of high-class literary craftmanship. There is little that is fortuitous in a good Novelle; and while the dangers of over-

[19] Cf. E.K. Bennett, *A History of the German Novelle from Goethe to Th. Mann*, 1934; Johannes Klein, *Geschichte der deutschen Novelle*, 1954; F. Lockemann, *Gestalt und Wandlungen der deutschen Novelle*, 1957; Benno von Wiese, *Die deutsche Novelle von Goethe bis Kafka*, 2 vols., 1962.

interpretation are always there, it would be a superficial and insensitive critic who would not be encouraged to read with care and insight between the lines of the printed text.

Few Novellen had appeared in German literature before Kleist wrote his *Erzählungen*. Goethe's *Unterhaltungen deutscher Ausgewanderten* was published in 1795 and some Romantic 'Märchen' had appeared by the time Kleist published his first story, but that is virtually all. It was really only after the middle of the nineteenth century, with the writings of the Poetic Realists, that the Novelle established itself as a leading genre in German literature. Kleist's stories stand at the beginning of the development of the German Novelle. With them Kleist was attempting something that had not been done before, and it is a measure of his success that no historian of the German Novelle would dream of ignoring him. He would perhaps have noted this with a wry smile. When he published his two volumes of stories he was to some extent motivated by the need to make some money, however little, and Clemens Brentano, who like most of his other contemporaries had little idea of Kleist's genius, reports[20] that he felt humiliated at having to switch from drama to the, to him, less lofty form of narrative prose. This may or may not have been the case. Kleist was working on *Das Erdbeben in Chili* and *Die Marquise von O.* at the same time that he was writing plays, at a comparatively buoyant period of his life. The narrative form clearly attracted him; and he must have known that what he was attempting was something out of the ordinary, bound to startle and to shock. He need certainly have felt no sense of humiliation. The stories are masterpieces in their own right; in their own way and within their own terms by no means inferior to his plays.

The main features of the stories are dealt with in Chapter 8. Suffice it to say here, by way of introduction, that they are concerned with the themes of truth, knowledge and self-knowledge; with human emotions, particularly love, and the range of emotions and the extremes of behaviour of which an individual is capable when caught in an unusual situation; with human institutions, particularly those of the state, the

---

[20] In a letter to Achim von Arnim, 10 Dec. 1811.

law and organised religion; and with the insecurity of life, depicted as it so often is against a background of conflict, and the instability caused by the intrusion of chance in human affairs. The events in the stories, frequently of an extraordinary nature, are often presented paradoxically, and their outcome is not without ambiguity. Their unexpected and apparently inexplicable nature is heightened by Kleist's technique of starting with an extraordinary situation, the preliminaries to which are then explained by means of flashbacks. Many of the stories revolve round a mysterious and baffling situation, and this is described as it is experienced by different characters at different times, a technique that enables Kleist to hide behind the characters and events as an apparently impartial chronicler. The stories start with a paradox; and their ending is often paradoxical.

2
Das Erdbeben in Chili

Es kann kein böser Geist sein, der an der Spitze der Welt steht: es ist ein bloß unbegriffener![1]

'In Santiago, the capital of the kingdom of Chile, at the very moment of the great earthquake of 1647, in which thousands of people perished, a young Spaniard by the name of Jeronimo Rugera, under arrest on some criminal charge, was standing by a pillar in the prison cell where he had been confined, and was about to hang himself.' With this arresting sentence Kleist begins his story *Das Erdbeben in Chili*, the tragic tale of two lovers, set against the background of the great earthquake in Santiago of 13 May 1647. The opening sentence is characteristic of Kleist:[2] time and place are stated, a main character is introduced, a background of general destruction is indicated, and an extraordinary situation is presented, namely, that of a prisoner about to hang himself while an earthquake kills thousands of his fellowmen. The startling and paradoxical opening sentence is matched by the paradoxical nature of the closing one, where a survivor of the lynching that killed the two lovers is left with his own son murdered and the child of the dead lovers in his arms, a substitution he feels in his heart of hearts almost compelled to welcome. In fifteen packed pages[3] a story of love and violence is told, and a host of themes touched on, relevant to the story and characteristic of Kleist's work as a whole. It is a fitting story with which to begin this study of Kleist's narrative works, just as *Der*

---

[1] 'It cannot be an evil spirit that presides over the world; it is merely one that has not been comprehended.' Letter to Karl Freiherr von Stein zum Altenstein, 4 August 1806.
[2] Cf. Chapter 8 below, pp. 156-7.
[3] Sembdner, vol. 2, pp. 144-59.

Zweikampf is a fitting one with which to end it.

The plot can be briefly summarised. A young Spaniard, Jeronimo Rugera, falls in love with Josephe, the daughter of a rich noble in Santiago. To protect his daughter the nobleman puts her in a convent; but the lovers contrive to meet there and make love in the convent garden. Months later, on the feast of Corpus Christi, Josephe, taking part in a solemn procession of nuns and novitiates, sinks down on the steps of the cathedral in labour and shortly afterwards gives birth to a child. The affair occasions great scandal. Josephe is sentenced to be executed, and Jeronimo is imprisoned, to await sentence and punishment. At the moment when the execution is due to take place the city is destroyed in a great earthquake. Both Josephe and Jeronimo escape alive, and meet again in a wooded valley outside the city. The following day a *Te Deum* is announced in the one surviving church in the city, and the two lovers set out with a party of survivors to worship in the church and give thanks to God for their deliverance. The crowded congregation is inflamed by a sermon in which the priest attacks the morals of the city, mentions in particular the case of Josephe and Jeronimo, and says the earthquake is the vengeance of God on the evildoers. The lovers are seen in the church; and they are lynched, along with some of their friends, on the steps outside the church. Their child survives, and is adopted by Don Fernando and his wife, whose own son has been slaughtered in the church under the mistaken impression that it was the child of the two lovers.

The story was first published in Cotta's *Morgenblatt für gebildete Stände*, nos. 217-21, September 10-15 1807, under the title of *Jeronimo und Josephe. Eine Scene aus dem Erdbeben zu Chili, vom Jahre 1647*. It was subsequently published in the first volume of the *Erzählungen* under the terser and more effective title of *Das Erdbeben in Chili*. It is not known what source Kleist used for his story, though some details may have been furnished by descriptions of the Lisbon earthquake of 1755.

Das Erdbeben in Chili is a highly concentrated story. So much is packed into its few pages, so many incidents adumbrated and themes touched upon, that the story outgrows the space it occupies on the printed page, and against a kaleidoscopic background of events a tragic picture of man in society is depicted and the fate of two lovers shown in a world very much out of joint. A scandalous courtship, a natural disaster and a violent upsurge of human emotion culminating in the lynching is seen against the larger issue of the position of man in a universe apparently dominated by chance. All this is contained in just three paragraphs,[4] the shorter middle one forming a bridge linking the two longer ones and providing a contrast in mood to them. The violence of the first and third paragraphs is heightened and ironically set off by the idyllic setting and lyrical sweetness of the middle one, and the tragic impact of the final disaster is increased when contrasted with the prospect of happiness suggested in the second paragraph. The first two paragraphs end on a conciliatory note. At the end of the first the lovers are miraculously reunited, and at the end of the second, impressed as they are by the kind and friendly attitude of the survivors of the earthquake towards them, they look forward to a life together in Chile. By rounding off the paragraphs in this way Kleist heightens the tragic irony. There are three main characters, the two lovers and Don Fernando, who does not appear until the second paragraph. Yet it is almost misleading to speak of characters, for they are hardly individualised, but are rather subordinated to the events in which they are engulfed. The individual characters merge into the background of the mob. The magnitude of the catastrophes, the earthquake and the lynching, dwarfs the characters caught up in them.

The dramatic impression made by the story is heightened by the fact that it is concentrated within approximately twenty-four hours, with a brief prologue accounting for the plight of the lovers at the beginning and a short epilogue at the end. The story is not narrated in strict time sequence. Kleist starts with the earthquake and shows by means of exposition and flashback how the opening situation was arrived at. The

---

[4] Sembdner says that the division into three paragraphs in the final printed version of the *Erzählungen* is fortuitous, being dictated by typographical considerations; he reverts in his edition to the 1807 *Morgenblatt* version with its many paragraphs. There may be sense in this. On the other hand the story does clearly fall into three sections, coinciding with the three paragraphs of most printed versions. Anyone objecting to the use of the word 'paragraph' in this chapter can substitute for it the word 'section'.

earthquake is the starting point – its central importance is indicated in the title – and Kleist comes back to it again and again, in fact the earthquake is mentioned again five times.[5] The earthquake is never described objectively; it is presented as it affects individuals, either at the moment it occurs or then in their recollection. There is no static picture of the earthquake, it is presented dramatically. First, the escape of Jeronimo from prison and his subsequent experiences during the earthquake are related. He then meets Josephe, and she in her turn tells what happened to her during the earthquake. So again the reader is taken back to the opening situation, and the earthquake is experienced for a second time through someone else's eyes. There is a deliberate similarity in the way Jeronimo and Josephe are made to react to the catastrophe, as they experience alternating hope, despair, threatened or actual loss of consciousness, and hope regained, and the theme of the earthquake is repeated with only slight, though significant variations. A parallelism of structure therefore marks the first paragraph. In the second paragraph the theme occurs twice more, as the survivors recount their experiences during the earthquake. First of all, disasters and portents of a more general nature are told, how the streets were full of women in childbirth and monks with crucifixes were rushing through the streets proclaiming that the end of the world was at hand. Then stories of individuals are recounted, of heroic deeds of bravery and self-sacrifice amidst the general destruction. The subsidiary contrasting themes of superstition and individual heroism are thus sounded, and the part they occupy in the final tragic denouement prepared for By means of this technique the earthquake is continually in the reader's mind, and this leads up to the climax in the final paragraph, when the earthquake is taken up for the fifth and final time, in the inflammatory sermon of the Dominican priest, and echoed in the eruption of mass violence, when the enormity of the natural disaster is equalled or even surpassed by the savagery of the lynch mob. Linked with the theme of the earthquake are individual words, used as 'Leitmotive' to create a sense of the

---

[5] In just the same way the central incident in *Das Bettelweib* is recounted five times, cf. below, p. 83.

inevitability of the tragic climax. Repeated mention is made of the 'Richtplatz', the 'Gefängnis' and the 'Glocken',[6] and these ominous words of 'execution square', 'prison' and 'bells' recur during the idyllic section of the second paragraph, awakening feelings of presentiment in the reader that are not dispelled by the melodious sounds of the nightingale as the lovers enjoy their fleeting moments of happiness together.

Das Erdbeben has a closely-knit, almost fugal, structure, and this formalistic approach then contrasts with the emotional content of the story, which is one of unparalleled violence, pessimism and tragedy. This is how Kleist very often achieves his effects, namely, in the unique mixture of intellectual precision and emotional tension, and it is this that is a feature of his prose style.[7]

The story is tragic. A pair of lovers meets a frightful end. What force lies behind the tragedy? Is it fate, or is it chance? The element of chance, of 'Zufall', plays an important part in Kleist's works, and his characters are continually exposed to this entirely arbitrary and irrational force. The words 'Zufall' and 'zufällig' occur frequently in *Das Erdbeben*. It is the result of a 'glücklicher Zufall' that Jeronimo and Josephe consummate their love in a convent garden; it is the result of chance that a rope is left in Jeronimo's cell for him to hang himself from; it is because of a 'zufällige Wölbung'[8] formed by two collapsing houses that Jeronimo is able to crawl to safety; it is chance that a man escaping from a house should be suspected of looting and summarily strung up; it is chance that Donna Constanze should be mistaken for Josephe and murdered in the church; indeed, the earthquake itself is a manifestation of chance. Yet the impact made by chance is reduced by the formal artistry of the work, which imposes a

---

[6] Recalling the vivid impression the bells of Würzburg made on Kleist, cf. letters to Wilhelmine von Zenge of 11/12 September 1800 and 13/18 September 1800, where the phrase occurs: 'Auch hier erinnert das Läuten der Glocken unaufhörlich an die katholische Religion, wie das Geklirr der Ketten den Gefangnen an seine Sklaverei' – 'Here too the ringing of the bells is a continual reminder of the Catholic religion, just as the rattling of his chains reminds the prisoner of his slavery'.

[7] Cf. remarks on style in Chapter 8 below; also remarks on music and mathematics, below p. 95 ff.

[8] The symbol of the arch or vault, 'Wölbung', is stressed by Kleist in his letter to Wilhelmine, 16/18 November 1800.

kind of order on chaos and persuades the reader to accept details he might otherwise question, bestowing on them an impression of inevitability.

But then perhaps they *are* inevitable. To the priest in the church the earthquake is not a chance event, but a punishment sent by God. When Jeronimo escapes from prison it seems as if his prayers have been answered and he thanks God for his deliverance. When Josephe rushes into a burning building to rescue her child it is 'as if all the angels in heaven protected her', 'als ob alle Engel des Himmels sie umschirmten'. Perhaps the hand of God directs what happens. But if so, he is inscrutable, as Sylvester Schroffenstein complains in Die Familie Schroffenstein,[9] and he is cruel too, for the lovers, saved by their prayers from the earthquake, meet an even more terrible fate at the hands of their fellowmen.

Yet it may be misleading to ascribe the tragedy to the workings of fate, chance or a supreme being. Society as a whole and social institutions, corrupted by the degenerating effect of civilisation, may be responsible. In this work, more perhaps than elsewhere, Kleist shows the influence on him of the doctrines of Rousseau.[10] Human institutions and the conventions of society inhibit the natural development of human feelings and are a corrupting influence. When freed from the restraints of social conventions men become quite different and are seen in a much more favourable light. The earthquake provides the means of release. It occasions a remarkable change in men's behaviour. When the survivors congregate in the fields and valleys, away from the city, they have, under the impact of the natural catastrophe, become united, as Kleist says, 'into one family'. 'Es war,' he writes, 'als ob die Gemüter seit dem fürchterlichen Schlage, der sie durchdröhnt hatte, alle versöhnt wären',[11] the earthquake, despite the misery it had caused, has enabled the spirit of man

---

[9] *Die Familie Schroffenstein*, Act V: 'God of justice! speak clearly to man, so that he may know what he must do!'

[10] Kleist encouraged his fiancée Wilhelmine to read Rousseau; cf. letters 22 March 1801, 14 April 1801, 3 June 1801.

[11] 'It was as if the hearts of all men were reconciled after the shattering impact of this fearful blow.'

to blossom 'wie eine schöne Blume' ('like a beautiful flower'). An idyllic picture of the survivors is painted: 'Auf den Feldern, soweit das Auge reichte, sah man Menschen von allen Ständen durcheinanderliegen, Fürsten und Bettler, Matronen und Bäuerinnen, Staatsbeamte und Tagelöhner, Klosterherren und Klosterfrauen, einander bemitleiden, sich wechselseitig Hilfe reichen, von dem, was sie zur Erhaltung ihres Lebens gerettet haben mochten, freudig mitteilen, als ob das allgemeine Unglück alles, was ihm entronnen war, zu einer Familie gemacht hätte'.[12] A striking contrast is drawn. Human life and human relations as they might be are compared with human life as it actually is in society. The idyllic valley to which the lovers retreat is compared to the Garden of Eden, and it contrasts strongly with the prison where Jeronimo had been confined.

The prison as a setting is much favoured by Kleist.[13] He frequently locates the action in a prison or some confined space, providing a sense of constriction symbolic of a restricted attitude on the part of characters or of society. Jeronimo sits in his prison as Josephe is taken to execution. Littegarde, in *Der Zweikampf*, lies in her prison cell and nearly abandons herself to despair. Kohlhaas is put under house arrest and waits powerless as the legal machinery gets under way. Gustav, in *Die Verlobung in St. Domingo*, is confined for a great part of the story to a darkened room. For the marquis in *Das Bettelweib in Locarno* the castle becomes a prison, closing in on him and driving him to his final act of despair. Elvire, in *Der Findling*, escapes from reality by retreating to her bedroom, but the confinement of this sanctuary does not protect her from the destructive attentions of Nicolo. The asylum is a kind of prison for the mad brothers in *Die heilige Cäcilie*, providing a release from the world around them. The

---

[12] 'In the fields, as far as the eye could see, all sorts and conditions of men could be seen jumbled together, princes and beggars, gentle ladies and peasant women, state officials and day labourers, monks and nuns, commiserating with one another, succouring one another, gladly sharing whatever possessions they had salvaged to keep alive, as if the general disaster had united all those who had survived it into one single family.'

[13] Kleist had first-hand experience of prison, being captured by the French as a suspected spy and imprisoned in Fort Joux and Chalons-sur-Marne in 1807.

means of release from the 'prison' setting symbolically portrayed in the stories may vary. In *Das Erdbeben* it is the earthquake.

When Jeronimo escapes from prison and stumbles through the ruins away from the heart of the city he reaches a small eminence just outside the city gates and collapses in a faint on the ground. His return to consciousness is carefully and minutely described. At first he sees only the countryside before him, the 'blühende Gegend', 'luxuriant region', outside Santiago, and its beauty overwhelms him. A feeling of bliss possesses him, and he rejoices in being alive. But with returning consciousness comes memory and an awareness of pain and grief, and he turns round to see the city in ruins behind him. A contrast is made between the beauty of the countryside and the ruined city. Innocent enjoyment of life gives way to an awareness of sorrow and suffering, peace and harmony yield to the troubled world of civilised society and inhibiting institutions where man is a prisoner. The social institution Kleist singles out for particular criticism is the institution of religion.

Kleist's stories are full of references to religion and religious institutions. The issues posed by religion and the moral demands made by organised religion quite obviously occupied him very much. As an institution religion is harshly attacked in *Das Erdbeben*. It distorts human feelings, inhibits them, and imposes vetoes and restraints on them. Offences against its code of morals are punished by the arm of the law. It thinks in terms of punishment and sentence. The sermonising priest in the church is quick to talk in terms of a 'Weltgericht', of the 'Last Judgement', the law is called upon to punish Josephe for her offence against public morality, the bells that toll for her execution are symbolic of an institution that deals in public executions and auto-da-fés. Such an institution brings out the worst in people. The 'pious daughters of the city', eager to see a public execution, are indignant that Josephe is not to be burned, but merely executed; monks rush around the ruined city indulging in an orgy of superstition; the priest, denouncing the morals of the city, talks 'im Flusse priesterlicher Beredsamkeit', carried away by 'the flow of priestly eloquence'; and the climax is reached when people

Das Erdbeben in Chili

gathered together in a church to give thanks to God for their deliverance from the earthquake call for vengeance on Josephe and Jeronimo: ' "Steinigt sie! steinigt sie!" die ganze im Tempel Jesu versammelte Christenheit!'[14] Hypocrisy and blood lust behind the mask of Christianity – well might Kleist end the sentence with an exclamation mark. The head of this institution in Santiago is the archbishop, and it is doubtless fitting that after the earthquake his corpse is dragged out of the ruined cathedral.

Opposed to all this is another view of religion and religious values. Religious feeling is not discounted, it is on the contrary upheld by Kleist. Both Josephe and Jeronimo are capable of genuine religious emotion, of prayer straight from the heart and a warm desire to give thanks to their creator for mercies received. It is true that the answer to their prayers is ambiguous, indeed cruelly ironic, since they escape the earthquake to meet death by lynching. But this does not diminish the validity of the religious emotions they experience when they pray. The feelings of love they experience for each other are branded as sinful by organised religion, whereas their intrinsic worth is underlined by Kleist. Implicitly Josephe is compared to the Virgin Mary. When Jeronimo sees her by a spring in the valley washing her child he cries out 'O Mutter Gottes, du Heilige!' as he is reunited to her – slender evidence, one might feel, for mentioning Josephe in the same breath as the Virgin Mary, but the inference is there and it is one that is developed more explicitly in other stories.[15] The figure of the Virgin occurs in Kleist's works as a symbol of purity and spiritual innocence, and here this figure is linked with Josephe and the basic purity of her love thereby stressed. The innocence and purity of love is captured in the scene in the wooded valley, compared as it is to the Garden of Eden, where the lovers spend their brief idyll together.[16] This idyll is

---

[14] ' "Stone them! Stone them!" the whole Christian throng assembled in the temple of Jesus!'

[15] Cf. *Marquise von O.*, ch.5, p.68, and *Die Verlobung in St. Domingo*, ch.3, p.45. 'O Mutter Gottes, du Heilige!' – 'Holy Mother of God!'

[16] Cf. letter to Wilhelmine, 3/4 September 1800, where, describing a valley not far from Dresden, Kleist writes: 'Solche Täler, eng und heimlich, sind das wahre Vaterland der Liebe' – 'Such valleys, narrow and secluded, are the true fatherland of love.'

then abruptly shattered by the events in the Dominican church.

Organised religion and law operate hand in hand. Josephe offends against the moral code of the society to which she belongs, and she also offends against the 'klösterliche Gesetz', the convent law, and is punished by it. The course of true love does not run smooth in Kleist's works, it has continually to contend with tabus of one kind or another, with vetoes, social conventions, and legal institutions. Josephe, however pure her love may be, falls foul of the moral standards of society. Don Fernando may be impressed by her dignity and grace, her 'Würdigkeit' and 'Anmut'; to the citizens of Santiago she is a sinner and a whore, a 'Sünderin' and a 'Klostermetze'. This gaping discrepancy in values is brought home by means of a series of paradoxes. The place chosen by the lovers as the 'setting for their complete happiness', the 'Schauplatz ihres vollen Glückes', is a convent garden; during the feast of Corpus Christi, of all times, a nun, of all people, collapses in labour – on the steps of a cathedral, of all places; a Te Deum is used as the background for a lynching. The point is amply driven home.

The tragedy is, then, caused as well by the very nature of human society and the laws and conventions which its members are required to respect. Can one go further and attach some responsibility to individual characters? After all, it is Jeronimo who changes his resolve to leave the country and informs Josephe he intends to stay. And it is Josephe who insists on returning to the city to attend the service of thanksgiving. But this element of responsibility, though indicated, is slight and hedged with irony. In Josephe's case it is true religious feeling that gets the better of prudence, and it is ironical that this proves her undoing. Jeronimo changes his mind because of the extreme kindness and friendship everybody shows to Josephe and himself; he is deceived by appearances and forgets that back in the city, where freedom from restraining convention no longer obtains, people will be moved by feelings of prejudice, hypocrisy and false morality. In other words, it is the frailty of human institutions and the deceptive nature of the world that misleads the lovers. Ultimately, however, it may be wrong to attempt to pin down the responsibility for the tragedy on any particular cause. Kleist rarely commits himself. The narrative method he follows is to trace the course of events as they appear subjectively to the characters themselves, to reproduce their alternating hopes and fears, and to assess events from their relative and shifting standpoints.[17]

The effect of the story is tragic. A pair of young lovers is murdered, another woman is killed by mistake, and a child belonging to another couple is mistaken for the love-child of Josephe and Jeronimo and is sickeningly slaughtered. A vista of chaos is opened up. Does anything remain?

Something certainly does remain, namely, the child of Josephe and Jeronimo. It is rescued from the lynching and adopted by Don Fernando and his wife. Kleist goes out of his way to mention it in the closing sentence, and its survival must therefore presumably be of some significance. It is true that the final sentence is highly conditionally phrased. Alas, Kleist often does end his works in a teasingly ambiguous manner – *Amphitryon, Die Marquise von O.* and *Prinz Friedrich von Homburg* spring readily to mind – and the critic of his work must juggle with paradoxes as best he can. Opinions differ as to the significance of the survival of the child in *Das Erdbeben*. For some critics it represents a certain mitigation of the tragedy, a symbol of the enduring value of true love.[18] Others, notably Walter Silz, have objected to this, pointing out that its survival is pure chance and that the fact that Don Fernando loses his own child and is left with somebody else's only underlines the crazy disorder of the universe and is a final comment on a world gone mad.[19] It is difficult to endorse this view. It seems far more likely that the child survives as a symbol of human love, indicating as a love-child that this love, however tragic its outcome, was something real and valid. The fact that it

---

[17] Cf. J.M. Ellis, 'Kleist's *Das Erdbeben in Chili*', *Publications of the English Goethe Society*, 33, pp. 10-55, (revised version in *Narration in the German Novelle*, Cambridge, 1974), and Wolfgang Kayser, 'Kleist als Erzähler' in *Die Vortragsreise*, Bern, 1958, and *German Life and Letters*, n.s. VIII. These are good articles. Critics whose judgments on Kleist are heavily weighted one way or the other need to be treated with considerable caution.

[18] Benno von Wiese, *Die deutsche Novelle*, vol. 2, 1965; K.O. Conrady, *Germanisch-Romanische Monatsschrift*, NF, 1954, 185-95.

[19] Walter Silz, op.cit., ch. 1.

survives only by chance is immaterial. Its survival is as real, or then as fortuitous, as was the initial love affair between Jeronimo and Josephe, and the very fact of this fortuitousness does not automatically eliminate any symbolic significance. The world is governed by chance, which operates without regard to the people whose lives it affects. The archbishop, a 'bad' person, is killed in the earthquake, but so is the abbess, a 'good' person. Human feelings, however, and the integrity of human emotions are important and they count, whatever their fate in the external world. The pure, as it were 'divine' love of Josephe is mirrored in the remarkable sequence of events appertaining to the child, and it suggests that Kleist has singled out the child for special treatment. It is conceived in the garden of a Carmelite convent; it is born on the day of Corpus Christi; it is saved from the earthquake by the protective hand of the abbess and by 'ein Wunder des Himmels', for Josephe undergoes an ordeal by fire, a 'Feuerprobe', to save it,[20] and all the angels of heaven protect her; it is baptized, as it were, in a spring in a wooded valley; and it is rescued from lynching by Don Fernando, the 'divine hero'. Is it in fact mere chance that the child is saved? All the forces of heaven appear to conspire to save it, and Kleist makes sure that it is saved.

The child is an important symbol, and may well reflect Kleist's wish, frequently expressed in his letters, to be the father of a child. The importance of a parent's attachment to a child is stressed. In the case of Josephe her maternal feeling gives her strength to escape from the earthquake and not succumb to despair, and her love for her child helps her to emerge unscathed from a burning building. The symbol of the child then links up with another theme indicated in this astonishingly rich story, the theme of the family. Josephe, Jeronimo and their child form a family group as they rest at night under the pomegranate tree, with Josephe in Jeronimo's lap and the child in hers. It is almost as if Kleist were reproducing some pictorial representation of the Holy Family

---

[20] The idea of an 'ordeal by fire' is variously expressed in *Der Findling* (Elvire's rescue by Colino), *Der Zweikampf* (the fate awaiting Trota and Littegarde), perhaps *Die Marquise von O.* (rape and the burning fortress), and most obviously in the ordeal of Käthchen in the play *Das Käthchen von Heilbronn*.

resting on the flight into Egypt. And this idealised picture of the family is then projected on to the human race; for the survivors of the earthquake who congregate outside the city are compared with one big human family. It is a splendid wish dream, but one which does not stand up to reality. Here again Kleist shows the disparity between the ideal and what happens in reality. The discord in the world is reflected in the discord within the family. Josephe's father acts to stifle her love for Jeronimo by immuring her in a convent, and he learns of her liaison because of the 'hämische Aufmerksamkeit seines stolzen Sohnes', the 'malicious watchfulness of his proud son', Josephe's brother. Family discord shows itself even more drastically in the case of Jeronimo. He is clubbed down in the cathedral 'mit einem ungeheuren Keulenschlage', 'with a monstrous blow from a club', by his own father. Such is the tragic nature of the world.[21] But this does not impair the validity of ideals. The selfless courage and assertion of human dignity by Don Fernando in the church at the end remains as something positive, and wins him the lovers' child, even though he is powerless to prevent the slaughter of his own child. And the symbol of the child remains as a vindication of human love, even though when the child grows up it may turn out to be just as pernicious as Nicolo in *Der Findling*.

Das Erdbeben is written in a style unique in German literature.[22] Within the short space that the story occupies Kleist is able to gain a remarkable variety of stylistic effects. There is dry, terse narrating and a deliberate eschewing of rhetorical embellishment, so that often an atmosphere of pitiless finality is engendered, as in the laconic account of Josephe's death: 'Meister Pedrillo schug sie mit der Keule nieder' ('Meister Pedrillo felled her with the club'). Sometimes, in complete contrast, Kleist indulges in lyrical effusion, as when night falls on the secluded valley where the lovers have sought refuge: 'Indessen war die schönste Nacht

---

[21] Similarly in *Die Familie Schroffenstein* fathers kill their children, in this case by mistake. There is some affinity between this play and *Das Erdbeben*. Indeed the names of the characters in the earlier version *Die Familie Ghonorez* correspond to those in the story, cf. Sembdner, vol. 2, note on p.903.

[22] The following remarks to some extent anticipate the remarks on style in Chapter 8 below.

herabgestiegen, voll wundermilden Duftes, so silberglänzend und still, wie nur ein Dichter davon träumen mag.'[23] The heroic style is used to describe Don Fernando fighting off the bloodthirsty mob: 'Mit jedem Hiebe wetterstrahlte er einen zu Boden; ein Löwe wehrt sich nicht besser.'[24] There is the trick of a long series of clauses introduced by the same conjunction, producing a cumulative effect and leading up, in an account of the earthquake, to the incident of how an innocent man was hanged in the general breakdown of law and order. There is the extraordinary description of the earthquake as it appears to Jeronimo, where one frightening event follows another as nine consecutive clauses are introduced by the word 'hier', the 'hier's piling up on top of one another and the pace quickening in the second sentence, until the final 'hier', isolated by a semi-colon, is reached to deliver the ultimate comment and final indictment of heaven for permitting such things to happen.[25]

This is hardly a realistic style. It is far more a grotesque, a nightmarish effect that is aimed at. Things happen as if in a dream. Jeronimo asks a woman if she has heard if Josephe has been executed: 'Eine Frau, die auf einem fast zur Erde gedrückten Nacken eine ungeheure Last von Gerätschaften

[23] 'Meanwhile the most beautiful night had fallen, full of miraculous, mild fragrance, with a silvery sheen and so tranquil, such as only a poet might dream of.' The poet is Kleist.

[24] 'With every lightning thrust he made one bite the dust; a lion does not fight better when at bay.'

[25] The passage is worth quoting: 'Hier stürzte noch ein Haus zusammen und jagte ihn, die Trümmer weit umherschleudernd, in eine Nebenstraße; hier leckte die Flamme schon, in Dampfwolken blitzend, aus allen Giebeln und trieb ihn schreckenvoll in eine andere; hier wälzte sich, aus seinem Gestade gehoben, der Mapochofluß an ihn heran und riß ihn brüllend in eine dritte. Hier lag ein Haufen Erschlagener, hier ächzte noch eine Stimme unter dem Schutte, hier schrien Leute von brennenden Dächern herab, hier kämpften Menschen und Tiere mit den Wellen, hier war ein mutiger Retter bemüht, zu helfen; hier stand ein anderer, bleich wie der Tod, und streckte sprachlos zitternde Hände zum Himmel' – 'Here a house was collapsing and, scattering its debris in all directions, drove him into a side street; here the flames, flashing like lightning through clouds of smoke, shot forked tongues at him from every gable and sent him headlong into another street; here the River Mapocho, bursting its banks, came roaring towards him and hurled him into a third street. Here lay a pile of battered corpses, here there still groaned a voice from under the ruins, here people screamed from burning roofs, here men and animals fought with the waves, here a brave rescuer was busy trying to help; here there stood another person, pale as death, and, speechless, stretched out trembling hands towards heaven.'

Das Erdbeben in Chili 27

und zwei Kinder, an der Brust hängend, trug, sagte im Vorbeigehen, als ob sie es selbst angesehen hätte: daß sie enthauptet worden sei.'[26] A woman loaded down with possessions and two children at her breast, a casual remark framed in a conditional clause – this is a hallucinatory means of representation. This kind of description reaches its climax in the dreamlike vividness of the final scene in the church. Vast candelabras cast shadows in the darkened church, the priest depicts the horrors of the Last Judgement, voices cry out in the gloom, recognising the lovers and their party and demanding their blood, snatches of dialogue break up the sentences, figures appear, such as a naval officer known to Don Fernando, and then equally bafflingly disappear, no one recognises Don Fernando, well-known person though he is, the identity of Josephe and Jeronimo becomes confused, Donna Constanze is mistaken for Josephe and is murdered, from out of the blue a voice in the mob cries out 'Dies ist Jeronimo Rugera, ihr Bürger, denn ich bin sein eigner Vater!' ('This is Jeronimo Rugera, citizens, for I am his own father!'), and the owner of the voice kills Jeronimo. The identity of persons is called in question, individuals merge in the mob, all becomes impersonal, names and the pronouns 'he' and 'she' are replaced by the pronoun 'it', by 'a voice', by 'a stranger'. As the climax builds up and the final orgasm of violence is reached, figures become larger than life, positive and negative qualities are taken to extremes, the conflict moves on to a superhuman plane, Don Fernando is now 'the divine hero' confronting Meister Pedrillo, 'the leader of the satanic horde', it is as if heaven and hell stand opposed. The final moment of horror is reached when Meister Pedrillo seizes Don Fernando's son by the legs, swings him round and round, and smashes him against the corner of a pillar. With this the immediate nightmare is over, people reappear, a kind of normality is re-established.

The style gains in dramatic intensity by Kleist's treatment of time. Sometimes a whole stretch of time is glossed over or

---

[26] 'A woman, practically touching the ground under the colossal weight of household goods she bore on her neck, and carrying as well two children at her breast, said, as she went by, as if she had herself witnessed it: that Josephe had been beheaded.' Cf. Silz, op.cit., ch.1.

summed up in a phrase or two, notably on the opening page, when in one sentence the reader is told how the lovers consummated their love in the convent garden, and in the next sentence Josephe is collapsing in labour on the steps of the cathedral. Compression could hardly go further! At other times Kleist dwells on a moment of time at length, as in the repeated description of the earthquake. There is speed of narration on the one hand, and on the other the constant returning to the central moment of time. The dramatic urgency is then further built up by the compression of the action in just over twenty-four hours, by the switching of tenses and by the alternating use of direct narration and reported speech, the one rooted in the present, the other looking back to the past, all this helping to produce the impression of simultaneity and increasing the range of effects.

This dramatic style is then enhanced by the use of images. Some of them are descriptive and highly lyrical. The human spirit, under the impact of the earthquake, opens up 'like a beautiful flower'; as the lovers repose under the tree 'die Nachtigall flötete im Wipfel ihr wollüstiges Lied' ('in the top of the tree the nightingale piped its sensuous song'); when Don Fernando's wife has recovered from her grief at the loss of her son 'sie fiel ihm mit dem Rest einer erglänzenden Träne eines Morgens um den Hals' ('she embraced him one morning, one last tear-drop still glistening in her eye'). There are passages where an almost plastic kind of description, a sort of visual representation, is aimed at. There are many such examples: the interior of the church, with the packed congregation and boys, hat in hand, perched expectantly on picture frames on the walls, like so many baroque cherubs; Josephe suckling her infant; the groups of homeless refugees gathered around fires in the meadows outside the city; Don Fernando, sword in hand, at bay outside the church. It is as if Kleist had in mind paintings he had seen in the Dresden art gallery,[27] and was weaving these visual impressions into the story. This is an important element of his style. On the one hand the dramatic impetus of the narrative; and on the other hand these more static descriptive details. One remembers the

---

[27] Cf. Chapter 3 below on *Die Verlobung*, pp. 37-8.

priest denouncing the sinners in the church; but one remembers as well the detail of the white surplice framing his hands as he stretches them towards heaven. It is the fusion of the retarding elements in the style with those that precipitate the reader onwards that goes to make up Kleist's unique kind of dramatic prose.

Das Erdbeben has, as will in due course become evident, many features in common with the other stories. The role of chance and the apparent fortuitousness of events, the theme of love, an extra-marital love that comes into conflict with society, the hostilities, normally suppressed, that break out within a family, the way that normally decent law-abiding citizens, once an established pattern of behaviour is disrupted by an extraordinary event, indulge in a frightful outbreak of violence, the role of religion, and the almost sadistic subjecting of human beings to a cruel fate. There is the deliberate use of paradox, a prisoner trying to hang himself while thousands perish, a string of murders committed in the name of Christianity, and the basic irony that underlies it all, whereby the lovers escape the fury of the earthquake only to be cruelly deluded into encountering the fury of their fellowmen. There is the narrative method of telling the story as it is experienced by this or that character, with the kaleidoscopic varying of perspective that this entails.

Structure, form and content blend in *Das Erdbeben in Chili* to produce a work which is unquestionably a masterpiece. The tightly-knit character of the story may be illustrated by one small touch. Towards the beginning there occur the sentences already referred to where nine clauses commence with the word 'hier'. They reach their climax in the last phrase, where a man, pale as death, mutely raises his trembling hands towards heaven. At the end of the story, when Don Fernando sees the corpse of his son lying at his feet, he raises his eyes 'voll namenlosen Schmerzes', 'full of nameless grief', towards heaven. The gesture in both cases is basically the same. What does it mean? Is it grief at what has happened, is it man accusing God for permitting such enormities, is it the speechless reaction of someone faced with horror beyond his comprehension? Perhaps it is all of this, the ultimate comment on the world put forward by Kleist in this startlingly original story, a world in which finer human emotions, though they exist and are real, are faced with destruction. The world of Goethe and Schiller, measured and ordered despite its tragic undertones, seems very far away. How different is the world of *Das Erdbeben*.[28] A vista of chaos, of threatening nihilism, is opened up, but kept in check here by the order, the artistic perfection with which it is presented.

---

[28] Not so different from our own, according to Arnold Zweig, 'Nochmals der Novellist', 1946, quoted by Sembdner, *Nachruhm*, p.656, where he says: 'In order to realise what is generally valid about these larger-than-life figures the reader only has to substitute for the earthquake in Santiago the aerial bombardment of Rotterdam, Warsaw or Dresden, and to substitute for the mass instincts aroused by the clergy of that age the national-socialist mob reactions of our own times.'

3
Die Verlobung in St. Domingo

Du hättest mir nicht mißtrauen sollen![1]

The background of *Das Erdbeben in Chili* is one of violence and slaughter, rising in a crescendo to the tremendous climax of the lynching on the steps of the cathedral. There is violence and slaughter in *Die Verlobung in St. Domingo*, but there is more besides. If *Das Erdbeben* is not unlike a musical composition, a tightly-knit work in which the themes of the opening movement are gathered together in the tragic finale, then the general effect of the *Verlobung* is that of a painting, a sombre affair for the most part in black and white, in which against a dark background isolated figures stand out somewhat, caught by a pale, fitful gleam of light, before being engulfed again in the prevailing darkness. Indeed, the comparison with a painting may not be fanciful, but may serve to underline the technique of composition that characterises this particular story and sets the tone for it. Black is opposed to white; negroes, originally from the Dark Continent, are out to exterminate the white Europeans; night is opposed to day; scenes are set in darkened rooms or against shadowy backgrounds fitfully illuminated by the light of distant fires and flickering torches; the forces of evil, of hell, appear to be ranged against those of good, of at least a surface Christianity; the outward setting of dark and light, of night and day, has its counterpart within the hearts of the two main characters, the 'night' of confusion and misunderstanding, the 'day' of truth and inner certainty. Yet again a tragic story of love is set

---

[1] 'You ought not to have mistrusted me!' – Toni's dying words to Gustav, and the punchline of the story.

against a background of mass violence and the extremes of inhumanity and humanity, of frightful revenge and supreme self-sacrifice.

Die Verlobung in St. Domingo was first published in the periodical *Der Freimüthige* in Berlin in March and April, 1811, and then appeared in book form in the second volume of the *Erzählungen* published in 1811. It is a story which takes place on the island of Haiti in 1803, at the time of the bloody revolt of the negro slave population, under their ferocious leader Jean-Jacques Dessalines, against the white (French) colonists, which results in the expulsion of the French in November, 1803, and the proclamation of Dessalines as emperor. One night, when the revolt is at its height, a white fugitive, a Swiss officer named Gustav von der Ried, seeks refuge at a plantation which formerly belonged to a white settler but has now been taken over by a Negro, Congo Hoango, who has slaughtered his white master and all his dependants and is now the implacable enemy of anyone who is white. He is away when Gustav knocks at the door of the house asking for help; and Babekan, Congo's mistress, and her daughter Toni admit the stranger, intending to keep him there until he can be suitably put to death by the returning Congo. Toni, an attractive half-caste girl, has the job of beguiling unsuspecting white fugitives, who are then set upon and butchered to death by Congo and his followers. This time events take an unexpected turn. For Toni and Gustav fall in love and consummate their 'Verlobung', their 'betrothal', that night. And instead of being willing to betray Gustav to Congo Hoango, when he returns, Toni is prepared to elope with him and with the band of relatives who are waiting for him in a nearby wood and who are dependent on him for help. Unfortunately Congo Hoango returns with his men the following night earlier than expected, and Toni, to cover up her betrayal of him which Babekan has already suspected, ties up Gustav in his sleep to his bed and hands him over to Congo Hoango, while at the same time alerting Gustav's friends waiting not far away for news of him. Help does come, Congo Hoango and his men are overpowered, and Gustav is set free. But his love for Toni has turned into hate, because he thinks she has betrayed him, and his first act on being released is to seize a pistol and shoot her. When he finds out, too late, that she had remained faithful to him and had been forced by necessity to give the appearance of betraying him, he turns the pistol on himself and blows his brains out.

There are various possible sources for the story. Rainsford's *Historical Account of the black Empire of Hayti, comprehending a view of the principal Transactions in the Revolution of St. Domingo*, London, 1805, appeared in German translation in Hamburg, 1806, and may well have been known to Kleist, as too may Dubrocas' *Geschichte der Empörung auf St. Domingo*, published in *Minerva* in 1805. He was familiar (letter to Ulrike, 16 December 1801) with August Lafontaine's novel *Klara du Plessis* (1794), and this could have furnished a detail or two of the experiences of Gustav during the French Revolution prior to his arrival in St. Domingo. Far more important is the fact that during his stay in Paris in 1803 Kleist may well have read newspaper accounts and articles dealing with the negro revolt, which naturally excited lively interest in the French capital. Furthermore, one of the leaders of the revolt captured by the French, Toussaint l'Ouverture, ended his days (1803) in wretched captivity in the very fortress, Fort Joux, where Kleist was confined in 1807 when arrested by the French under suspicion of spying.[2] It is indeed likely that Kleist drew on his recollection of historical events, which for him were of course very contemporary events, just possibly adding to them echoes of his own experiences when living on the Lake of Thun in 1802. It is impossible to say when the story was written. In the last line of the story mention is made of the year 1807. It was first published in the last year of Kleist's life. But it may well have been conceived and drafted before then, in fact any time during the years 1803 to 1806, when his most tragic works were conceived or written. The important thing is that the story is set against a background of contemporary events, fully justifying the 'Nun weiß jedermann' ('as everyone knows') with which the author starts the story proper.

Die Verlobung is very carefully and closely constructed. Unity of place is observed, the scene being set in the house, formerly belonging to the white planter and now occupied by Congo

[2] Cf. letter to Ulrike, 23 April 1807.

Hoango, and in its immediate precincts. The fact that the unity of place is observed is not fortuitous. It helps to build up the atmosphere of oppressive confinement which motivates in part Gustav's fears and suspicions. The unity of time is all but observed. The action is contained within some thirty-six hours, from shortly before midnight of the first night to some time after midnight of the second night, with dawn breaking and the sun rising on the final tragic ending. The action, with the 'Verlobung', the betrothal, as its centre point, revolves around the tragic love of Gustav and Toni, set against a background of strife and violence, of open warfare between blacks and whites. Toni and Gustav stand to some extent midway between this struggle. For Gustav, although a white, comes from neutral Switzerland, and the idyllic setting of the memorial under the shadow of the Rigi in Switzerland to commemorate him and Toni contrasts sharply with the strife-ridden island of St. Domingo where the story takes place. And Toni, though apparently pledged at first to the cause of the negroes, has in fact more white blood in her than black, for she is the child of the mulatto Babekan and a white man and was born in Paris. The story is told in a straightforward fashion, introduced by a prologue describing the emergence to prominence of Congo Hoango, and ending with an epilogue in which the survivors return eventually to Switzerland and settle down there in peace. But the thread of the narrative is interrupted by three flashbacks, all of considerable importance in the elucidation of the basic themes of the story. The first flashback occurs when Babekan tells Gustav how she conceived and gave birth to Toni in France, as the result of a liaison with a white man who subsequently publicly betrayed her, denying all knowledge of her. The second flashback occurs when Gustav tells Toni and Babekan of an incident during the bloody seizure of Fort Dauphin by the negroes. A negress, who had been cruelly ill-treated three years before by a white settler, offered this settler refuge from the vengeance of the negroes, took him into her bed and suffered for a time his amorous advances, only then to announce to him that she had yellow fever and had infected him, so that he could go and give it to all his fellow white men. The third flashback is recounted by Gustav to Toni. He tells her she resembles a former fiancée

of his, Marianne Congreve, who during the Terror had
sacrificed herself for him and been guillotined in his place,
even going to the extent of publicly denying all knowledge of
him when he arrived at the scene of the execution intending to
die instead of her. There are as well implicit parallels in the
story. The violence of the negroes in revolt is matched by that
of the revolutionary mob during the French Revolution. At the
beginning of the story Congo Hoango repays the kindness and
trust of his master Herr Villeneuve by butchering him to
death; at the end of the story Gustav repays the love of Toni
by shooting her. The father of Toni deliberately betrays
Babekan; Gustav unwittingly betrays his betrothal to Toni.
The story is, then, carefully constructed.

'Zu Port au Prince, auf dem französischen Anteil der Insel
St Domingo, lebte zu Anfang dieses Jahrhunderts, als die
Schwarzen die Weißen ermordeten, auf der Pflanzung des
Herrn Guillaume von Villeneuve, ein fürchterlicher alter
Neger, namens Congo Hoango.'[3] This is the opening sentence
of *Die Verlobung*, and one characteristic of Kleist, for in it he
sets the time and the place, introduces the general theme of
violence, and names the character around whom much of it
centres. 'When the blacks were murdering the whites' – the
motifs of black and white are played on and hammered home
right from the beginning. It is dark and stormy when Gustav
arrives at midnight seeking help – 'in der Finsternis einer
stürmischen und regnigten Nacht' – and he, a stranger in the
'blackness of the stormy and rainy night', like some
Kafkaesque figure in his isolation, stretches out his hand
through the 'Dunkelheit' ('darkness') imploring help and
asking Babekan 'Seid Ihr eine Negerin?' to which she replies
'Nun, Ihr seid gewiß ein Weißer, daß Ihr dieser stockfinstern
Nacht lieber ins Antlitz schaut als einer Negerin!'.[4] The effect
is cumulative: 'Finsternis', 'Negerin', 'Dunkelheit', 'Nacht',
'stockfinster', while the lonely white man pleads for help, sees

---

[3] 'At Port-au-Prince, in the French part of the island of Santo Domingo, there lived on the plantation of Guillaume de Villeneuve at the beginning of this century, when the blacks were murdering the whites, a terrifying old negro, whose name was Congo Hoango.'
[4] 'Are you a negress?', to which she replies, 'Well, you must certainly be a white man, seeing that you would rather face this pitch-black night than a negress!'

to his horror dark shapes flitting about in the yard, and is then drawn into the house by Toni, who holds a lantern so that its rays shine on her face and illumine her fairer skin in the encircling gloom, and who swears 'by the light of the sun', 'bei dem Licht der Sonne', that there is no-one else in the house but herself and her mother.

This contrasting of white with black, examples of which are legion, is further reinforced by the timing of the action of the plot. For all the important events in the story take place at night, more often than not at midnight, as is so often the case in Kleist's works. The massacre of the whites at Fort Dauphin begins at midnight, the band of white refugees under Herr Strömli, of whom Gustav is one, march by night and rest by day, it is nearly midnight when Gustav knocks at the door seeking help, his 'Verlobung' with Toni takes place during the night, against a lurid background of torches and beacons on the horizon behind the house as the troops of the black General Dessalines march past in the distance, Congo Hoango returns during the night, the night when Toni sees their only salvation in tying Gustav to his bed. The action takes place during two nights, with the day serving as an interval between them. But even the daytime turns out to be a form of night, for Gustav, on Babekan's orders, in the interests of his own safety as she says, has to have the shutters of his windows closed, so that the room is cast into darkness, into 'Nacht' as Kleist calls it, only partly dispelled by the wretched candle that Babekan has difficulty in lighting. The effect of this contrasting of black and white, of night and day, is to create in the first instance a sombre pictorial effect. But, with the oppressive sense of confinement thereby engendered, it also reflects the dark threatening forces building up tension in the story; and it has the psychological effect of sowing the seeds of anxiety, doubt and suspicion in the mind of Gustav, contributing to the motivation of his murder of Toni. Occasionally a shaft of light may penetrate the gloom, banishing for a moment the shadows and holding out the promise of a conciliatory ending to the story. When Toni gazes at Gustav as he lies asleep the illusion of a fleeting happiness is suggested by the moonlight which shines on his face. But the moonlight proves treacherous, darkness

Die Verlobung in St. Domingo

intervenes, and tragedy ensues. It is only at the end of the story, when Toni and Gustav are dead, that the darkness yields to light, and then the sunlight comes streaming into the room, the scene of their tragic end.

The motif of black and white is reflected in the colour of people's skins, obviously enough. Here too this is differentiated and there are various shades and tones, for Babekan has some white blood, though in her case negro blood predominates, and Toni is more white than black. And the motif of colour, of light and shade, is carried through very consistently in the language. Babekan, referring to the colour of her skin, speaks of 'der Schatten der Verwandschaft' that links her to the negroes, while Gustav on the other hand says of her 'Aus der Farbe Eures Gesichts schimmert mir ein Strahl von der meinigen entgegen'. Babekan talks of the 'Schimmer von Licht, der auf meinem Antlitz, wenn es Tag wird, erdämmert', and says of Toni 'Was kann meine Tochter, die in Europa empfangen und geboren ist, dafür, daß der volle Tag jenes Weltteils von dem ihrigen widerscheint?' When Toni, after her 'Verlobung', has associated herself with Gustav and his friends, it is entirely fitting that she should tell Congo Hoango 'Ich habe euch nicht verraten; ich bin eine Weiße.'[5]

The pictorial elements, the chiaroscuro effects, are an important feature of *Die Verlobung*. In connection with this it may be worth stressing the importance of painting for Kleist's work in general. Some paintings obviously impressed him greatly, as is clear from references to them in his letters.[6] When he visited the gallery at Dresden in 1801 the pictures there made a lasting impression on him,[7] and he would have had plenty of opportunity to renew acquaintance with them

---

[5] Translation of the phrases in this paragraph: 'the shadow of kinship'; 'A touch of light shines from the colour of your face mirroring a gleam of my own'; 'the glimmer of light that dawns on my face at the break of day'; 'how can my daughter, who was conceived and born in Europe, help the fact that the full light of day of that continent is reflected in her own face?', 'I have not betrayed you; I am a white.'

[6] Notably in letters to Wilhelmine von Zenge, 3/4 September 1800, 4 May 1801, 21 May 1801; to Luise von Zenge, 16 August 1801; and to Marie von Kleist, June, 1807.

[7] Letter to Wilhelmine, 21 May 1801. He was also impressed by the Louvre when he was in Paris.

during his stay in Dresden from 1807 to 1809. Throughout his creative life he was in contact with painters or with their works, from his friendship with the painter Heinrich Lohse in 1802 to his articles and comments on painting in the *Berliner Abendblätter*. Sometimes a direct link can be traced with his work. It was a painting that provided the initial impetus to the writing of his comedy *Der zerbrochne Krug*, and a painting was very possibly in his mind when writing his play *Prinz Friedrich von Homburg*.[8] But generally speaking the influence of painting on him would appear to be of a more indirect nature. His stories are full of scenic details, arresting descriptions within the narrative flow that force the reader at least momentarily to linger over them as if contemplating a painting. It may be that it is part of the dramatist's inspiration to view things scenically. What is certain is that the intrusion of almost plastic effects into the story is a feature of Kleist's style, however dramatic the presentation may ultimately be.

The motif of black and white in *Die Verlobung* is not just a pictorial embellishment or stylistic adjunct to the story; it also helps to underline some of the themes in it, both in general and as they affect the two main characters. White and black might at first be thought to correspond to right and wrong, good and evil, Christian and pagan, and superficially there is much in the text to strengthen this impression. But through all the savagery and horror it soon becomes clear that, in terms of guilt, blacks are not as black and the whites not as white as may at first appear.[9] Congo Hoango takes a fearful revenge on Herr Villeneuve, the white master who has so favoured and befriended him; but it is 'eingedenk der Tyrannei, die ihn seinem Vaterlande entrissen hatte' – 'in memory of the tyranny which had torn him from his fatherland' – for he is a former slave from the Gold Coast. In other words, the white men share a collective guilt in the general fate of the black slaves, and Gustav has to concede this when talking to Babekan, indeed he says it goes back several centuries and he

---

[8] Cf. Richard Samuel (ed.), *Prinz Friedrich von Homburg*, 1962, where the painting is reproduced.

[9] Cf. the article by Peter Horn, 'Hatte Kleist Rassenvorurteile? Eine kritische Auseinandersetzung mit der Literatur zur *Verlobung in St. Domingo*', *Monatshefte* 67, 1975.

finds it indefensible. Herr Villeneuve is built up at the beginning of the story as a kind and humane master; but Babekan reveals that, after her affair with Herr Bertrand, the father of Toni, she was ordered by Herr Villeneuve to be given sixty lashes of the whip, and since that day has been permanently incapacitated. Guilt and blame are apportioned equally, they are, as it were, inherent in the state of the universe. The white colonists abused their power and ill-treated the negroes; the wronged negress takes a terrible revenge on her former master and gives him yellow fever; the negroes abuse their newly-won freedom and take revenge on the whites; Herr Bertrand betrays Babekan, and Gustav shoots Toni. Against this background of guilt and blame the conflict between black and white assumes symbolic proportions, dwarfing the particular individuals it engulfs, indicating a fundamental state of conflict and division in the universe itself, reaching back beyond the memory of any individual.

Violence and revenge recur throughout *Die Verlobung*. Here, as in other stories, Kleist shows how, once established law and order has broken down and the fragile structure of civilisation is shattered, primitive feelings come welling to the surface and man, to use the image in *Michael Kohlhaas*, reverts to the jungle.[10] The pattern of human feelings in Kleist's works often resembles an iceberg, the conscious feelings visible above the surface masking the vast complex of unconscious feelings invisible beneath. When these feelings do erupt, then the actions they occasion, 'unmenschlich' though they may be, cannot be judged by the morality of the 'normal' world. On the individual plane, there is not much difference in the emotional responses that lead Congo Hoango to kill Herr Villeneuve and Gustav to shoot Toni. And on the collective plane, the violence of the French revolutionary mob matches the cruelty of the negro slaves, whose 'Wahnsinn der Freiheit' was called into existence by 'die unbesonnenen Schritte des Nationalkonvents'.[11] A Leitmotif word in the story is 'Rache',

---

[10] Cf. Chapter 7 below on *Michael Kohlhaas*, p. 131.

[11] Negroes in the French part of Santo Domingo had been given their freedom and accorded equal rights by the National Convention in Paris in 1794. Hence the 'frenzy of freedom' called into existence by the 'heedless steps of the National Convention'.

and this 'revenge' is not only individual revenge, but is also revenge variously described as 'die Rache Gottes', 'die Rache des Himmels' and 'die Rache der bestehenden Landesgesetze', 'the vengeance of the existing laws of the land', negro laws that have replaced white laws and that demand equally violent retribution. Kleist was writing with the French Revolution and the negro revolt on Santo Domingo very much in his mind; and the contemporary relevance of such events can hardly fail to escape the notice of the modern reader.

The conflict between black and white merges into a conflict on the individual plane. Latent in the story and appearing every now and then is the basic conflict between the sexes and the corresponding dualism of love and hate. In every case men are shown in an unfavourable light, for them love is something superficial and opportunistic. For women, on the other hand, love involves suffering, self-sacrifice and total commitment. Herr Bertrand, the father of Toni, has Babekan as his mistress, but then publicly denies her, and she is subsequently flogged; the fugitive planter cruelly ill-treats the negress with yellow fever, who then perpetrates her revenge on him; Gustav's irresponsibility leads, albeit unwittingly, to the guillotining of his fiancée Marianne Congreve; and his motives in seducing Toni are a curious mixture of love, sensual desire, and opportunistic calculation. In a universe torn with strife, love, as a state of lasting spiritual fulfilment, seems out of place and impossible of attainment. It is linked with deceit; for Toni is encouraged by Congo Hoango to practise the outward signs of love in order to lure white men on to their destruction. It is linked with illness, the plague-like contagion the negress gives her would-be lover. It is linked with death; for Congo Hoango tells Toni that if she gives herself completely to a white man he will kill her, and this 'Todesstrafe', this 'death penalty', is, ironically enough, inflicted on her by the man she loves and to whom she has given herself.

Over and above the general impossibility of love in a universe full of conflict and strife there is, in *Die Verlobung*, a personal tragedy of love, the love of Gustav and Toni, and it is around these two characters that the story centres.

The climax of the story comes when Gustav shoots Toni

and then shoots himself.[12] The question immediately poses itself: why does Gustav commit this frightful act, and how does Kleist motivate it and make it credible? In keeping with the taut compression of the story there is no description of what Gustav looks like or of his past history, apart from the Marianne Congreve flashback. The reader is told that he has a small property on the banks of the River Aare in Switzerland, but this detail is only inserted to provide an idyllic contrast with the terrible reality of the situation in which he now finds himself. What Kleist does describe is Gustav's emotional responses to different situations, because in so doing he is motivating Gustav's highly emotional response to Toni's supposed treachery. He acts in an unthinking manner. It was his 'Unbesonnenheit', his thoughtlessness, in criticising the revolutionary regime that led to the guillotining of his fiancée. His instability is reflected in the fact that after that event he passed 'from one fainting fit to another' – 'er fiel aus einer Ohnmacht in die andere'. He is extraordinarily impetuous in the way he trusts in Babekan and confides in her; 'Euch kann ich mich anvertrauen', 'I can confide in you', he declares, when, had he thought rationally, he would not have had such trust. He is astonishingly talkative and discloses the whereabouts of Herr Strömli's party in what is an irresponsible manner. He is clearly emotionally highly strung; he grasps Babekan's bony hand and while she speaks rains kisses on it. He is disturbingly forward in the way he approaches Toni. He is struck by her appearance, puts his arm around her, presses her to him, and in no way behaves like a man who is on the run for his life. Obviously he reacts emotionally and not rationally to the circumstances in which he finds himself.

He is attracted to Toni for two reasons. In the first place she is young and good-looking, and adept at the arts of coy flirtation. And in the second place she bears a strong resemblance, at least in Gustav's eyes, to Marianne Congreve, and the memory of Marianne and how she sacrificed herself for him is very present in his mind when he regards Toni and

---

[12] The shooting is roughly similar to, though infinitely more messy than, Kleist's own suicide.

colours the attraction he feels for her with sentimental affection. Furthermore, the story of Marianne Congreve which Gustav tells has a transforming effect on Toni and awakens in her unaccustomed feelings, a 'menschliches Gefühl' as Kleist calls it, and this 'human feeling' increases her attractiveness in the eyes of Gustav. His feelings for her are a mixture of desire and sentiment based on echoes from the past, an opportunistic wish to safeguard his position in the house, and a nervous susceptibility born of the tension of his particular situation and the atmosphere in Congo Hoango's house where he now finds himself. Does he love Toni? Presumably, for he calls her his 'bride', seals their union by giving her a cross given to him by Marianne Congreve, whispers her name in his sleep, and is so shattered by what he construes as her betrayal that he kills her and afterwards himself. Yet, like the white lover of Babekan, he betrays the 'Eidschwur', the solemn oath he made to her, his love cannot survive the circumstantial evidence with which he is confronted.

'Du hättest mir nicht mißtrauen sollen!' are Toni's dying words to Gustav. Gustav's murder of Toni is motivated not only by his own impetuous, emotional way of behaving; it is motivated too by his lack of trust in her. His lack of trust is amply provided for by Kleist. When he arrives at the plantation he is a 'stranger', an 'officer' in a hostile army, and this is stressed, for he is continually referred to as 'der Fremde' and 'der Offizier', isolation and estrangement being conjured up by these words. He arrives in the dark and is horrified to see dark figures flitting about and the gates of the yard being shut behind him. His imagination, says Toni, was full of Moors and Negroes, 'ganz von Mohren und Negern erfüllt'. Babekan's story of how Toni's father publicly washed his hands of her fills him with a sense of unease, the story of the revenge perpetrated by the negress with yellow fever fills him with 'ein widerwärtiges und verdrießliches Gefühl', 'a feeling of repugnance and vexation', so much so that 'ein Gefühl der Unruhe legte sich wie ein Geier um sein Herz', 'a feeling of uneasiness settled like a vulture on his heart', and this image of the vulture as a bird of ill omen is echoed again when Kleist says that in Toni's arms the feelings of uneasiness vanish 'wie ein Heer schauerlicher Vögel', 'like a host of awesome birds'. The fact that Babekan finds it necessary to lock him up in his room during the daytime plunges him understandably enough 'in einen Wirbel von Unruhe', 'in a turmoil of restlessness'. So that, in view of all this, it is not surprising that when he finds himself roped to his bed and sees Toni entering his room along with Congo Hoango and other negroes he should lose faith in her and think she has betrayed him. The importance of the three flashbacks now becomes obvious. Babekan's story of Herr Bertrand and his own of the negress with yellow fever engender a feeling of unrest and suspicion, show the betrayal of one person by another, underline the element of deceit and revenge. The recital of the story of Marianne Congreve helps for a time to make him forget such fears, and reinforces the attraction Toni has for him. When however he gives way to distrust he no longer sees in her the embodiment of his former love Marianne, but instead associates her in his mind with the negress, black gains the upper hand in his mind over white. The process is underlined by the repetition of a stylistic device. Three times Kleist makes Gustav go to the window of a room and look out, tormented by emotions of uncertainty and sentimental memories of former associations.[13] The first occasion is after he has told the story of the negress to Babekan and Toni; the second is after he has told the story of Marianne to Toni; and the third is after he has shot Toni, discovered her innocence and loving self-sacrifice, and stares out of the window before blowing his brains out. The inference is obvious. His inability to distinguish between the emotional attitudes of the negress and Marianne Congreve as embodied in the character of Toni, to distinguish between black and white, leads to the double tragedy at the end. Such is the artistry with which Kleist, by the repetition of such apparently irrelevant detail, anticipates the final outcome of the story.

Gustav's act is, then, motivated by his own emotional make-

[13] This motif occurs in a letter to Wilhelmine, 22 November 1800, which starts as follows: 'Liebe Wilhelmine. Deinen Brief empfing ich grade, als ich sinnend an dem Fenster stand und mit dem Auge in den trüben Himmel, mit der Seele in die trübe Zukunft sah' – 'Dear Wilhelmine. I received your letter just as I was standing pensively by the window, my eyes staring at the overcast sky, my soul staring into the overcast future.'

up and the mistrust born of the chaotic circumstances in which he finds himself. Can one in all conscience blame him for losing faith in Toni? After a dream in which he breathes her name he wakes up to find he is bound hand and foot by her. Surely the weight of circumstantial evidence is so great that superhuman insight would have been needed to see through it? Gustav's act may be explained by psychological and circumstantial reasons; but behind it all Kleist is in this story advancing a metaphysical view of the world that is almost unrelievedly tragic. The world is in a state of uproar and chaos, violence and anarchy pierce the thin facade of law and order, the inadequacy of rational processes leaves man at the mercy of his emotions, appearances deceive and human beings in their isolation are the prey of misunderstanding and deceit, groping their way in a universe governed by chance. Key words such as 'Verrat', 'Schein' and 'Täuschung', 'betrayal', 'appearance' and 'deception', figure largely in the story. In such a world of disorder and deceit, where the tragic conflict is mirrored in the splitting up of people into the two hostile camps of black and white,[14] there is no room for a lovers' idyll.

Yet there might have been. Had Gustav possessed enough faith in Toni, enough to make him disregard the voice of reason, forget the memory of things past and ignore the evidence of his own eyes, then all might have ended happily. For it is this quality of 'Vertrauen', of implicit, steadfast and unreasoning trust, that Kleist puts forward as the one way whereby it may be possible for man to find his way out of the tragic labyrinth in which he is lost.[15] Complete faith in the integrity of another human being, based on love, may help to pierce the confusion of appearances and lift man out of the chaos of emotional anarchy of which otherwise he is the inevitable victim. Such a quality demands almost a superman,

---

[14] Well expressed by Babekan, however hypocritical her attitude may be: 'Ist es nicht, als ob die Hände *eines* Körpers oder die Zähne *eines* Mundes gegen einander wüten wollten, weil das *eine* Glied nicht geschaffen ist wie das andere?' – 'Isn't it just as if the hands of *one* body or the teeth of *one* mouth were violently raging against one another, because *one* limb isn't created the same as the other?'

[15] Kleist frequently insisted on boundless 'Vertrauen' from Wilhelmine, particularly in a letter written at the beginning of 1800, *Werke*, II, p.501 ff.

Die Verlobung in St. Domingo 45

it is an all but absolute ideal, incapable of realisation. It is realised in *Der Zweikampf*, where as a result tragedy is averted. Gustav is more fallible and incapable of rising to such heights.

Toni possesses this quality, for her love, called into being by the central experience of the 'Verlobung' that quite properly provides the story with its title, is something transforming, an existential commitment, that conditions her reactions to the past, the world around her, and her future hopes. Up to the arrival of Gustav she has used her charms to entice white men into the house, where they are then slaughtered by the negroes, she has, then, been party to the general prevalence of deception and betrayal, even if as a fourteen-year old girl she is not fully conscious of the horror of it all. The presence of Gustav affects a gradual transformation in her. When he tells the story of the negress she is ill at ease – for the first time she is able to see her own acts objectively, for the revenge of the negress is not much worse than the fate she indirectly brings on the white men. She might in a sense be identified with the negress. When she hears the story of Marianne Congreve and the way she had sacrificed herself for her fiancé Gustav she is overcome by a 'menschliches Gefühl', and it is under the impact of the 'human emotions' released by this story that she gives herself to Gustav. The experience of love, bound up as it is for her with the risk of the 'Todesstrafe' threatened by Congo Hoango, makes her conscious of herself and the position she is in, makes her mature. She now belongs completely to Gustav and the whites, the white blood in her takes precedence over the black. The experience of love has the impact of a deep religious experience. Toni is given a cross by Gustav to mark their 'Verlobung', she prays to an image of the Virgin Mary, symbol of pure, selfless love, and confesses all her past sins to her. Toni's love cleanses and purifies her. Her outward beauty becomes transformed into a spiritual beauty, at the end reference is made by Kleist in Schillerian terms to her 'beautiful soul', her 'schöne Seele'. To Congo Hoango and Babekan, however, she is a 'traitress', a 'Verräterin', and Gustav, unable to distinguish the real quality behind her apparent betrayal and seeing blackness where there is whiteness, calls her a whore. But she remains faithful to him in death, she is 'treu' to the man to whom she is 'verlobt'. When Gustav told her of Marianne Congreve and the way she died for him, he said of her that she was 'die treueste Seele unter der Sonne', (lit. 'the most faithful soul under the sun'). It is this faith and loyalty, this 'Treue', that Toni acquires once she has fallen in love with Gustav, this is the outward manifestation of her 'Vertrauen'. From embodying, to some extent, the qualities of the negress with yellow fever, she, the illegitimate offspring of a white man and a mulatto, takes on after the 'Verlobung' the virtues of Marianne Congreve. And herein lies the tragic irony of the story. For Gustav sees in her at first the resemblance to Marianne Congreve, only afterwards, misled by appearances, to confuse her in his mind with the figure of the negress.

'Der Himmel, wenn mich nicht alles trügt,' says Gustav as he clasps Babekan's hand, 'hat mich mitleidigen Menschen zugeführt'.[16] He is sadly mistaken. The story is full of such irony. Gustav trusts Babekan, but does not trust Toni. His violence at the end matches that of Congo Hoango, his failure to keep faith with Toni matches the betrayal of Herr Bertrand. So full was Gustav's mind of Moors and Negroes, says Toni, when describing his reactions when she first opened the door of the house to him, that had a lady from Paris or Marseilles opened the door he would have taken her for a negress. He does confuse black and white, and at the end only sees the negress in Toni. Irony in the *Verlobung* underlies the themes of distrust and the deceitful nature of appearances, a state of affairs in which even heaven seems to connive. It is a sombre view of the world Kleist presents in this story, and it would be even more depressing were it not for the artistic skill with which it is told. This conscious artistry gives the story a form and a shape, and to that extent keeps the tragic attitude expressed in it within bounds. Nor is that all. Some human qualities are upheld and rescued from the prevailing gloom, characters such as Toni and Gustav are not just puppets, powerless in the grip of blind chance or fate, but human beings to whom the experience of love is a real and transforming one, affording the individual the opportunity of transcending the confusion of appearances, an opportunity

---

[16] 'Heaven, if I am not completely deceived, has led me to merciful people.'

which can be seized by Toni, but not by Gustav. The story ends tragically, but the quality of 'Treue' which Toni acquires, and which the other fiancée of Gustav had, is still valid and to some extent mitigates the tragedy, just as the survival of the child in *Das Erdbeben* mitigates, though of course it does not alter, the tragic ending of that story.

After the death of Toni and Gustav, all the more shattering because of its suddenness, the story ends on a peaceful note. Sunshine illumines the scene, as the bodies of the lovers are sunk in a common grave. The white survivors make their way to Port au Prince and thence to Switzerland. There Herr Strömli buys a property in the shadow of the Rigi and amidst the bushes of his garden erects a monument to Toni and Gustav. The tragedy merges into an idyll. The 'Treue' of Toni is not forgotten: 'und noch im Jahr 1807 war unter den Büschen seines Gartens das Denkmal zu sehen, das er Gustav, seinem Vetter, und der Verlobten desselben, der treuen Toni, hatte setzen lassen.'[17]

---

[17] 'And in the year 1807, amidst the bushes of his garden, the monument could still be seen that he had had erected to the memory of Gustav, his cousin, and the latter's bride, the faithful Toni.'

4

Der Findling

Kein Priester begleitete ihn, man knüpfte ihn, ganz in der Stille, auf dem Platz del popolo auf.[1]

Of all the stories Kleist wrote *Der Findling* may reasonably be held to be the most sombre and depressing. In other stories that end tragically, such as *Das Erdbeben* and *Die Verlobung*, some ray of light does manage to pierce the enveloping gloom, some human qualities are salvaged from the wreckage. There are no such crumbs of comfort in *Der Findling*, where the tragedy is absolute and unresolved. Out of the goodness of his heart a worthy middle-class tradesman, happily married with wife and child, adopts a foundling child whom he finds by the side of the road. By the end of the story the man's son is dead, his wife is dead, the foundling has been murdered by him, he is strung up in a deserted Piazza del Popolo for this crime, and he goes eagerly to hell, hoping there to find his victim and carry out further revenge on him. All the good human virtues are questioned and perverted, and human institutions, such as law and religion, seem to aid and abet the satanic foundling. It is a bleak and chilling view of life that Kleist presents in this story, which is compressed into some sixteen pages of print.[2]

Antonio Piachi is a prosperous trader in Rome, married to a young wife Elvire, who as an adolescent girl was rescued from a burning building by a Genoese nobleman Colino at the cost of his life. His memory she still holds sacred. Piachi has an eleven-year old son by a former marriage. This son dies of the plague when accompanying Piachi on a business trip to

---

[1] 'No priest accompanied him, he was strung up, very quietly, in the Piazza del Popolo' – the last sentence of *Der Findling*. The first clause is an allusion to the last sentence of Goethe's novel *Die Leiden des jungen Werthers*.
[2] Werke, II, pp. 199-215.

Ragusa. Piachi returns to Rome with a boy he found by the roadside outside Ragusa and adopts this foundling, Nicolo, in place of the son he has lost. He showers benefits on Nicolo and in due course makes over to him his whole business, intending to live a life of quiet retirement with his wife. Nicolo has two disturbing faults: a narrowminded bigotry, which makes him fair game for the monks who have an eye to his fortune, and a highly-developed sensuality, which wins him the favour of Xaviera Tartini, the discarded mistress of a bishop. He has mixed feelings of lust and hate towards his foster-mother Elvire, who at first he thinks is attracted to him and who he later discovers retreats to her room to worship the image of her dead rescuer Colino. Nicolo bears a strong physical resemblance to Colino. One day, while Piachi is away, he dresses up in the uniform of a Genoese knight and surprises Elvire in her room, hoping to take advantage of her confusion to rape her. His plan misfires. Elvire falls into a faint and soon after dies as a result of a fever caused by the incident; and Piachi returns unexpectedly early to catch Nicolo red-handed as he bends over the swooning Elvire. He orders Nicolo out of the house, whereupon Nicolo, a latter-day Tartuffe, orders *him* out of the house, for Piachi had made it over to him. The government, hand in glove with Nicolo's friends in the church, confirms that Piachi has no legal claim to the property and tells him to leave Nicolo alone. Anger at this and at the death of his wife drives him headlong to Nicolo's house, where he finds the foundling, attacks him, crushes his skull against a wall, and stuffs the document with the government's pronouncement into Nicolo's mouth. He then hands himself over to justice and is condemned to be hanged. The law of Rome at that time required that no criminal could be executed until he had received absolution. But Piachi refuses absolution, for he wants to be sure of going to hell, so that he can pursue the ghost of Nicolo there. Eventually a blind eye is turned to the provisions of the law, and Piachi is strung up in a deserted, and therefore rather ironically named, Piazza del Popolo.

Der Findling was published in the second volume of the *Erzählungen* in 1811. It would appear to be one of Kleist's earliest works, even though he may well have written much of it to provide copy for the second volume of stories.³ The structure overall seems looser, the style more discursive. Elvire, albeit not unlike the Marquise von O. and Littegarde in *Der Zweikampf*, is a more shadowy figure less finely drawn. Piachi is, as it were, a raw version of Michael Kohlhaas, seeking justice via a revenge that is erected by the end of the story into an absolute principle transcending the limitations of time and space imposed by this world. The role of chance and the unrelieved pessimism at the end echo the atmosphere of Kleist's early play *Die Familie Schroffenstein*. *Der Findling* is told in a straightforward manner, and the only interpolated incidents are the account of the adolescent Elvire's rescue by the patrician Colino, and Nicolo's shortlived venture into the respectability of marriage to Constanze Parquet, a niece of Elvire, who dies in childbirth. The story contains some good scenes, the midnight burial of Constanze Parquet being a splendid example, but they tend to stand on their own, and overall there is less concentration and build-up of tension than in some of the other stories. All this may point to its relatively early conception. The fact remains however that it first appeared in 1811, and conjectures as to when it was drafted and written must remain more or less inspired guesswork.

It may be possible to trace distant echoes of works by other writers in *Der Findling*.⁴ But the work to which it owes most is quite clearly Molière's *Tartuffe*, and indeed in the text Nicolo is explicitly compared once to Tartuffe. A comparison of the two works is highly illuminating. Tartuffe is a bigot and a sensualist; so is Nicolo. He has designs on his patron's wife, hopes to marry his patron's daughter, and his presence leads to an estrangement between that man and his son; Nicolo has lustful feelings towards his foster-mother, marries his foster-mother's niece, and takes the place in the family of his foster-father's son. Tartuffe orders Orgon out of the house he has got

---

³ Sembdner, *Werke*, II, p.907, quotes the beginning of a story by C. Baechler in the *Gemeinnützige Unterhaltungsblätter* of 24 April 1810, which has marked similarities to the beginning of *Der Findling*, and suggests that Kleist may have been influenced by it. This would mean that Kleist wrote the finished version of his story after that date.

⁴ Sembdner, *Werke*, II, p.907, mentions Lessing and the Roman writer Hyginus; Kurt Gassen, *Die Entwicklung der novellistischen Kompositionstechnik Kleists bis zur Meisterschaft*, Diss., Leipzig, 1911, suggests A.G. Meissner's story *Diego de Colmenares*, contained in *Skizzen*, 2 Sammlung, 1783.

from him, and Nicolo does the same to Piachi, and in both cases lawyers give their support to these proceedings. Here the similarities between the two works end. Molière's comedy is set within a particular social context, and the portrayal of character and the criticism of social attitudes does not rest on a metaphysical basis. Furthermore, Tartuffe is finally unmasked, thanks to the deus-ex-machina intervention of an all-wise monarch, and the comedy ends with a genuflection to Louis XIV. How different is Kleist's tragic story! *Der Findling* does not enjoy the security of a social order ultimately based on law and reason – Berlin in 1811 was different from Paris in 1669. A nihilistic atmosphere predominates, with all the main characters dying, and with the plague at the beginning finding its counterpart in the vista of hell at the end. The irrational elements of human behaviour are stressed, and events are apparently conditioned by chance. The psychological relationships between the three main characters are given an added, far more problematic twist. The whole basis of human existence is questioned, and the final sense of desolation is underlined by the silent execution in a deserted Piazza del Popolo.

This execution is reminiscent of an anecdote written by Kleist and published in the *Berliner Abendblätter* on 30 November 1810. It is worth quoting in full, both to demonstrate the, here literal, gallows humour and sense of paradox Kleist injects into his wonderfully concise and pregnant anecdotes, and also to show how such an incident, piquantly and paradoxically related to achieve a telling, momentary effect, can be expanded and its potential developed on the wider plane of a Novelle broaching issues of metaphysical and social import:

> A Capuchin monk accompanied a Swabian on a very rainy day to the gallows. On the way there the condemned man raised frequent complaints to God that he had to undertake such a dismal walk in such wretched and cheerless weather. The Capuchin, seeking to offer him Christian comfort, said to him: you oaf, why are you making such a fuss, you only have to go there, while I've got to turn round in this weather and come all the way back. – Whoever has experienced how desolate, even on

a fine day, returning from the place of execution can be, will not find what the Capuchin said so stupid.

Der Findling centres around three fascinating characters. In this story Kleist again shows the incalculable nature of human reactions and the extremes of conduct indulged in by apparently normal human beings. Nicolo is the embodiment of evil, a satanic character and aptly named, if the fanciful notion of a critic that his name derives from Old Nick is to be believed.[5] He is a foundling, picked up by chance, and constitutes an imported element in the story. As in *Die Verlobung* with Gustav and in *Die Marquise von O.* with Graf F., so here an established pattern is broken up by the emergence of a foreign body, something alien. Nicolo too is a 'Fremder'. His entrance into the story is via death, for he is infected by the plague and gives it to Piachi's son, thus killing him. The plague is symbolic of him, the symbol of something diseased, undermining and destructive.[6] He has no roots and no allegiances. He looks both evil and handsome, with black hair and black eyes: 'Er war von einer besonderen, etwas starren Schönheit, seine schwarzen Haare hingen ihm, in schlichten Spitzen, von der Stirn herab, ein Gesicht beschattend, das, ernst und klug, seine Mienen niemals veränderte.'[7] Evil is attractive. Yet the corruption in him is on occasion shown in the 'häßliches Zucken seiner Oberlippe'.[8] His whole attitude is summed up in the description of his journey with Piachi back to Rome. He reacts taciturnly to the questions addressed to him by Piachi. And while from time to time tears fill Piachi's eyes as he thinks of his dead son, Nicolo silently takes a handful of nuts out of his pocket, puts them between his teeth, and cracks them open one by one. He is shown every kind of favour and kindness by Piachi and Elvire; and he

---

[5] Cf. Dietmar Nedde, *Untersuchungen zur Struktur von Dichtung an Novellen Heinrich von Kleists*, Diss., Göttingen, 1955, p.36.

[6] Cf. the negress in *Die Verlobung*, Graf Jakob der Rotbart in *Der Zweikampf*, and the play *Robert Guiskard*.

[7] 'He was handsome in a singular, rather set way, his black hair fell neat and straight over his forehead, shading a countenance whose earnest, intelligent features remained fixed and unchanging.'

[8] 'The ugly twitching of his upper lip.' Ulysses' upper lip also twitches in *Penthesilea*, line 2497.

repays them in the same way Congo Hoango repaid Herr Villeneuve. Nicolo has two main faults. Piachi disapproves of his bigotry, his tendency to associate with monks and ministers of the church – not for nothing is this substitute for Piachi's son called 'Gottes Sohn' i.e. the priest's son. But at the end of the story Piachi is just as deaf to the voice of reason and just as stubborn and singleminded as Nicolo was; in other words, after the encounter with Nicolo he takes over Nicolo's fault. And the other fault of Nicolo is the one that Elvire, significantly enough, disapproves of, namely, his sensuality, his all too precocious 'Hang für das weibliche Geschlecht', his 'partiality for the female sex'. But this fault is one that he will direct against her.

This is highly interesting. As a result of the contact with Nicolo, the chance foundling, both Piachi and Elvire are going to be exposed to the faults they find in him. One might go further. Nicolo may well represent a satanic, evil element. But one is bound to probe more deeply into the characters of Piachi and Elvire and to ask if perhaps they project their faults on to the foundling boy, faults that might never have been exposed had not Nicolo come along.

Nicolo is the victim of lust, and when only fifteen years old the unstable youth falls a prey to the bishop's ex-mistress Xaviera Tartini.[9] This lust is something destructive and sterile, associated with death, as is well brought out in the macabre episode when his wife is buried without his knowledge and he comes to the church where the funeral is being held expecting to keep an appointment with his mistress. His passions oscillate between lust and hate. He applies his intellect to his own evil ends and, as with Goethe's Mephistopheles, mere intellect without a leavening of nobler human emotion proves negative and destructive. He finally thinks in terms of an incestuous relationship with his foster-mother; and he turns his foster-father out of house and home. To this end the institution of earthly law and justice is

---

[9] The name Tartini is an ingenious allusion to the celebrated sonata 'Il Trillo del Diavolo', the 'Devil's Trill', written by Giuseppe Tartini (1692-1770). Tartini married the ward of a cardinal, was angrily pursued and was subsequently forgiven by him. For the metaphysical aspects of *Der Findling*, see Werner Hoffmeister, 'Heinrich von Kleists *Findling*', *Monatshefte* 58, 1966.

perverted, and this is symbolically underlined by Piachi's ramming the legal resolution down the throat of the murdered Nicolo. An aura of destruction and nihilism accompanies Nicolo, he is the satanic element in life, the 'höllischer Bösewicht', the 'infernal villain', who bursts into the calm and placid middle-class life of Piachi and Elvire.

Elvire is the spiritual sister of the Marquise von O. and Littegarde, another woman in whom the angel-devil aspects of love and passion are mirrored. But in Elvire's case this dichotomy is made to appear decidedly more suspect. She is, to quote phrases used of her during the course of the story, 'good', 'admirable' and 'loyal', she is physically 'beautiful', she is a 'paragon of virtue', has 'fine, sensitive feelings' ('ein schönes und empfindliches Gemüt'), and also has a 'pure soul', a 'reine Seele'. She seems the very paragon of a virtuous Christian lady. She is not strong, and has periodic attacks of fever, when she retires to her room and is not seen for some days. There is a mystery about her, she seems to harbour some secret. Nicolo calls her a hypocrite, a 'Scheinheilige'. And in a sense she is, for she leads a double existence, as the wife of Piachi, and as someone who cherishes a secret love. In her bedroom is a portrait of Colino, in his attire as a Genoese knight, a portrait specially lit by a concealed light and covered by a red silken curtain. It is Elvire's practice to retire to her bedroom, to draw back the silken curtain from the portrait, and to prostrate herself in adoration before it, calling in heartbroken tones on her beloved, the dead Colino. Extraordinary behaviour for a virtuous, happily married, middle-class lady! Elvire lives in the past, she worships at the altar of the dead Colino, the romantic knight who saved her from a burning building on the edge of the harbour, as she stood poised between death in the flames of the building and death in the unfathomable deep. Characteristic of Kleist are these symbols of fire and water, here meant to indicate the sensual awakenings of adolescence, the flames of desire and the threatening ocean of the unconscious. For three years Elvire tended Colino, until heaven stepped in and he died, 'durch eine unbegreifliche Schickung des Himmels', 'through the unfathomable workings of divine providence', as Kleist drily remarks, though the efforts of the doctors in digging bones out of his head may also have been responsible. And Elvire virtually dies with him. She never awakens sexually. She marries a businessman old enough to be her father, and the whole relationship is built up not so much on passionate love as on the quiet affection of a father-daughter relationship. Small wonder that Elvire succumbs to a 'hitziges Fieber', a violent fever, immediately following their marriage. The nervous attacks that any memory of Colino occasions can only be assuaged by her retiring to her room, where she can gaze on his portrait. Piachi never talks about this, and a veil of secrecy covers the whole affair. The couple pursue their quiet life together, and under normal conditions it is a perfectly happy marriage, though hardly a passionate one. One might hazard the guess that in their case the demon sex is, as it were, kept discreetly and firmly under lock and key.

And then, as it were, sex incarnate walks in through the front door in the person of Nicolo, the physical double of Elvire's romantic rescuer – but Nicolo is no romantic, and Elvire soon senses this. She regrets his 'Hang für das weibliche Geschlecht', deplores his unhealthy attachment to Xaviera Tartini, is glad when he is apparently safely married off to a niece of hers; and she awakens in Nicolo a lustful passion which is something she has never before had to face, because such desires have been relegated to a very low place in her own subconscious. In Colino and Nicolo the angel and devil[10] aspects of love are embodied, and their close relationship and interdependence is underlined by the fact that their names are anagrammatically linked. Both represent, as far as Elvire is concerned, extremes, distortions of the twin aspects of love, on the one hand an unreal romantic vision, on the other the embodiment of evil lust. Elvire cannot face up to reality. Her life is one-sided, it is basically false, because it is directed to the past, to the idealising (the 'Vergötterung') of a romantic vision. Her life is spent in the worship of a picture[11] of a man who has been dead twelve years, and the emotional side of her life, inasfar as it is not consumed in this sterile way, is

[10] On the angel and devil aspects of love see the chapter on *Die Marquise von O.*, p.69.
[11] For a fascinating variation on this theme see the story by Thomas Hardy, *Barbara of the House of Grebe*.

suppressed. The Marquise von O. has the inner strength eventually to come to terms with the angel-devil aspects of love. The Colino/Nicolo dualism is too much for Elvire. When Nicolo perpetrates his cruel trick and, dressed as Colino, steps out of the picture frame and advances on Elvire, the reality of it is too much for her and it kills this 'short-sighted' ('kurzsichtig') woman. She falls unconscious, succumbs to another 'hitziges Fieber', and dies. The 'hitziges Fieber' of her wedding night has finally overtaken her and brought about her death.

And what of the third party in this unnatural triangle? Piachi deplores Nicolo's bigotry; yet at the end of the story he is a creature with one obsession, that of revenge, and he is deaf to the voice of reason and the precepts of religion. An astonishing change has been wrought in this man by the impact of the satanic outsider on his life. No doubt he is infected with the plague from the first moment he sets eyes on Nicolo and Nicolo clasps his hand beseeching help, even though he shows no signs of physical illness. Certainly this contact produces effects later, as the spiritual contagion emanating from Nicolo invades his household. Piachi is a good, kindly man whose roots are in the world of business and material possessions – it is on a business trip that he loses his son and returns instead with the substitute Nicolo. He lives a cosy, comfortable existence with his wife Elvire, to whom he shows kindness and affection. But this is a limited, narrow kind of life, adequate as long as its even tenor is not disturbed, but vulnerable to threats from outside. Its very self-sufficiency is a challenge to evil and the force of passion, an invitation to fate to step in and show up its limitations. What right, one might ask, has Piachi, like Orgon in *Tartuffe*, to be so blind to the possibility of things going wrong that he piles benefits on his obviously unstable foster-son, thus courting disaster? He pays for his folly and blindness, well-intentioned though it may be. When disaster does strike he is a man transformed. Kleist shows here the extremes of behaviour human beings are capable of and how thin, as in the case of Piachi, is the line that divides middle-class bourgeois respectability from violence and a satanic lust for revenge. Perhaps the 'plague' was always part of Piachi, and Nicolo, far from infecting him

Der Findling

with it, was the agent that brought it to the surface. Once he arrives the whole world of Piachi crumbles and is seen to be, in its own way, a sham. Why does Piachi kill Nicolo and wish to pursue his revenge even beyond the grave? Perhaps it is the businessman's anger at being tricked out of his property; or the citizen's indignation at the corrupt legal system that cynically condones injustice. Perhaps it is a sense of guilt at being initially responsible, if only indirectly, for the death of his son and for adopting the substitute foundling. Perhaps it is jealousy of a sexual rival, concealed behind the mask of offended bourgeois respectability. Perhaps it is anger at his own folly and idiocy. Kleist nowhere explicitly states such reasons. But he is a clever enough writer to drop hints that make these speculations in the reader's mind possible and perhaps permissible. Whatever the reasons for Piachi's conduct, at the end of the story his whole world is in ruins. There is no Louis XIV to pick up the pieces and put them together again.

Such an approach to the characters might suggest that Kleist was writing a psychological story. This would be misleading. There can be no doubt that Kleist does probe into the psychology of his characters in a far more subtle and conscious way than he is usually given credit for, and merely to treat his stories as metaphysical blueprints would be absurd. Character certainly interests him; but so do events and the problematic view of life and society mirrored in them. *Der Findling* is concerned with wider issues, which may be briefly summarised here, for they occur in some form or other in most of the stories. There is the way in which two apparently 'normal' people react when something utterly unexpected intrudes into their lives. Things are not what they seem to be, and characters, albeit unconsciously, lead a life of deception and self-deception. There is the motif of a secret, that of Elvire, cruelly brought to the light of day. Characters find it difficult to communicate, the world of Piachi and Elvire is to some extent built on a deception, a conspiracy of silence, and when reality bursts in on this world it kills the one and makes the other a monster of revenge. The range and extremes of human behaviour are brought out in the motif of the Doppelgänger, Nicolo is the mirror image of Colino, a chance arrangement of letters produces now the one name, now the other. The motif of rape occurs here, as it does in *Die Marquise von O.*, causing the death of Elvire and indirectly that of Nicolo.

Chance plays a considerable role in *Der Findling*, and the phrases 'zufällig' and 'es traf sich', 'by chance' and 'it so happened', occur frequently. It is chance that Piachi happened to be making a business trip to Ragusa at the time the plague broke out. It is chance that Nicolo wears the costume of a Genoese nobleman before he ever knew of the existence of Colino. It is chance that Piachi returns from yet another business trip unexpectedly early to discover Nicolo on the point of assaulting Elvire. It is chance that there is an anagrammatic link between the names Nicolo and Colino. The very title *Der Findling* underlines the role of chance, for it is mere chance that Nicolo is picked up by the side of the road. But it might equally well be maintained that the apparent intrusion of chance conceals the workings of a purposeful fate, and the operation of 'Zufall' brings out what is already implicit in a particular individual and social situation. Human institutions are not shown in a favourable light in *Der Findling*. Organised religion in the 'Kirchenstaat' of Rome is a pretty shoddy affair, manifesting itself in a world of greedy monks, bishops and their concubines. There is a grim kind of humour in the satirical way a priest is described at the end of the story trying to make Piachi receive absolution, depicting 'mit der Lunge der letzten Posaune' the 'last trump' and the horrors of hell. The institution of law is likewise the target of criticism. The lawyers, dubiously motivated, support Nicolo's claim to Piachi's house. There is irony in the fact that the law requiring criminals to receive absolution before execution has in the end to be quietly ignored, so that Piachi is perforce illegally hanged.[12] There is the theme of revenge, the vehicle through which Piachi seeks justice when human institutions fail and man, as it were, reverts to the jungle,[13] a revenge that goes

---

[12] Cf. the comic counterpart to this, the anecdote *Der verlegene Magistrat*, published in the *Berliner Abendblätter* on 4 October 1810, where a magistrate has to let an offender off scot-free rather than invoke the appropriate penalty, long since out-of-date, namely, the death penalty. Cf. p.88.

[13] Cf. Chapter 7 below on *Michael Kohlhaas*, p.131 and p.144 ff.

beyond the spatial and temporal limitations of this world as Piàchi goes hounding his prey along the corridors of hell.

These themes occur in *Der Findling* and it is not difficult to identify them. There may be blemishes in some of the motivation of the story, and the narrative may be more discursive than in other stories by Kleist. For all that it makes an extraordinary impact. The spectacle of evil, and the chaos and sense of desolation it occasions, is brought home in a very immediate fashion to the reader. As in *Die Marquise von O.*, so here a sheltered family milieu is the setting for the action. And here it is not, as in *Die Marquise von O.*, protected. It is blown sky-high.

5
Die Marquise von O.

Ich will keine andre Ehre mehr als deine Schande[1]

If a member of the aristocracy, a marchioness for example, put an advertisement in the personal column of a daily newspaper stating that she had without her knowledge become pregnant and that out of consideration for her family she would marry the father of the child she was to bear, if he would be so kind as to come forward, such an announcement might well cause a stir, even in the second half of the twentieth century. How much more startling an effect an announcement of this sort might have had on readers one hundred and fifty years ago! Yet this is precisely the situation with which Kleist chooses to open *Die Marquise von O.*, a story which first appeared in the second number of the journal *Phöbus* in February, 1808. Subscribers to the journal were already reeling under the impact of what Kleist called the 'organic fragment' of *Penthesilea*, which had appeared in the first number. And now they were regaled in the second number with the story of an aristocratic lady raped whilst unconscious and her reactions to the pregnant state in which she so inexplicably finds herself. They were shocked and scandalised. 'No young lady,' wrote Dora Stock, 'can read it without blushing', and Henriette von Knebel, writing to her brother from Weimar, said that it was a disgusting story, longwinded and boring to a degree.[2] Perhaps Kleist was taken aback by this reaction from outraged readers. He was certainly not amused; and he took revenge on the narrow-minded attitude of the public in a biting epigram:

---

[1] 'The only honour I want is your disgrace' – spoken to the Marquise by her mother after the two have been reconciled.
[2] Cf. Sembdner, *Lebensspuren*, pp. 173, 179 and 184.

Dieser Roman ist nicht für dich, meine Tochter. In Ohnmacht!
Schamlose Posse! Sie hielt, weiß ich, die Augen bloß zu.³

The readers of *Phöbus* may have had the last laugh, for the journal soon ran into financial difficulties and was wound up after twelve numbers had appeared. The offending story was then published in the first volume of the *Erzählungen* in October, 1810.

The story is as follows. The marchioness, a widow with two children, lives with her parents in the town of M. in northern Italy, where her father is commandant of the fortress. On the outbreak of war the garrison is attacked by hostile Russian forces at night, and overrun by them. The marchioness is forced by an outbreak of fire to seek shelter in another wing of the beleaguered fortress. She is intercepted by soldiers who drag her off with the obvious intention of assaulting her, when a Russian officer arrives in the nick of time to save her. She faints; and when she recovers consciousness the officer sees to her immediate needs and then rushes back into the heat of battle. Weeks pass, peace returns to the district as the campaign moves further south, and news arrives that the Russian officer, a count, has been killed in battle. The marchioness, usually a paragon of health, begins to have intermittent periods of sickness. One Sunday, to the astonishment of the family, the Russian count appears on the doorstep, is greeted in a surprised but friendly manner by those present, and promptly asks the marchioness to marry him. After initial consternation he extracts a very conditional promise from the lady and hastens off to his regiment, intending to return as soon as possible. More time passes, and the marchioness becomes convinced that she is inexplicably pregnant, a suspicion only too readily confirmed by a doctor and midwife. As a result of this her parents turn her out of the house and she retires to a small property of her own in the country. It is at this point she inserts the notice in the paper with which the story commences. The count comes back to

---

³ 'This novel is not for you, my daughter. Unconscious! Shameless trick! She merely closed her eyes.' *Werke*, I, p.22.

find this changed state of affairs. Shortly afterwards another notice appears in the paper, to the effect that if the marchioness is present at her father's house at 11 a.m. on a certain day the man she is looking for will throw himself at her feet. Fresh consternation! The marchioness, by now reconciled with her parents, is present at the appointed time with them and her brothers when in walks – the count! At this the marchioness reacts as if the devil had appeared in person, refuses to have anything to do with the count, sprinkles her family with holy water and rushes out of the room, leaving behind an astonished family and a shattered count. A marriage is arranged and takes place, but the count has to renounce all marital rights and is denied access to the marchioness. Gradually, by virtue of his correct behaviour, he is admitted to the family circle and the marchioness relents in her attitude to him. A year later a second, happier, wedding is held, and the couple live happily ever after. The marchioness tells the count why she reacted so violently at 11 a.m. on the fateful day: he would not, she says, have appeared to her as a devil then had he not, the very first time they met, seemed to her to be an angel.[4]

The theme of a woman being raped while unconscious and the consequences of this may appear to be somewhat scandalous. Yet it is a theme that appears elsewhere in literature and Kleist would not have had to look very far for sources for his story, always supposing he needed any. The idea of rape while the victim is unconscious or apparently dead would appear to be one of the archetypal themes of literature, reflecting possibly some suppressed desire or morbid fantasy on the part of men. Literature and folklore is studded with tales of divine and semi-divine offspring more or less immaculately conceived, heroines overpowered whilst unconscious by lustful gallants, drunken suitors and chance males miraculously rendered invisible, girls ravished while apparently dead only to clamber out of their coffins and produce children in due season, not to mention the incubi and

---

[4] The German sentence, characteristically conditionally phrased, is: 'Er würde ihr damals nicht wie ein Teufel erschienen sein, wenn er ihr nicht, bei seiner ersten Erscheinung, wie ein Engel vorgekommen wäre.'

succubi in which mediaeval legend abounds. Kleist may well have been familiar with the piquant story of a woman raped in her sleep told by Montaigne in his essay on drunkenness; he may have read Cervantes' *La fuerza della sangre*, where a Spanish nobleman rapes a young gentlewoman whilst she is unconscious, though there is no reason to suppose that he had or that he was influenced by it; but he is almost certain to have been familiar with a story 'Die gerettete Unschuld' which appeared in the *Berlinische Archiv der Zeit und ihres Geschmacks* in April, 1798, a story which deals with the rape of an apparently dead girl by a Bavarian merchant and the consequences of this, and which contains several phrases which appear almost word for word in Kleist's story.[5]

Sex and violence, and the mystery of divine conception are topics that deeply engaged Kleist's attention. They occur in four of his plays. The conflict between the sexes that underlies human love is one of the basic themes of *Penthesilea*, where the emotional crisis is mirrored in imagery oscillating between martial savagery and lyrical sweetness.[6] The attempted seduction of an innocent girl by a club-footed satyr in the shape of Judge Adam provides the basis for the comedy in *Der zerbrochne Krug*. The rape of the German girl Hally by Roman soldiers is cruelly and calculatingly exploited by Hermann in *Die Hermannsschlacht*. Alkmene is unknowingly seduced by the god Jupiter in *Amphitryon*, a play that deals with the human and divine aspects of love, the mystery of conception and the purity of a woman destined to bring forth the demi-god Heracles. The rehabilitation of an innocent girl seduced by a nobleman is given anecdotal treatment in *Sonderbare Geschichte, die sich, zu meiner Zeit, in Italien zutrug*, a story that appeared in the *Berliner Abendblätter* on 4 January, 1811 and that forms a humorous pendant to *Die Marquise von O*. Nicolo attempts to assault his foster-mother in *Der Findling*. Rape, seduction, the

---

[5] Alfred Klaar, *Heinrich von Kleist, Die Marquise von O. Die Dichtung und ihre Quellen*, Berlin, 1922, gives the text of 'Die gerettete Unschuld', and also Montaigne's essay on drunkenness, Essais, II, cap. 2, which is a possible source. In this essay a widow is raped by a young servant who finds her asleep after having drunk a great deal; she becomes pregnant, has it announced from the pulpit that she will marry the man who made her pregnant, marries the servant, and they live happily ever after.

[6] Cf. my article 'The Imagery in Kleist's *Penthesilea*', *PEGS*, 31, 1961.

mental torture of a woman exposed to a predicament with which her knowledge of the world is unable to cope, these are themes that occur in Kleist's works and they occur in *Die Marquise von O*.

The story is very carefully constructed. A flashback technique is used. After the startling opening sentence the events that lead up to the Marquise's decision to insert the announcement in the newspaper are recounted, and this takes up just over half the story.[7] The rest is concerned with the consequences of the Marquise's action, and the final solution of the whole affair. The story, then, falls readily into two parts: the rape and its physical consequences, and the discovery of the man responsible for the whole business. But this outward division of the story in fact reflects a more subtle division which corresponds to the inner processes going on within the mind of the Marquise. For the story centres around two conflicts with which the Marquise is faced and with which she has to come to terms. In the first place she has to accept the fact of her pregnancy and the resulting rupture with her family, and still retain a faith in herself and her own spiritual purity. This she does after a struggle. The second conflict she has to face, and an equally difficult one, is her relationship to Graf F. She may be convinced of her spiritual purity; but she still has to be confronted with her seducer and to face up to the ambivalent nature of love and the fallible nature of human action. These two conflicts are marked by two external events, around which they centre, namely, the actual rape, and the 'fürchterliche Dritte', the 'fearful third day of the month' when the Marquise has to meet the man who raped her.

In this way the story acquires an almost architectonic balance, as it revolves around the two crises in the mind of the Marquise. The basic structure is then modified and diversified by interpolated scenes and incidents which serve to pinpoint dominant themes in the story and to illustrate the characters of some of the persons appearing in it. Twice the count calls on the Marquise and her family as they sit in the family sitting-room; once at the beginning of the story when he so unexpectedly asks the Marquise to marry him, and then

---

[7] Twenty-three pages out of forty in Sembdner's edition, *Werke*, II.

at the end when he keeps his appointment at 11 a.m. on the third of the month, and a marriage of convenience is arranged. The two scenes are parallel yet contrasting, a formal pointing of issues dominant at the time they occur. Three scenes illustrate the character of the count: in one he describes how as a child he had thrown mud at a swan as it swam on the lake, and how the swan had submerged itself in the waters of the lake and re-appeared in all its glistening purity; in another Kleist tells how, immediately after the rape, the count helped put out a fire, rolling barrels of gunpowder to safety and running around with a dripping fire hose in his hand; and the reader is told how news reached the family that the count had died in battle with the words on his lips 'Julietta! Diese Kugel rächt dich!', 'Julietta! This bullet avenges you!' – the Marquise is called Julietta. Childhood urges, the flaring up of passion during the siege of the fortress, and apparent atonement through death in battle; and at the end of the story the spectacle of the count patiently waiting outside the church for a sign of forgiveness from the woman he has married. The whole development of a character is summed up in scenes like these. The problem of truth and the conflict between conscious awareness and intuitive knowledge is pinpointed in the scene between the Marquise and the midwife who pronounces her pregnant. The relationship between the Marquise and her father is marked by two scenes, one in which he tries to shoot her and the other in which he is reconciled to her, both scenes charged with sexual symbolism. Significant phrases link the story. When the count rescues the Marquise from the licentious soldiery he appears to her like an angel from heaven; at 11 a.m. on the 'fürchterliche Dritte' he seems to her the incarnation of the devil; and angel and devil are linked together in the paradoxical sentence with which the story closes.

The structure of the story is complicated by the fact that it is narrated from various standpoints. In the first place it is told from the standpoint of the narrator himself, who comments explicitly and implicitly on the action and characters. But it is told as well from the varying standpoints of the count, the Marquise's father, her mother and the Marquise herself. This technique of changing perspectives gives variety to the story, in itself arresting enough, and ensures that the basic problems are treated in a more subtle and complicated manner against a background of shifting planes of reality. These problems are brought more sharply into relief by the time factor in the story. The narrative centres around two moments in time, the rape and the fateful third of the month, and is marked by the flashback technique starting with the newspaper announcement and then explaining the events leading up to it. Events are thus related with one eye to the past and one eye to the future, details gain significance through what has happened or what will happen and a curiously ambivalent presentation of reality results.[8] The actual progress of the plot, however, is conditioned by the state in which the Marquise finds herself. Whatever the themes in the story – psychological, spiritual, metaphysical – they are in the last resort dependent on a physiological process, the pregnancy of the Marquise. This sets a very real time limit on the story and is the fact that knits it together.

One final fact may be noted which governs the way the story is told. Here, as in so many of his plays and stories, Kleist uses the device of a secret, a puzzling situation, around which everything revolves, a technique exploited most obviously in *Der Zweikampf*. This detective-story device is employed in *Die Marquise von O.* – but with a difference. For here the secret is an open secret. The reader cannot long remain in doubt as to who in fact is responsible for the Marquise's condition. The fact that the secret is an open one determines the way the story is told and gives it its distinctive stamp. It means that Kleist can indulge his gift of irony. The story of rape and violence, of the spiritual anguish of a woman called upon to face an incomprehensible situation, is, as will be seen more fully later, treated ironically.

Die Marquise von O. is concerned with the themes of knowledge and truth, of the conflict between appearances and the reality that lies behind them, of the conflict within a person between reason and emotion, rational knowledge and intuition. The Marquise has to maintain her faith in her

---

[8] Well brought out in the article by Walter Müller-Seidel, 'Die Struktur des Widerspruchs in Kleists *Marquise von O.*', *DVS*, 28 (1954), pp. 497-515.

integrity, despite the evidence with which she is confronted. The problem, drastically posed by Kleist, is most clearly stated in the masterly scene between the Marquise and her mother, following on the visit of the doctor. The Marquise says her conscience is clear, despite the pronouncement of the doctor, and her mother reassures her, saying 'Wenn dein Bewußtsein dich rein spricht, wie kann dich ein Urteil, und wäre es das einer ganzen Konsulta von Ärzten, nur kümmern?' Yet the Marquise feels the sensations of pregnancy and so says 'Hab' ich nicht mein eignes, innerliches, mir nur allzuwohlbekanntes Gefühl gegen mich?' She insists that her conscience is as pure as that of her two children; but suggests that for all that her mother should summon a midwife. 'Eine Hebamme!' the mother cries, 'Ein reines Bewußtsein, und eine Hebamme!' – and words fail her. The problem of appearances and reality could hardly be more sharply and paradoxically stated. A pure conscience – and a midwife.[9]

The teasing problem is pursued further. The mother tells her daughter that for her to claim to be innocent is to deny all the laws of nature, and says that such a story is nothing less than a 'Märchen von der Umwälzung der Weltordnung', a 'fairy-story standing the whole order of the world on its head'. The same idea is echoed by the very matter-of-fact midwife when she says that the only person she has heard of who conceived unwittingly was the Virgin Mary. Yet when the mother later becomes convinced of her daughter's innocence she is prepared to believe in a miracle rather than credit any impure action on her part. She addresses her as 'du Reinere als Engel sind', 'more pure than the angels', says she is 'von Unschuld umstrahlt', 'irradiated with innocence', calls her a saint, compares her to a supernatural being, and caps it all by declaring 'ich will keine andre Ehre mehr als deine Schande'. Such is the astonishing reversal of values brought about by the innocence and integrity of the Marquise and such are the radical consequences of the count's intrusion into the life of

---

[9] Translation of the passages in this paragraph: 'If your consciousness proclaims your purity, how can a medical opinion, even if it were the opinion of a whole army of doctors, bother you at all?'; 'Do not my own innermost feelings, which are only too familiar to me, argue against me?'; 'A midwife! A pure conscience, and a midwife!'

this family that the mother is prepared to go back on the whole code of morality in which she has been brought up and find honour in her daughter's disgrace! The appearance is rejected in favour of the reality which lies behind it.

The purity and integrity of the Marquise is by implication compared to that of the Virgin Mary, echoing the allusions to the Virgin in *Das Erdbeben* and *Die Verlobung*.[10] Kleist is careful not to push the comparison too closely. There is after all a difference between a virgin who conceives by the Holy Ghost and a widowed mother of two children who is raped whilst unconscious. The Marquise's unborn child appears in her eyes to be 'all the more divine in origin because of the mystery surrounding its conception' – 'dessen Ursprung, eben weil er geheimnisvoller war, auch göttlicher zu sein schien'. Both this phrase and the remark of the midwife referred to in the previous paragraph were added by Kleist to the 1810 version of the story and make it clear that in alluding to the Virgin he was anxious to underline the fundamental purity of the Marquise, to broach the mystery of parthenogenesis, and to state, by reference to an absolute example, the value of inner purity and integrity in a world dominated by appearances. Faith in her inner purity is only won by the Marquise after a hard conflict that brings her to the brink of despair and leads to her isolation and rejection at the hands of her parents. She regains her faith in herself when she defies her father's orders to leave her children in his care and takes them with her to her country seat. Mother love gives her back her faith in herself, the unselfish action on behalf of the children restores her sense of perspective. The result is beautifully put by Kleist: 'Durch diese schöne Anstrengung mit sich selbst bekannt gemacht, hob sie sich plötzlich, wie an ihrer eignen Hand, aus der ganzen Tiefe, in welche das Schicksal sie herabgestürzt hatte, empor'.[11]

'Mit sich selbst bekannt gemacht' – herein lies the crux of Kleist's approach to the problem of knowledge. It is not only

---

[10] Cf. above, p.21, and p.45. The concept of divine conception is also broached in the final scene of the play *Amphitryon*.

[11] 'Having by means of these courageous exertions become aware of herself, she was suddenly able to take hold of herself, as it were, and raise herself up from the very depths into which fate had plunged her.'

the baffling contradictions between the world of appearances and the world of reality that he is concerned with, large though this aspect of the problem looms in his work. Over and above this there is the problem of self-knowledge, the consciousness that a character may have of his or her integrity, based not only on blind, unreasoning faith, but also on an awareness of the fragile and fallible nature of the world and the conflicting emotions of the human personality, a self-knowledge won through hard experience after an encounter with despair and the goal to which many of Kleist's characters, consciously or unconsciously, proceed.[12] This self-knowledge the Marquise has gained, she has survived the crisis within herself and accepted unquestioningly the 'mysterious and inscrutable scheme of things', submitting to 'der großen, heiligen und unerklärlichen Einrichtung der Welt'.

But this is not the end of the story. 'Mit sich selbst bekannt' the Marquise may be. But she still has to come to terms with the count. And this leads to the consideration of another basic issue in *Die Marquise von O.*, the problem of human emotions, particularly the emotion of love.

Love has featured in the stories already dealt with, where it has ended in tragedy, either owing to the impossibility of true love flowering in a convention-ridden society or to the inability of a person to let his trust in the person he loves rise superior to the confusions and misunderstandings of the world in which he lives. But there is more to the treatment of love than this, and a hint has been given in the Nicolo/Colino relationship in *Der Findling*. The clue to the problem is contained in the final sentence of *Die Marquise*, where the count is said to have appeared now as an angel and now as a devil.

In talking of the angel-devil aspects of love Kleist is indicating the contrasting extremes of attitude and conduct through which this emotion may be manifested and of which the character concerned may or may not be conscious. The extent to which a character develops may hinge on whether he

---

[12] As does Homburg in *Prinz Friedrich von Homburg*; Penthesilea in the final scene of *Penthesilea*; and Littegarde in *Der Zweikampf*.

or she becomes aware of these extremes of emotion and learns to accept them, thus creating a balance, an emotional equilibrium. If such a balance is achieved then it may well turn out that what a character interpreted as extremes only appeared to be so, they were the projections of his or her own one-sided view of things. It is interesting to see how Kleist discusses human nature, both from the point of morals and emotions, in a little-noticed essay published under a pseudonym in the *Berliner Abendblätter* between 29 October and 10 November 1810. In this 'Allerneuester Erziehungsplan', as the essay is titled, Kleist proceeds from the fact that in physics different charges of electricity, positive and negative, plus and minus, attract one another, and that if an electrically charged body is placed next to an uncharged one a flow of electricity from one to the other will result in a state of equilibrium being established. Kleist then applies this physical law to the moral world, saying that if a person of neutral qualities comes into contact with a person of, say, plus qualities he will be activated by the contact, but in the opposite way, i.e. he will acquire minus qualities, and a field of plus and minus (or positive and negative) qualities will then be set up. This law of plus and minus he then applies not only to moral qualities of good and bad, but also to the realm of feelings, emotions, traits of character. Good qualities in one person provoke bad qualities in another, love provokes hate, human relationships are governed by the 'law of contradiction', 'das gemeine Gesetz des Widerspruchs'. This 'Polarverhältnis' ('polar relationship') in human nature, as he calls it, is most important when it comes to assessing Kleist's characters. They tend to be more complicated than at first sight they appear to be. Apparently neutral, they may swing over into extremes of plus or minus. And, at least in the case of some of them, their development may be concerned with establishing a balance, reconciling, as it were, plus with minus. The idea of equilibrium, of establishing a balance, is important for Kleist, and is shown in his use of imagery concerned with balance and equilibrium and in his fondness for the contrasting algebraic symbols of plus and minus.[13]

---

[13] Cf. my article ' "Plus and Minus" in Kleist', *Oxford German Studies*, vol.2, 1967.

Die Marquise von O.

Kleist may appear to be a poet of extremes. He is also concerned with balancing out the extremes within a particular character.

The angel aspect of love is embodied in those idealised heroes who appear as knights in shining armour to defend some lady in distress, such as Colino, Graf F. (as he first appeared to the Marquise), and Friedrich von Trota in *Der Zweikampf*. Love becomes spiritualised and wears a halo, it is supremely unselfish, it establishes a link with the divine. But there is also the devil aspect of love, love as sex, as passion, as lust, which sweeps away reason and conventions, a threatening destroyer, embodied in characters such as Nicolo, Graf Jakob der Rotbart (in *Der Zweikampf*), and the Graf F. who rapes the Marquise. Similar contrasts are found in the plays, for example in *Penthesilea*, where love is equated now with the sun god, and now with the passions of wild animals, or in *Amphitryon* and *Der zerbrochne Krug* where the divine and devilish aspects of love are embodied, in part at least, in the god Jupiter and the club-footed Adam. And who are the ladies to whom love presents such frightening aspects? How harmless, conventional and bourgeois they are! There is Elvire (*Der Findling*), a woman living on past memories of her dead Colino. There is Littegarde (*Der Zweikampf*), a retired widow, about to enter a convent. And there is the Marquise von O., a widow with two children living with her parents. These are the women so cruelly put to the test. They are lifted out of their sheltered existence and confronted with the reality of an emotion with which they had previously been acquainted only in its more tender and self-effacing form. The Marquise has to face such a test. Who is she?

She is a widow, devoted to the memory of her husband, dead some three years, the mother of two children, whom she has 'brought up well', 'wohlerzogen' as Kleist goes out of his way to say. She lives 'in der größten Eingezogenheit', 'in the greatest seclusion', and is firmly determined never to marry again. She lives a conventional life with her children, her brother and her parents, dabbling a little in cultural activities, trying her hand at painting, reading books. Such a life of conventional withdrawal, where excess of emotion is carefully kept at bay, seems ideally suited to be the target of some unexpected invasion of passion. It may be an exaggeration to talk of represssions. But in retrospect the carefully regulated widowhood of the Marquise seems almost a hostage to fortune, a temptation to fate. Her purity is stressed, as is her selfless love for her children, and the humility with which she accepts the pregnancy so strangely forced upon her. But the pride which leads her to resolve on a life of 'ewig klösterliche Eingezogenheit', of 'eternal monastic seclusion', once she has had the bastard child, and the 'feeling of self-sufficiency', the 'Gefühl der Selbständigkeit', that encourages her to put the announcement in the newspaper may be double-edged, courting disaster. Her feelings to the count are by no means clear. One need not take the epigram Kleist wrote on the whole business too seriously and speak of her desire, conscious or unconscious, to be raped.[14] Some initial attraction she no doubt feels towards Graf F. When he makes his startling proposal of marriage she says she likes and dislikes him ('er gefällt und mißfällt mir'), but is prepared, because of the service he rendered her (!) during the siege, to marry him, and her eyes shine ('ihre Augen glänzten') as she says this. But when the count arrives to see her at her country retreat, disturbing the peace she has so carefully built up, she tries to keep him at arm's length, although by now she might well make an intelligent guess as to the true state of affairs. She is unwilling to face up to reality and recognise rape for what it is. This accounts for the violence of her reaction when the count does actually present himself as the guilty party, appearing now to her as a devil, as someone contaminated with the plague ('pestvergiftet'), so that she sprinkles her family and herself with holy water against his influence. The confrontation with reality catches her off balance. The basic instability and inadequacy of her ideas and experience stands revealed. The emotion of love is equated by her with absolutes. At first the count has 'appeared' to her as an angel. And consequently she swings to the opposite extreme and he now 'appears' to her as a devil. She has to learn to accept both

---

[14] Dorrit Kohn, in her stimulating article 'Kleist's *Marquise von O.*: The problem of knowledge', *Monatshefte* 67, 1975, investigates the conscious and subconscious levels of awareness on the part of the Marquise.

sides of the count and the emotions he embodies, to accept him as a complete and loved person, fallible as the world is fallible, this world with its 'gebrechliche Einrichtung'. Fires were raging in the fortress when the count rescued her from the soldiers, symbolic fires indeed in view of what happened immediately afterwards. These 'fires' the Marquise has to come to terms with. The world is no place for absolutes, angel and devil, rescuing knight and sinful lover are merged in one and the same person, a loving and loved human being. This is the education the Marquise undergoes. At the end of the story she has retained her inner purity, her consciousness is widened, she is completely integrated with the world of reality. The balance is restored.

In *Der Findling* the angel-devil aspects of love are embodied in two persons, Colino and Nicolo, and the interdependence of these Doppelgänger is stressed by their being anagrammatically linked. In *Die Marquise von O.* the two aspects are located in one man, the count.

Graf F. is a young Russian officer, brave, impetuous, sensuous and honourable. The fact that he is Russian underlies the foreign element, the touch of the exotic that he brings into the story. His bravery during the siege of the fortress is stressed, along with disregard of personal safety as he fights the fires and rolls away the barrels of gunpowder. His sensuousness is indicated in the motif of fire and flames that accompanies him, the 'feurige Fluten' the swan Thinka glided over when he threw mud at it, the background of fire as he rapes the Marquise, his scarlet face as he protests his love for Julietta, blushing as he does so. His impetuosity is brought out in the way he woos her, though the reader knows he is hurrying against a time limit imposed by pregnancy. Mention is made of his 'heftiger, auf einen Punkt hintreibender Wille' and his 'auf Kurierpferden gehende Bewerbung', and the family are agreed 'daß er Damenherzen durch Anlauf, wie Festungen, zu erobern gewohnt scheine',[15] though the irony of these words is lost on them. His sense of honour is also

---

[15] 'His willpower, which was headstrong and quite single-minded'; 'post-haste courting at the double'; 'that he seemed accustomed to capture ladies' hearts, like fortresses, by storm.'

indicated. He regrets his 'einzige, nichtswürdige Handlung', his 'one base action', and tries to remedy it. He accepts death in battle as an atonement. His tendency to blush, a characteristic Kleistian touch, also indicates a sense of shame.

The soldiers who assaulted the Marquise during the siege are ordered to be shot by the general in command. They attempted to do what the count actually did, and their execution is by implication a condemnation of his own misdemeanour. On the same day they are shot the count is caught in a skirmish with enemy forces and apparently receives a mortal wound. Later, when he so unexpectedly turns up at the family home to woo the Marquise, the family protests he is supposed to be dead and he asserts he is very much alive. To all intents and purposes he has risen from the dead. This motif of rebirth is crucial for the understanding of the character of the count. He becomes in effect a new man, and this is borne out at the end, when, his impetuosity cured by months of patient waiting, he is at last forgiven and welcomed into the bosom of the family – and himself becomes a family man, the father of a string of young Russians.

The theme of love is treated variously as it affects the Marquise and the count, and both acquire self-knowledge in the process. Love is depicted in other ways as well. There is the maternal love of the Marquise for her children, a love that strengthens her faith in herself. And there is the issue of parental love, the emotional ties between the Marquise and her parents. This too is treated by Kleist in terms of extremes. When the mother hears the midwife's pronouncement on the Marquise's condition and fails to discover from her daughter who the father is she reacts melodramatically, cursing the day she gave birth to Julietta and sweeping in high dudgeon out of the room. But when convinced of her daughter's innocence she goes, as has been seen, to the other extreme, calling her a saint and revelling in her disgrace in the teeth of what the world will say. Even more extraordinary is the way the relationship of the Marquise to her father is depicted. There is a strong hint of an unconscious incest motif. On the death of her husband she returned to live with her father – 'zu ihrem Vater zurückgekehrt'. He runs the family. He loves her, but carefully avoids showing this – he never let her sit on his lap, the reader is informed. He is clearly annoyed by the count's courtship, and just as clearly jealous of him. His conduct, under the impact of something that breaks through all his conventional standards, expresses itself in extremes of love and hate. He fires a revolver at his daughter – a sexual act, one might say – he tries to rob her of her children, and resorts to extreme language of hate and violence when speaking of her. But when he is reconciled to her his remorse shows itself in an extreme expression of overt love, physically expressed and described in detail almost painful to read as he bends over the Marquise to kiss her, fondles her, and plays with her hand at table.[16]

Yet another instance of barriers being broken down and another insight into human love and passion is given in this picture of the amorous father, the army officer, embracing his daughter, a widow with two children, like a lover; and it is a picture that contrasts oddly with the bourgeois background against which it is set, with his wife cooking his favourite dishes for supper, putting hot-water bottles in his bed, and peeping through the keyhole to see how father and daughter are getting on!

When the Marquise consults a doctor she asks him 'scherzend', 'jokingly', what he thinks. He tells her she is pregnant. She asks him not to 'scherzen'; and he retorts that he wishes she had always shown herself so disinclined to joke, 'zum Scherze'. But it is hardly a joke, and the Marquise is faced not only with social ostracism and exclusion from the family circle, but also with abandonment to despair and loss of faith in herself. This contrasting of 'Scherz' and 'Ernst' brings out the underlying irony of the story. The irony is its hallmark, and it is this that makes it a great story.[17]

There is in the first place the basic irony of the situation. A member of the aristocracy advertises in a newspaper to find out who is the father of her child. Yet she had no need to do this, did she but know it, for the count has already presented himself and asked for her hand in marriage. When she does find out it is the count who raped her, the scene in the family

---

[16] No doubt strongly influenced by the erotic scene between father and daughter in Rousseau's *Nouvelle Héloïse*, Letter 63.

[17] The intermingling of 'Scherz' and 'Ernst' is also a feature of *Der Prinz von Homburg*.

sitting-room ironically reproduces the earlier scene when he proposed to her. The story is based on a paradox, the rape of the Marquise by her rescuer, which is a mystery to her and an open secret to the reader. There is the irony of the conventional, bourgeois setting, which, although it acquires a spurious veracity by being set in Italy and having the names of people and places abbreviated to avoid giving offence, still smacks far more of Frankfurt-an-der-Oder and Kleist's own world. It is deliberately made prosaic, realistic, somewhat flat; and this contrasts with the emotional reality of the spiritual conflict. But it is the setting that – ironically – has the last word, as the count settles down, his wings a little clipped, into the bosom of the family. Irony is produced by the way Kleist handles the language. There is a constant use of military metaphors, counts take ladies as well as fortresses by storm, they woo at the double, and the father of the Marquise not only has to surrender his fortress to the count but his daughter too. The military metaphors are reinforced by imagery of fires, both real and emotional, which further heightens the irony. There is the curiously unreal effect, also ironic in the circumstances, of the frequent use of indirect speech. In the scene where the count appears out of the blue to make his proposal of marriage there are over thirty clauses introduced by the word 'daß', and the impression of reality at one remove gained by this device is highly effective.

Irony is used to show the illusory nature of knowledge. The commandant once says irritably of the Marquise 'She did it in her sleep' ('Sie hat es im Schlaf getan'). He all but speaks the truth, inasmuch as she is raped whilst unconscious. Perhaps there is even a deeper truth in what he says. It is always possible, if not likely, that the Marquise unconsciously wished for some such thing to happen – hence the allusion to Morpheus[18] – and the translation of an unconscious wishdream into reality would then account for her violent reaction to the count when she discovers what he did. Chance

[18] Early on in the story the Marquise guilelessly remarks to her mother that she just felt something very akin to a pregnancy sensation, and jokingly says she will give birth to a child whose father is Morpheus or one of his attendant dreams. Mother and daughter laugh. In the very next paragraph the count arrives – Kleist's clever way of dropping a broad hint as to who the father really is.

remarks in this story have ironic undertones as Kleist weaves his web of truth and illusion. When the Marquise hears of the count's dying words she is sorry for the Julietta referred to, little realising she is the lady in question. On more than one occasion the family speak of the obligation ('Verbindlichkeit') they are under to the count. Mention is made of the many excellent qualities ('viele vortreffliche Eigenschaften') he displayed on the night the fortress was stormed. The mother tests her daughter by pretending the father of her child had called at the house the day before – and so he had, for the count had called, though she knows nothing of this. It is fantastic how Kleist carries on this game, ringing the changes on truth and deception via the medium of irony and double-entendre, even down to apparently irrelevant details. It is fitting, for example, that immediately after the rape the count should appear 'sehr erhitzt im Gesicht' (very hot in the face), although this may be understandable in view of his exertions in putting out the fire. Indeed, the irony of the story may be summed up in a single punctuation mark. The business of the rape, not an easy thing for a writer to motivate and recount, is indicated by a single dash in the middle of a sentence; following which the count assures the Marquise everything will be alright, puts on his hat, and plunges back into the fray. He puts on his hat – 'indem er sich den Hut aufsetzte' – the monstrosity of the offence is made to appear almost comic by Kleist's gratuitous adding of this detail.

Indeed, the irony does at times swing over into comedy bordering on the grotesque, resembling in this respect certain parts of *Michael Kohlhaas*.[19] The scene where the count calls unexpectedly on the Marquise and her family illustrates this. It follows immediately after a passage in which the Marquise had spoken of possible symptoms of pregnancy, and the sequence is doubtless not fortuitous. The family thought the count was dead, but here he is, and everyone calls out his name, 'Graf F.', the valet, the Marquise and her father all echo his name, preparing the perfect stage entrance. And in he comes, like a young god, though a trifle pale – as well he might be – and straightaway asks the Marquise if she is well.

---

[19] Cf. the scene with the knacker from Döbbeln in *Michael Kohlhaas*.

After repeated enquiries the Marquise says she has been a little off colour, but she hopes this will be of no consequence, to which he replies, joy colouring his face, that he also hopes not, and would she please marry him! A comic scene, with irony breaking through in the loaded enquiry after her health and the grotesque situation of a man walking, as if risen from the dead, into a family sitting-room and asking the woman he has raped, without any preamble and almost casually in a subordinate clause, to marry him. A strange comic prelude to the spiritual anguish the Marquise will shortly have to undergo and a remarkable contrast to the other occasion when he will walk into the same room, appearing to the Marquise as a devil and certainly not as a young god.

In another scene the remorse of the Marquise's father is described, after he has been convinced of her innocence and of how he has misjudged her. Another domestic setting, with the Marquise and her mother together in the drawing room. Then an extraordinary noise is heard, the sound of far-off sobbing, a sound that comes nearer, until the father, a colonel in the army, comes crying into the room and stands there, in the middle of the room, bent double, howling so much that the walls echo with the noise, shaking convulsively between each sob, so that in the end his daughter runs to him and constrains him to sit down. The scene borders on farce, the description is so grotesque as almost to move beyond the real world. Yet a few lines later there is to be a highly sensuous account of the father caressing his child like a lover. Once again Kleist indulges his liking for extremes, spicing the potentially tragic situation with touches of melodrama and relieving the profoundly serious issues with an element of comedy.

Indeed, melodramatic touches abound in *Die Marquise von O.* On hearing of the midwife's diagnosis the mother exclaims 'Go! Go! Worthless creature! Cursed be the hour I gave birth to you', and flounces out of the room. The scene between the Marquise and her indignant father could be taken out of grand opera. When the mother is convinced of her daughter's innocence she sinks to her knees before her. Her daughter also sinks to her knees, so both are on their knees gazing emotionally at one another. When the count is revealed as the man who raped the Marquise the melodramatic sprinkling of holy water is followed by a scene between the count and the father where melodrama is combined with the very down-to-earth business of fixing up a marriage: 'The commandant laid his hand on him; his eyelashes twitched, his lips were as white as chalk. "May the curse of heaven depart from this head!" he cried. "When are you thinking of getting married?"' The examples could be multiplied. Irony borders on the grotesque, the paradoxical comes close to farce.

When the Marquise consults the midwife she is in an agony of bewilderment and despair. The midwife goes stolidly about her business, talks of young widows getting pregnant who imagine they live on desert islands, and says – Kleist here varies the military metaphor – that the young pirate who landed at night will soon show up, thereby ironically anticipating what actually happens. This is cold comfort for the Marquise, who faints on hearing her worst suspicions confirmed, the second time she faints in the story, the first time being just before she is raped. There follow the remarks about conception by the Virgin Mary. After giving the Marquise some useful tips about the forthcoming delivery the midwife then departs. Kleist's method in this story could hardly be better illustrated. The problem of appearance and reality, the issue of the conventional judgments of society and the contrasting purity of soul symbolised in the figure of the Virgin, all this is portrayed in a curious mixture of irony and near-tragedy with a down-to-earth midwife as a central character.

Irony is, then, the basic statement and attitude of *Die Marquise von O*. The abyss of despair is bridged over, and tragedy is averted. A solution is reached, based on self-knowledge wrested from despair and on an awareness of the range of human emotion and the fragile, fallible nature, the 'Gebrechlichkeit', of the world. The extremes are reconciled, and a state of equilibrium is achieved. The scandalous beginning is balanced by the happy end, with its ironic, enigmatic final sentence. The alien Russian officer settles down and raises a family in Italy.

6

Paradox and the Irrational

(i)   *Das Bettelweib von Locarno*

Die Welt ist eine wunderliche Einrichtung; und die göttlichsten Wirkungen gehen aus den niedrigsten und unwahrscheinlichsten Ursachen hervor.[1]

At the foot of the Alps, near Locarno in northern Italy, there stood an old castle, belonging to a marquis, which now, coming from the direction of the St. Gotthard, can be seen lying in ruins and ashes: a castle with high and spacious rooms, in one of
5   which, on a bed of straw, spread out for her, a sick old woman, who turned up begging at the door, had been put by the lady of the house, who had pity on her. The marquis, who, returning from hunting, chanced to enter the room, where he used to keep his gun, irritably ordered the woman to get up out of the corner,
10   where she was lying, and find a place behind the stove. The woman, as she got to her feet, slipped with her crutch on the polished floor, suffering a severe injury to her back; so severe indeed, that although, exerting herself unutterably, she was able to get up and walk diagonally across the room, in the direction
15   prescribed for her, she then, amidst groans and moans, collapsed behind the stove and breathed her last.

Several years later, when the marquis, due to war and failure of crops, had got into severe financial straits, a Florentine knight turned up, wanting to buy the castle from him, because of its
20   beautiful situation. The marquis, to whom the transaction meant a great deal, bade his wife put the stranger up in the above-mentioned room, which was vacant and which was furnished in a very beautiful and splendid fashion. How taken

---

[1] 'The world is a most odd set-up; and the most divine effects result from the lowliest and most unlikely causes.' This is taken from *Brief eines Malers an seinen Sohn*, *Werke*, II, 328f.

aback the couple were, however, when, in the middle of the night, the Florentine came downstairs to them, pale and agitated, solemnly and steadfastly avowing that the room was haunted, that something, invisible to the eye, had got up in the corner of the room, making a rustling noise, as if it had been lying on straw, had with audible steps slowly and haltingly crossed the room, and had then, amidst groans and moans, collapsed behind the stove.

The marquis, horror-stricken, without quite knowing why, laughed at the knight with forced heartiness, and said he would gladly get up straight away and spend the night with him in his room, to put his mind at rest. But the knight asked the marquis if he would be so good as to permit him to pass the remaining hours in an armchair in his room, and, when morning came, he had his carriage brought, paid his respects and left.

This incident, which caused a very considerable stir, frightened off several would-be purchasers, much to the marquis's annoyance; so much so that, in view of the fact that the rumour started circulating, strangely and inexplicably, amongst his own domestic staff that something walked the room at the midnight hour, he determined, anxious to scotch the rumour with one decisive step, to investigate the matter himself the very next night. When darkness fell, accordingly, he had his bed made up in the afore-mentioned room, and, without falling asleep, waited for midnight to come. But what was his consternation when, at the witching hour, he did indeed hear the mysterious noise; it was as if someone got up from a pile of straw, that rustled beneath him, went diagonally across the room, and amidst sighs and gasps collapsed behind the stove. The marchioness, when he came downstairs the following morning, asked him how the investigation had gone; and when, looking around him with apprehensive and uncertain gaze and bolting the door, he assured her that it was a fact that the room was haunted, then she had a feeling of horror and fright, such as she had never before had in her life, and she besought him, before he let the matter become known, to subject it once more, in her presence, to a coldblooded investigation. Both of them, however, together with a faithful servant, whom they had taken with them, did in fact the very next night hear the same inexplicable, ghost-like noise; and only the urgent desire to get rid of the castle, at whatever price, enabled them to suppress in the presence of their servant the terror which seized them, and to pass off the incident on to some trivial and fortuitous cause which it would certainly be possible to discover. On the evening of the third day, when both of them, in order to get to the bottom of the affair, with pounding hearts once again climbed the stairs to the guest room, their watchdog, which had been let off its chain, chanced to be in front of the door of the room; so that the two of them, without giving any particular reason, perhaps with the involuntary intention of being accompanied by some third living creature, took the dog with them into the room. Husband and wife, with two lights on the table, the marchioness fully clothed, the marquis with sword and pistols, which he had taken from the cupboard, by his side, sit down about eleven o'clock on their separate beds; and while they try to pass the time in conversation, as best they may, the dog lies down in the middle of the floor and, all curled up, goes to sleep. Then, just as midnight was striking, the dreadful noise can be heard again; someone, visible to no human eye, gets up, on crutches, in the corner of the room; the sound of straw can be heard rustling under him; and at the first step: tap! tap! the dog wakes up, starts to its feet, its ears pricked, and growling and barking, just as if a person were walking towards it, the dog backs away towards the stove. At this sight the marchioness, her hair standing on end, rushed out of the room; and while the marquis, sword in hand, cries out 'Who's there?', and, getting no answer, like a madman slashes the air in every direction, she calls for her carriage, determined, that very instant, to drive off to the town. But even before she went clattering out of the gate, after gathering together a few belongings, she sees the castle going up in flames on all sides. The marquis, his nerves at breaking point with terror, had seized a candle, and, weary of life, set fire to it at every corner, panelled in wood as it was throughout. It was in vain that she sent people in to save the unfortunate man; he had already perished in the most wretched fashion, and to this very day his white bones, gathered together by the country folk, lie in the corner of the room out of which he had ordered the beggarwoman to get up.

This is a translation[2] of Kleist's story *Das Bettelweib von Locarno*, which first appeared in the *Berliner Abendblätter* on 11 October 1810, and was then published with only minor alterations in the second volume of the *Erzählungen*. There are no obvious sources for it, apart from a story told to Kleist by

[2] I have translated literally, in order to convey some impression of Kleist's syntax and use of punctuation. Figures in brackets on the following pages refer to line numbers of the translated text.

Friedrich von Pfuel,[3] though folk legend abounds in ghost stories and midnight hauntings. This too is a ghost story, occupying barely three pages of print, told to entertain the readers of the Berlin newspaper, and of no apparent further significance.

It is very expertly told, and its form and technique merit some attention.[4] The treatment of the central incident follows the same pattern as the treatment of the earthquake in *Das Erdbeben*, that is to say, the death of the beggarwoman is reported, and then relived again four times, through the medium of the Florentine knight; the marquis; the marquis, marchioness and the servant; and finally the marquis, marchioness and the dog; four variations on a theme. The location is set in the opening paragraph, and returned to in the closing sentence. But as the story progresses, the setting gradually becomes more constricted; the castle may have 'high and spacious' rooms, but the walls of the haunted room gradually close around the marquis and his wife as the nightmare engulfs them. The sequence of time is used to build up the tension. The opening is almost leisurely, with its reference to past and present. But then the tempo accelerates and culminates in the hauntings on the three successive nights, with the narrator switching from past to present tense to describe the happenings of the final night, before then reverting to the past tense for the epitaph of the final sentence. Characters as such hardly exist. The marquis may be thoughtless and inconsiderate, though not necessarily cruel,[5] and the marchioness charitable towards the poor, but no real attempt is made to depict them as characters, they are rather caught up in events – not surprisingly in a short ghost story.

The success of the story depends on the way it is told, on the style Kleist uses. It is highly economical, direct and to the point. There is particular stress laid on phrases describing

---

[3] Cf. Sembdner, *Lebensspuren*, p.277.

[4] Brilliantly analysed by E. Staiger, 'Heinrich von Kleist *Das Bettelweib von Locarno*', *Meisterwerke deutscher Sprache*, 4th ed., 1963; and by Jürgen Schröder, '*Das Bettelweib von Locarno*. Zum Gespenstischen in den Novellen Heinrich von Kleists', *Germanisch-Romanische Monatsschrift* 48 (1967), pp.193-207.

[5] Egon Werlich, 'Kleists *Bettelweib von Locarno*', *Wirkendes Wort* 15 (1965), pp.239-57, overstresses the inhumanity of the marquis in a desire to find a highly 'moral' meaning to the story.

sounds, the rustling of straw, the sighs, moans and groans of the old woman, the barking of the dog, and these are repeated to produce a compelling auditory effect. Nouns and adjectives are used frequently in pairs, and the cumulative effect of this is to achieve almost the incantatory effect of a spell, the invocation of something irrational and supernatural. Subjects – the marquis, the marchioness – are isolated by interpolated clauses from their verbs, and the isolating effect of this reinforces the final climax of two human beings face to face with the supernatural. The daring, eccentric syntax of the sentence setting the scene for the final haunting (1.75 ff.) is a splendid example of this: 'das Ehepaar' amidst a world of objects, lights, swords and pistols, far removed from the verb 'setzen sich' with which it is remotely, though not entirely grammatically, connected, pinning its faith as it were on familiar, inanimate objects as it awaits the manifestation of something from another world. This impression of isolation, of discontinuity, is further underlined by Kleist's highly individual use of punctuation, above all of commas. Every phrase, every subdivision of a clause is comma'd off, to mark off the separate pieces of the jigsaw, the individual fragments of a world whose rationality and logic is being threatened and undermined.

The narrator nowhere intrudes in this story. The narration is completely impersonal, deadpan. Incidents are told in a matter-of-fact way, people react and die like animals. The narration is taut and terse, and odd details go unexplained in a sometimes maddening way. Why should a beggarwoman be sheltered in the best guest room of this castle, with its 'high and spacious rooms', and the marchioness permit straw to be scattered around in such a grand apartment? Does the castle have plenty of guest rooms, or just one, and why do the owners apparently sleep on the ground floor? These and other questions can be asked; but there seems little point in cavilling at the odd inconsistency in this short story, and indeed it could be argued, albeit with some perversity, that the inconsistencies contribute to its predominantly irrational element. Kleist narrates the story factually and dispassionately, like some scientific experimenter, or, to use his own terms, like someone who can not only use a metaphor but also assemble the terms of a mathematical formula.⁶

Does the story have a metaphor, a content, that goes beyond the actual events formulated by the detached narrator? Is it, to use the language of literary criticism, a Novelle or a blown-up anecdote?

Some phrases in the story certainly stand out and suggest that there is more to it than just a story about a spook. The role of chance is hinted at – the marquis arrives by chance, 'zufällig', to find a beggarwoman in his best guest room. The beggarwoman walks across the room in the direction 'prescribed' for her, and the word 'vorgeschrieben' suggests a more absolute directive than might be indicated by the marquis' brusque command. Both marquis and marchioness experience feelings of dread that go far beyond the normal range of human emotion – 'der Marchese, erschrocken, er wußte selbst nicht recht warum' (1.32), 'so erschrak sie, wie sie in ihrem Leben nicht getan' (1.57/58). At the end the marquis sets fire to the room and to the castle because he is 'müde seines Lebens' (1.95/96).

Das Bettelweib is a story of punishment for an offence, of justice and revenge. This punishment is carried out by the introduction in the story of a supernatural source. Kleist does not introduce this supernatural element in order to exploit the world of ghosts and the 'night-side' of nature⁷ in a Romantic fashion. This supernatural element is a development of his insistence on the role of chance, the breakdown of rationality, and the erection of justice into an absolute principle. It is a development of the irrational nature of the behaviour of the lynch mob in *Das Erdbeben* and the desire of Piachi in *Der Findling* to pursue his quest for revenge beyond the boundaries of the rational world. The element of

---

⁶ Cf. below p.97. Cf. also *Werke*, II, 338: 'Man könnte die Menschen in zwei Klassen abteilen; in solche, die sich auf eine Metapher und 2) in solche, die sich auf eine Formel verstehn. Deren, die sich auf beides verstehn, sind zu wenige, sie machen keine Klasse aus' – 'People could be divided into two classes; those with a good knowledge of metaphors and those with a good knowledge of formulae. Only few are expert at both, too few to form a class of their own.'

⁷ Kleist knew various Romantic writers and was familiar with G.H. Schubert's *Ansichten von der Nachtseite der Wissenschaft*, 1808, and indeed attended Schubert's lectures in Dresden. There seems to be no evidence that Kleist borrowed directly from Schubert.

the irrational appears too in *Die heilige Cäcilie* and in the figure of the Zigeunerin in *Michael Kohlhaas*, but it is immanent in the earlier stories. The supernatural is an extension of the role of chance. It can too, when it appears in the guise of a miracle, represent the culmination of the development to perfection of human qualities, and this, as will be seen, is what occurs in *Der Zweikampf*.

Das Bettelweib shows the breakdown of the rational world and the impotence of human volition in the face of this. The marquis and marchioness, in this respect typically Kleistian characters, are made to experience feelings of incomprehensible terror and dread, they peer into a world of irrational horror, and are brought to the brink of despair and madness. This horror and its dislocating effect is well brought out in one of Kleist's favourite words 'Entsetzen' ('terror', 'horror'), which he uses as well in the sense of 'Ent-setzen' ('dislocate'). Two features in this story stand out particularly. There is the brilliant introduction of the dog for the final vigil, the breakdown in the rational world receiving its ultimate confirmation via the reactions of the dumb creature. And there is the one and only use of direct speech in the story, when with perfect timing Kleist has the marquis cry out 'wer da?', an abandoned cry of isolation and helplessness echoing in the room before he futilely slashes the air with his sword, a cry of a human creature in need reminiscent of the figure of Gustav seeking help in the midnight gloom in *Die Verlobung in St. Domingo* or even of some character in a story by Kafka exposed to incomprehensible forces undermining the stability of the familiar world. Small wonder that the marquis is 'müde seines Lebens' and, his punishment grotesquely disparate to the triviality of the offence, succumbs to despair and madness.

Inasmuch as it contains the hints of such themes *Das Bettelweib von Locarno* is more of a Novelle than an anecdote. But it is foolish to consider works of literature in terms of fixed literary categories, and it is prudent to be on guard against the dangers of over-interpretation. *Das Bettelweib* is a story expertly told by a narrator,[8] a scientific observer of the human

---

[8] Walter Silz, op.cit., ch.2, compares Kleist's story with Grillparzer's retelling of it. The differences between the two writers is brought out very clearly in this comparison.

scene, who shrewdly calculates his effects and indicates themes that extend far beyond the bare three pages it occupies in his printed works.

(ii) *The Anecdotes*

Die Geschichte ... könnte in Erz gegraben werden.[9]

Kleist wrote several anecdotes for publication in the *Berliner Abendblätter*, where they were eagerly read and much praised by discerning critics.[10] He needed them to provide copy for his paper, and but for this fact they might never have seen the light of day. Some of them can be accounted miniature masterpieces of the genre.

The anecdote as a literary form first became popular in Germany during the sixteenth century, when many collections of them were published, owing much to the influence of Poggio and written first in Latin and later in the vernacular. Interest in the anecdote was then revived during the Romantic period of German literature at the beginning of the nineteenth century.[11] An anecdote may be defined as something that in the briefest possible way illustrates a particular side of a character or situation, something self-contained, a rounded whole, a cameo illuminating for a brief second the human situation. It may achieve its affect by means of wit, a play on words, or an intellectual paradox, and it can be satirical, farcical or frivolous. It may revolve around an intellectual 'Pointe' or a symbolic incident. Generally speaking it will be set against the background of everyday life, reproducing a single scene of the human drama. Within its short compass there is little room for psychological embellishment, and, since it is geared to making a striking effect, its characters tend to be exceptions, rather than the general run of human beings.

---

[9] 'The story ... could be engraved in bronze.' Letter to Prinz von Lichnowsky, 23 October 1810, where Kleist is speaking of one of his anecdotes.

[10] They were reprinted in many contemporary journals, and have been much praised by writers from Clemens Brentano to Franz Kafka, see *Nachruhm, passim*.

[11] Ref. article 'Anekdote' in Merker-Stammler, *Reallexikon der deutschen Literaturgeschichte*, 2nd. ed., 1958; Hans Lorenzen, *Typen deutschen Anekdotenerzählung. (Kleist – Hebel – Schäfer)*, Diss., Hamburg, 1935; J. Klein, *Geschichte der deutschen Novelle*, 1954, pp. 11-12.

One anecdote by Kleist has already been quoted,[12] and it might be helpful to quote another one, to show how he handles this particular form:

The embarrassed magistrate

A militiaman not so very long ago, without the permission of his officer, deserted his post in the municipal guard. According to an ancient law an offence of this kind, which in old days, because of the raids of the nobles, was a very grave one, is punishable by death. However, without the law having been expressly repealed, no use has been made of it for several hundred years: with the result that, without sentence of death being passed, anyone found guilty of violating it is, according to established custom, merely fined a sum of money which he has to pay to the city treasury. The fellow in question, however, who was doubtless by no means keen to pay up the fine, declared, to the great consternation of the magistrate, that, since it fell to his lot, he wished to die, in accordance with the law. The magistrate, sensing some misunderstanding, sent a deputy to the fellow to point out to him how much more advantageous it would be for him to pay up a few shillings fine, rather than be finished off by a firing squad. But the fellow insisted that he was weary of living and wanted to die: with the result that the magistrate, who did not want to shed any blood, had no other choice but to let the rogue off his fine and was glad enough when the latter declared that, in view of the changed circumstances, he was prepared to go on living.

The story is brief and to the point. It is rooted in everyday life. It has an element of wit. A rogue gets off scot-free by insisting on the letter of the law being carried out. A magistrate has to break the law, to prevent an injustice. The legal machinery is thrown out of gear by an individual who uses his wits.

Kleist's anecdotes are generally terse and lapidary – 'wert in Erz gegraben zu werden'. They are told in what is apparently a completely objective and detached manner. They dispense with unnecessary detail and make their point effectively with a minimum of effort. They frequently have an everyday, realistic background, featuring scenes from the life

---

[12] Cf. above p.51/2.

of the people, appropriately enough, since Kleist wanted the *Berliner Abendblätter* to be a 'Volksblatt' in the best sense of the word. They generally have a symbolic meaning, conveyed by Kleist's characteristic use of paradox, and they are spiced with wit and irony. The element of paradox, so predominant a characteristic of Kleist's brief but highly pregnant philosophical writings, is effectively conveyed by means of the 'Sonderbare Fälle' and 'Unwahrscheinliche Wahrhaftigkeiten', the 'singular events' and 'improbable truths', in which he delights. Many of the anecdotes are told against a background of death, but this is treated in a macabrely comic way. This gallows humour, already noticed in the anecdote of a Capuchin monk accompanying a delinquent to the place of execution, produces a grotesque effect where the wit acts as a foil to the sombre reality of death. Typical Kleistian themes occur in the anecdotes – the contrast between appearance and reality, the role of chance, the questionable nature of legal institutions – but they are hinted at, rather than explicitly stated, for the anecdotes, while containing deeper significance, are intended primarily to entertain.

Some examples of the anecdotes may be listed and their content briefly indicated. In *Tagesbegebenheit* a man objects to standing under a tree with another man during a storm; he gets the space all to himself, and is promptly struck by lightning and killed. Chance or poetic justice? In *Der Griffel Gottes* the costly gravestone of a countess is struck by lightning, so that the lettering on it is rearranged to form the words 'sie ist gerichtet', the judgement of God exposing the reality of her godless life behind the sham piety. In *Mutwille des Himmels* a Prussian general, due to a misunderstanding, is buried with his face covered with lather and half-shaven, a remarkable mixture of seriousness and farce. *Charité-Vorfall* is an anecdote full of wit and irony recounting how a man is continually being run over and physically mutilated by doctors, of all people. Coarse realism is a feature of *Anekdote aus dem letzten Kriege* where a drummer, sentenced to death by the enemy firing squad, lets down his trousers and asks to be shot in the behind, so that the drum of his body doesn't get any further holes in it! Two English boxers engage in a fight to the finish, and one is carried off dead – but the victor dies the following day.[13] In *Korrespondenz-Nachricht* a Königsberg actor is forbidden by the management to improvise on the stage; when a horse relieves itself on the stage, the actor turns round and tells it not to improvise. Other anecdotes contain some of the raw material for the *Erzählungen*, and indeed aptly illustrate the difference between a Novelle and an anecdote. The anecdote *Sonderbare Geschichte, die sich, zu meiner Zeit, in Italien zutrug* concerns the seduction of an innocent young girl by a nobleman and appears, on the face of it, to have much in common with *Die Marquise von O*. But whereas the latter story is concerned with the metaphysical and psychological aspects of the Marquise's dilemma, this anecdote is a witty description of how a trick is played to make an honest woman of the young lady, and nothing more.

Kleist's best anecdote, and a splendid example of the literary merit the form is capable of in the hands of a master, is the *Anekdote aus dem letzten preußischen Kriege*, published anonymously in the *Berliner Abendblätter* on 6 October 1810.[14] It is a story told to the narrator by the landlord of an inn near Jena and takes place shortly after the battle in which the Prussian army was so disastrously defeated by Napoleon, when the village in which the inn is situated has been evacuated by the Prussian forces and is awaiting occupation by the main body of the French army. A solitary Prussian cavalryman rides up to the inn and orders a glass of brandy. The landlord can scarcely believe his ears, since any sane man would be in a hurry to leave the village before the French arrived. But not only does the soldier enjoy his brandy, slowly savouring each drop; he orders a second and then a third glass, while the landlord is on tenterhooks, knowing that a second's delay spells certain death. Then the soldier slowly and calmly fills a pipe and starts to smoke it, carefully eyeing three French cavalrymen who appear at the entrance to the village. Then, scorning retreat, he utters a Turkish oath and attacks the three Frenchmen, scattering them to right and left, before turning round, riding past the landlord, bidding him

---

[13] Cf. Chapter 9 below on *Der Zweikampf*, p.175/6.
[14] Well analysed by Walter Silz, op.cit., pp. 40-4.

farewell, and with an exultant cry charging out of the village. It is a cliffhanger story, brilliantly told, with a mixture of long and short sentences, direct and indirect speech, full of dramatic gestures and incidental detail, a tale describing the bravery of an anonymous soldier, an ordinary person who uses ordinary language, yet quite extraordinary in the impact he makes. In this portrayal of the bravery and calm courage of a common soldier, a 'Kerl' as he is continually called, Kleist implicitly criticises by contrast the performance of the Prussian army at Jena and shows where the true strength of Prussia lies, thereby prophetically anticipating the Wars of Liberation he did not live to see.

This section on the anecdotes may be fittingly concluded by quoting another good anecdote, *Der Branntweinsäufer und die Berliner Glocken*. It too features a soldier, a very genuine Berliner – a hallmark of the characters in Kleist's anecdotes is that they are genuine, 'echt'. It is set against a realistic Berlin background, indeed the background plays a decisive role in the story. It revolves around the nice paradox that everything conspires against this unfortunate innocent – the familiar setting of his native town, religion in the shape of the cathedral bells, the very heavens themselves. It is remarkable also in that it is infused not so much by wit as by a genuine humour based on an observation and understanding of ordinary men in the street. Pommeranzen, Kümmel and Anisette, it should be noted, are three kinds of spirits:

The brandy drinker and the bells of Berlin

A soldier in the former Lichnowsky Regiment, a hopeless and incorrigible drunkard, vowed, after continually being chastised for this, that he would mend his ways and lay off the brandy. And indeed he kept his word, for three whole days: but on the fourth day he was picked up dead drunk in a gutter, arrested by a corporal and taken into custody. When his case was heard he was asked why he had not been mindful of his good resolution and had once again succumbed to the vice of drunkenness. 'Captain' he answered, 'it is not my fault. I was doing a job for a merchant, taking a box of dye-wood across the park; when the bells started ringing from the top of the cathedral '*Pom*meranzen! *Pom*meranzen! *Pom*meranzen!' Go on ringing, and to hell with you, I said, and remembered my

resolution and drank nothing. In the Königsstraße, where I
had to deliver the box, I stop and stand for a moment in front
of the town hall, to take a rest: when the bells start tinkling
from the top of the tower 'Kümmel! Kümmel! Kümmel! –
'Kümmel! Kümmel! Kümmel!' I say to the tower: Go on
tinkling till the heavens open – and I remember, upon my soul,
I remember my resolution, even though I was thirsty, and I
don't touch a drop. Then on my way home the devil takes me
across the Spittelmarkt; and just as I am standing in front of a
pub, with more than thirty customers in it, the bells start
ringing from the Spittelturm: 'Anisette! Anisette! Anisette!'
What's the price of a glass? I ask. The landlord says: sixpence.
I'll have one, I say – and what became of me after that I have
no idea.

(iii)   Die heilige Cäcilie oder Die Gewalt der Musik[15]

Dieses zu gleicher Zeit schreckliche und herrliche Wunder.[16]

Towards the end of the sixteenth century four Protestant
brothers meet in Aachen and, hearing that the feast of Corpus
Christi is to be solemnly celebrated in the nearby convent of
St. Cecilia, decide to gather together a band of followers and
cause havoc at the convent during the celebration of the mass.
They intend thereby to vie with the iconoclastic riots
prevalent at that time in the Netherlands. An old Italian mass
of particular beauty is to be performed by the nuns at the
convent to mark the religious feast; but the performance
appears at the last minute to be jeopardised by the sudden
illness of Sister Antonia who was to conduct the mass. At the
last minute she, or somebody exactly resembling her, arrives
to conduct it, and it is sung so beautifully that the entire
congregation, the four brothers and their band included,
remain silent and motionless, and no harm comes to the

---

[15] I am indebted to my colleague Mrs Hilda Brown for help in connection with this section.

[16] 'This terrible and at the same time glorious miracle', words used by the abbess to describe the miracle.

convent. The four brothers, however, live thereafter in a religious trance, from which they awake every midnight to sing for a whole hour the *Gloria in excelsis* in tones of shattering disharmony. They are pronounced to be insane, and live to a ripe old age within the walls of the asylum at Aachen, contemplating the Cross and raising their unearthly clamour to the glory of God at the midnight hour. The convent of St. Cecilia flourishes until, as a result of the Treaty of Westphalia, it is eventually secularised. The salvation of the convent from the designs of the four brothers is deemed by the Pope to be a miracle wrought by St. Cecilia, who had assumed the guise of Sister Antonia and through the power of music frustrated the violence that had been planned against the church.

Such is the plot of Kleist's story, which he explicitly calls 'eine Legende', a classification which prepares the reader for the occurrence of miraculous and supernatural events. It first appeared in a shorter version in the *Berliner Abendblätter* in November, 1810 (nos. 40-2) as a christening gift for Cecilia Müller, a daughter born to Adam Müller on 27 October 1810 and baptized in the French reformed church in Berlin, Kleist being one of the godparents. This version restricts itself to an account of the events leading up to the miracle in the church, the subsequent condition of the brothers, and their consignment to an asylum. The final version, more than twice the length of the first version, though still only a story some thirteen pages long,[17] appeared in the second volume of the *Erzählungen* published in 1811. From being in the first version a more or less straightforward account of a miraculous legend written for an occasion it becomes in the second version, as will be seen, a much more profound story centring around the two issues of the nature and power of music and the psychological condition of four apparently insane men.

The story was written in the last year of Kleist's life; but the experiences on which it is based reach back into the years 1800-1, crucial ones for his development as a poet. In a letter to Wilhelmine von Zenge from Würzburg (13/18 September 1800) Kleist describes a visit he paid to the local asylum. He was deeply moved by what he saw. One inmate whose

---

[17] *Werke*, II, pp. 216-28.

appearance particularly struck him was a monk, 'tiefsinnig', 'ernst' and 'düster', 'melancholy', 'earnest' and 'sombre', who had once got his words mixed when delivering a sermon and from that day on lived a life of agonised repentance under the impression that he had falsified the word of God – an example of religious fixation leading to mental derangement, of a human being trapped for life in the prison of his eschatological delusions. This visit must have left a lasting impression on Kleist.[18] In another letter to Wilhelmine from Würzburg (11/12 September 1800) Kleist described with obvious distaste the religious services in the Catholic churches of Würzburg. The chanting of the priests, the mumbling of the Latin prayers, the carefully rehearsed ritual, all this left him unmoved – 'überhaupt, dünkt mich, alle Zeremonien ersticken das Gefühl. Sie beschäftigen unsern Verstand, aber das Herz bleibt tot'.[19] Very different, however, is his reaction to a Catholic service in Dresden, described in a letter to Wilhelmine from Leipzig dated 21 May 1801: 'nirgends fand ich mich aber tiefer in meinem Innersten gerührt als in der katholischen Kirche, wo die größte, erhebenste Musik noch zu den andern Künsten tritt, das Herz gewaltsam zu bewegen. Ach, Wilhelmine, unser Gottesdienst ist keiner. Er spricht nur zu dem kalten Verstande, aber zu allen Sinnen ein katholisches Fest'.[20] This is an astonishing volte-face, particularly when one bears in mind Kleist's Protestant background in Frankfurt-an-der-Oder and the horror with which anything Catholic would have been received by his family. The aesthetic experience of the catholic mass, and in particular the powerful effect of the music, affected Kleist with something almost akin to religious conversion.

---

[18] M. Morris, *Heinrich von Kleists Reise nach Würzburg*, 1899, says that the description of another inmate is an invention of Kleist's, but the evidence he produces is slight in the extreme. The visit and the impression it made seem genuine enough, even though Kleist then writes it up in a somewhat literary way.

[19] 'And indeed, it seems to me, all ceremonies stifle feelings. They engage our intellect, but our hearts remain dead.'

[20] 'Never did I find my innermost being more deeply moved than in the Catholic church, where the most grandiose, uplifting music joins with the other arts in powerfully affecting our hearts. Ah, Wilhelmine, our services are not proper worship at all. They only speak to the cold intellect, but a Catholic festival appeals to all our senses.'

These experiences have clearly left their imprint on *Die heilige Cäcilie*, written some ten years later. More significant than any one experience, however, is the importance that music in general had for Kleist. Throughout his life Kleist was keenly interested in music. He played in a quartet in Berlin with his brother officers, and was a virtuoso on the clarinet and flute.[21] His capacity to react to situations in terms of music is graphically described in the letter to Wilhelmine of 19/23 September 1800, yet another of the crucial Würzburg letters: 'Zuweilen – ich weiß nicht, ob Dir je etwas Ähnliches glückte, und ob Du es folglich für wahr halten kannst. Aber ich höre zuweilen, wenn ich in der Dämmerung, einsam, dem wehenden Atem des Westwindes entgegengehe, und besonders wenn ich dann die Augen schließe, ganze Konzerte, vollständig, mit allen Instrumenten von der zärtlichen Flöte bis zum rauschenden Kontra-Violin. So entsinne ich mich besonders einmal als Knabe vor 9 Jahren, als ich gegen den Rhein und gegen den Abendwind zugleich hinaufging, und so die Wellen der Luft und des Wassers zugleich mich umtönten, ein schmelzendes Adagio gehört zu haben, mit allem Zauber der Musik, mit allen melodischen Wendungen und der ganzen begleitenden Harmonie. Es war wie die Wirkung eines Orchesters, wie ein vollständiges Vaux-hall; ja, ich glaube sogar, daß alles, was die Weisen Griechenlands von der Harmonie der Sphären dichteten, nichts Weicheres, Schöneres, Himmlischerisches gewesen sei, als diese seltsame Träumerei ... '.[22] The same ideas are described in almost

---

[21] According to Clemens Brentano, letter to Achim von Arnim, 10 December 1811, quoted in *Nachruhm*, p.77.

[22] 'Sometimes – I don't know if you were ever fortunate enough to have a similar experience and so can believe what I say to be true. But sometimes, when it is twilight and I am on my own and I feel the west wind breathing and drifting in my face as I walk towards it, I can hear whole concerts, in their entirety, with every single instrument from the tender flute to the rumbling sound of the double-bass. In particular I remember when I was a boy nine years ago walking towards the Rhine, the evening breeze in my face and the waves of water and the currents in the air both roaring in my ears, I remember having heard a melting adagio, with all its musical magic, all its melodic variations and the whole harmony that accompanied it. Its effect on me was like that of a complete orchestra, an entire Vauxhall; indeed it is my firm belief that anything ever dreamed by the Greek sages when they have spoken of the harmony of the spheres cannot have been more delicate, more beautiful, more heavenly, than this strange reverie.'

identical terms ten months later in a letter to Adolphine von Werdeck (28/29 July 1801), an indication not only of Kleist's 'Ideenmagazin' method of noting down impressions and repeating them but also of the importance he attached to this particular impression, even though its immediate impact is to some extent toned down by the literary manner in which he writes it up.

This receptivity to music remained with Kleist all his life; and only a few months before his death, in a letter to Marie von Kleist (spring/summer 1811), he underlined its importance for him when mooting the possibility of abandoning poetic pursuits for a year or more in order to devote himself entirely to the study of music: 'denn ich betrachte diese Kunst als die Wurzel, oder vielmehr, um mich schulgerecht auszudrücken, als die algebraische Formel aller übrigen, und so wie wir schon einen Dichter haben – mit dem ich mich übrigens auf keine Weise zu vergleichen wage – der alle seine Gedanken über die Kunst, die er übt, auf Farben bezogen hat, so habe ich, von meiner frühesten Jugend an, alles Allgemeine, was ich über die Dichtung gedacht habe, auf Töne bezogen. Ich glaube, daß im Generalbaß die wichtigsten Aufschlüsse über die Dichtkunst enthalten sind'.[23]

Many of the writers of the Romantic School were keenly interested in music and pondered on its relationship to the other arts. Kleist's youthful absorption in musical impressions has its counterpart in Wackenroder's writings, with which it would seem he must have been well acquainted;[24] C.F. Schubart linked music with mathematics, stating that 'die Tonkunst sei nichts anderes als eine Rechenkunst' and 'was den Generalbaß betrifft, so gehört er zur mathematischen,

---

[23] 'For I consider this art to be the root, or rather, to use the proper term, the algebraic formula of all the others, and just as we already have a poet – with whom incidentally I would not venture to compare myself at all – who has considered all his thoughts on the art he practises in relation to colours, so from the earliest days of my youth onwards I have related all my general ideas on poetry to notes and sounds. It is my belief that the most important pronouncements on the art of poetry are to be found in the figured bass.' The poet referred to is Goethe, whose *Farbenlehre* was published in 1810.

[24] Many interesting parallels are listed in Donald P. Morgan, *Heinrich von Kleists Verhältnis zur Musik*, Diss., Cologne, 1940, pp. 45-58. This dissertation contains much useful material, which needs however to be properly worked over.

und nicht zur ästhetischen Kunst';[25] Novalis remarked that 'die Sprache (sei) ein musikalisches Ideen-Instrument' and 'der Generalbaß enthält die musikalische Algeber und Analysis'.[26] The examples could be multiplied. The idea on the one hand of music in some way mirroring the music of the spheres, while on the other hand through its formal qualities, especially as shown in the figured bass, being linked with mathematics, the formal basis of the universe, all this is very much a part of Romantic, and indeed mediaeval, thinking and Kleist might well have been influenced by it, particularly during his Dresden days. But equally well he could have evolved such ideas himself, intuitively. They seem to accord well with the very essence of his poetic personality, the combination of highly-charged emotion and formal precision. The imaginative side of music on the one hand, and its strictly formal structure on the other, clearly appealed to a writer who as well as being interested in the arts was also keenly attracted to mathematics and the physical sciences, fields of human knowledge on which he constantly drew for much of his imagery.[27] The figured bass has a formal, quasi-mathematical base; but in its working out it allows of improvisation and imagination, and this combination of discipline and phantasy to some extent reflects the twin features of the soldier-poet Kleist, the man who wrote 'ich kann ein Differentiale finden, und einen Vers machen; sind das nicht die beiden Enden der menschlichen Fähigkeit?'[28]

It is possible that music had a greater influence on Kleist as a writer than is generally conceded, both as far as the emotional colouring and the structure of his works is concerned. It certainly provided him with one of his basic images. Some images lie at the heart of his work – the vaulted

---

[25] 'Music is nothing more than arithmetic' and 'as far as the figured bass is concerned, it is part of mathematics and not aesthetics', in C.F. Schubart, *Ideen zu einer Ästhetik der Tonkunst*, 1806, p.24 and p.295.

[26] 'Speech is a musical instrument of ideas' and 'the figured bass contains musical algebra and analysis', Novalis, *Fragmente*, ed. Kamnitzer, 1929, p.583.

[27] The influence of mathematics and the physical sciences on Kleist's imagery would be a good subject for a doctoral dissertation.

[28] 'I can work out a differential and put a verse together; are those not the two poles of human capability?' Letter to Ernst von Pfuel, 7 January 1805.

arch, which remains standing precisely because all its parts are simultaneously falling inwards, the angel guarding the gates of paradise, the image of the wreath, the imagery of the Garden of Eden. One such image, which occurs in a letter to Wilhelmine von Zenge of 13 November 1800 and is repeated eight months later in a letter to Karoline von Schlieben on 18 July 1801, and can therefore be considered to form part of his poetic 'Ideenmagazin', is that of the tones of the flute sounding through the hurricane and gradually dying away, the 'Flötenton im Orkan'. The lyrical sweetness of the flute and the dark menacing hurricane engulfing it – this mirrors a pattern often to be found in Kleist's works, the eye-of-the-hurricane technique as it were, where a brief moment of lyrical sweetness and harmony is sandwiched between outbursts of violence, a lovers' idyll interrupts for a brief spell the tragic process, the technique used for example in *Das Erdbeben in Chili*, *Die Verlobung in St. Domingo* and *Penthesilea*.

Formally too it may well be that Kleist's works owe something to the influence of music. Attempts have been made to compare his works to musical compositions. *Das Erdbeben in Chili* may be based on the pattern of the fugue.[29] A formal comparison has been made between *Robert Guiskard* and Bach's Brandenburg Concerto No.1.[30] *Prinz Friedrich von Homburg* has been interpreted impressionistically in terms of a musical score.[31] The musical elements in the language of *Penthesilea* are there for all to see. Clearly there is in any case an overlap between the structure of, say, a symphony or a fugue and that of a drama or dramatic Novelle. It is however not impossible that Kleist strove consciously to introduce principles of musical composition into his literary works, and it could be that the revolution in drama he sought to realise when working in vain on *Robert Guiskard* was the fusion of music and drama. Be that as it may, it seems highly likely that

---

[29] Cf. Kurt Günther, *Die Entwicklung der novellistischen Kompositionstechnik Kleists bis zur Meisterschaft*, Diss. Leipzig, 1911; Hermann Davidts, *Die novellistische Kunst Heinrich von Kleists*, Bonner Forschungen NF, V, 1913.

[30] Hans Klein, 'Musikalische Komposition in deutscher Dichtkunst', *Deutsche Vierteljahrsschrift* 7 (1930), pp. 680-716.

[31] Fritz Teller, 'Neue Studien zu Heinrich von Kleist', *Euphorion*, 20 (1913), pp. 681-727.

particular features of his plays and stories owe something to his profound interest in music. There is for instance his technique of 'variations on a theme', of stating a theme, of setting a scene more or less objectively, and then retelling it through the experiences of different characters, as with the earthquake in *Das Erdbeben in Chili* and the fate of the beggarwoman in *Das Bettelweib von Locarno*. This 'variation' technique is central to Kleist's mirroring of reality and his absorption with the problem of truth and knowledge. It enables him continually to shift viewpoints and perspectives, and it underlines the interrogations and cross-examinations with which his works are studded. Musical too is Kleist's use of leitmotif, of particular words and phrases which he repeats a number of times within a short space of time and which cleverly pinpoint central themes and attitudes in his works. There is, for example, the brilliantly contrived repetition of the phrase 'Dann wird er die Fanfare blasen lassen', 'then he shall sound the fanfare', in the 'Parolescene' in *Prinz Friedrich von Homburg*, where the desire for glory of the as yet immature prince is mirrored; there is the repetition of the verb 'stürzen' as Penthesilea falls to the ground in her vain pursuit of Achilles, a part of the height-depth symbolism in the play and an indication of her spiritual conflict; there is the thematic repetition of the word 'verstoßen' in the scene between Kohlhaas and Luther,[32] a word that sums up the whole issue of the social contract and the position of the individual vis-à-vis society; there is the punning repetition of words in *Der zerbrochne Krug* used to underline the theme of fallen man and the old Adam. Phrases such as these are used like musical motifs, and an examination of Kleist's style, particularly in his plays, shows that he was acutely aware of the sound of words, quite apart from their meaning. This may help to account for the fact that he tried to train himself in declamation and set store by the proper recitation of his works.

In the last resort it may be impossible to give precise chapter and verse for the influence of music on Kleist's works; indeed, any attempt to do so would in the nature of things be suspect. It can be argued that the technique of variations, the

[32] Cf. below p.131.

use of leitmotifs, and the awareness of the sound of words, as distinct from their meaning, are part of the make-up of a dramatic poet. But the least one can say in the case of Kleist is that his keen sensibility to music reinforced his creative inspiration as a dramatist and novellist.[33]

Die heilige Cäcilie has two main centres of interest: the miraculous way in which through the power of music the convent is saved from desecration; and the strange fate which befalls the four brothers. The story is told in five paragraphs, with a postscript added in a short final paragraph. It is tempting therefore to analyse the form of the story in terms of a five-act play, in which each main paragraph forms an act – the threat to the convent, the performance of the mass and its effect on the crowded congregation, the visit of the mother to her four sons in the asylum, the account of the events given by Veit Gotthelf the cloth-merchant, and the mother's visit to the convent and meeting with the abbess, together with the final winding up of the story. Such a division into acts, neat and tempting though it may be, seems unduly facile.[34] Most Novellen, doubtless because of their inherently dramatic content, can be broken up in this way; and dividing this story up into five sections obscures the fact that essentially it revolves around the two centres of interest indicated above, linked as they are by the dual nature of the power of music, which on the one hand preserves the convent and strengthens the Catholic religion, and on the other hand acts apparently as a judgment of God on the four erring brothers.

Once again there is the Kleistian situation of a mystery – the fate of the brothers – which has to be unravelled, and once again, in the presentation of the central issues of the story, a technique of themes and variations is used. This is the big difference between the final version of the story and the

---

[33] References to music in Kleist's works are catalogued in D.P. Morgan, op.cit., pp. 101-4; cf. also Franz Servaes, *Heinrich von Kleist*, 1902. The most illuminating remarks on Kleist's relationship to music are contained in Otto Ludwig's letter to Julian Schmidt, 3 July 1857, quoted in *Nachruhm*, p.292.

[34] It is a division undertaken by Günter Graf, 'Der dramatische Aufbaustil der Legende Heinrich von Kleists *Die heilige Cäcilie oder Die Gewalt der Musik*', *Etudes Germaniques* 24 (1969), pp. 346-59.

shorter, earlier version. In the first version, after the description of the events in the church, the effect on the brothers was described solely through the report of the innkeeper of the inn where they lodged. In the final version the character of the mother is introduced, who six years later, like a kind of detective, tries to find out what has happened to her four sons. Another character, Veit Gotthelf, formerly a young tearaway but now a respectable, conforming merchant, describes the events as he saw them, and the behaviour of the brothers is also seen through the reporting eye of the overseers at the asylum and the abbess of the convent, with the narrator of the story remaining more or less objectively in the background. This leads to a multiplication of viewpoints and perspectives, and the effect of the music and the miracle it wrought is seen on characters other than the brothers. The mother is converted back to Catholicism, Veit Gotthelf, perhaps because of business opportunism, returns to the Catholic fold, and the Archbishop of Trier, and after him the Pope, deems the whole thing to have been a miracle performed by St. Cecilia.

Symbols and gestures knit the story together. When the mother visits the convent she sees happy workmen, singing as they toil, increasing the height of the church spires by a third, while at the same time dark menacing thunderclouds slowly move away into the distance. This 'double spectacle' aptly symbolises the preservation of the church against the vain threat of the brothers, with the symbol of the storm, a favourite one with Kleist,[35] echoed again in the 'invisible lightning' by which the four men have been struck from on high. While the storm clouds recede in the sky the mother can see the luminous beauty of the rose window in the back of the church, a visual representation, one might say, of the 'Flötenton im Orkan'. The *Gloria in excelsis* is a leitmotif running through the story and links its two themes, being

---

[35] Cf. letter to Wilhelmine, 10/11 October 1800, and the imagery of storms *passim* in *Penthesilea* and in *Der Zweikampf*, in the description of the duel. Cf. also Caroline de la Motte Fouqué's review of the stories, 3/5 September 1812, quoted in *Nachruhm*, pp. 626 ff.: 'The storm, setting in majestic splendour, and the light cast by the rays of the evening sun, it is these that form the actual words of the riddle in all its fearful sternness.'

sung miraculously in the church and discordantly every midnight by the brothers. The power of music is demonstrated twice in the story, first when the mass is performed in the church, and secondly when the mother visiting the abbess is confronted with the score of the mass. The reaction of the brothers and of the mother is marked by significant gestures. The brothers, gathered in the church to desecrate the house of God, solemnly bare their heads once the music starts and order all their followers to do the same. The mother, confronted with the score, kisses the sheet of music in a gesture of humility and obedience to the inscrutable will of God. As a result of their experiences the brothers indulge in a Catholic adoration of the Cross, and the mother is received back into the Catholic church.

The power of music is described by Kleist – and, as one might expect in a story by him, it exerts a strange, ambiguous power. It is both divine and terrifying, creative and apparently destructive. It cuts through the appearances of the everyday world and penetrates to an absolute reality. Its effect is irrational, or rather transcends the rational world – hence the use of miraculous, legendary elements which, whatever they may owe to the Romantic vogue for the supernatural and mysterious current at the time Kleist was writing, are a logical development of his probing investigation into the non-rational aspects of life and human behaviour. The different layers of reality are reflected in his use of the Doppelgänger motif, whereby the figure of the nun Sister Antonia merges into the bodily presence of St. Cecilia. Kleist speaks of the 'feminine nature of the mysterious art' of music, 'die weibliche Geschlechtsart dieser geheimnisvollen Kunst', notes that the mass in question is distinguished for its particular 'Heiligkeit und Herrlichkeit', 'sanctity and splendour', describes how the nuns, as they performed it, felt 'ein wunderbarer, himmlischer Trost', 'a wonderful, heavenly solace' in their hearts, and their souls were uplifted 'wie auf Schwingen, durch alle Himmel des Wohlklangs', 'as if on pinioned wings through all the celestial realms of harmony'. Seen from this point of view the effect of music is something positive, a source of spiritual comfort, a divine harmony resolving the dissonances of the imperfect 'gebrechlich' world, indeed, a 'Flötenton im Orkan'.

As in Goethe's *Novelle* so here spiritual strength tames brute force and violence. This is its plus side. But it would appear to have a minus side as well. When the mother sees the score of the mass at the convent she is beset by conflicting emotions. 'Sie betrachtete die unbekannten zauberischen Zeichen, womit sich ein fürchterlicher Geist geheimnisvoll den Kreis abzustecken schien, und meinte, in die Erde zu sinken, da sie gerade das Gloria in excelsis aufgeschlagen fand. Es war ihr, als ob das ganze Schrecken der Tonkunst, das ihre Söhne verderbt hatte, über ihrem Haupte rauschend daherzöge.'[36] The word 'Gewalt' used to designate music takes on a more sinister meaning, its power is seen too as something disruptive, 'ent-setzlich' in the literal meaning of the word, and, in condemning the brothers to a life of religious madness, inscrutably harsh and cruel. Spiritual ecstasy, a 'feminine' art in its power to bring balm and comfort to the soul; notes and numbers, mathematics and metaphysics, the baffling formula of a dreadful absolute.

Yet are the brothers damned for life by an avenging deity? Irony and ambiguity is present too in this story, not surprisingly, since it deals with a force that is Janus-faced and whose totality embraces diverging extremes. Indeed irony surrounded the actual writing and publication of the story. Adam Müller's daughter Cecilia was baptized in a Protestant church in Berlin, this although Adam Müller had been received into the Catholic Church in Vienna on 30 April 1805. He found it prudent to conceal the fact in Berlin, because of his hopes of preferment in the Prussian civil service. Ironically Kleist's story appeared in the same number of the *Abendblätter* as Müller's article 'Vom Nationalkredit' which, because of its criticism of Hardenberg's financial reforms, caused government hostility towards the newspaper which forced it eventually to wind up, with considerable financial loss to Kleist. In the story the singing of the nuns is so beautiful that the entire congregation is transfixed; the singing of the

[36] 'She gazed at the unknown magical signs with which a dreadful spirit seemed mysteriously to mark out its circle, and thought she would sink into the ground when she found that it was open at the *Gloria in excelsis*. It seemed to her as if the whole terrible power of music, that had destroyed her sons, was reverberating over her head.'

brothers is so discordant that windows threaten to burst and neighbours recoil in horror from a noise resembling nothing so much as the distraught cries of the damned beseeching God for mercy. The brothers sing the *Gloria* and praise God; but they do this at midnight, the witching hour, when troublesome spirits are abroad. The fact that the church is saved is stressed; but for all that it is secularised following the Treaty of Westphalia.[37]

The greatest ambiguity however surrounds the fate of the brothers themselves. It may be that Kleist, the visit to the Würzburg asylum still fresh in his memory, was struck by the phenomenon of insanity and the mental imbalance brought about by a sudden swing from one emotional state to another. The figure of the mad monk, caught in the grip of a religious fixation and lost to the world outside, may have haunted him. His stories show how human beings, under the impact of a set of circumstances beyond the normal range of human experience, develop quite unexpected characteristics and oscillate from one extreme of conduct to the other. The background to this story is anything but 'normal', with its setting of religious riots, iconoclasm, human fanaticism, and the mutual hostility of Protestants and Catholics. The atmosphere in the church recalls the fateful *Te Deum* in the Dominican church in *Das Erdbeben in Chili*, though the outcome here is very different. The fact that it is the brothers who are singled out for such a revolutionary change in behaviour may be accounted for because they are from the outset emotionally unbalanced. Their youth and 'Schwärmerei' is stressed by Kleist, they spend the night before the planned attack drinking wine and eating, 'bei Wein und Speisen', fired by tales of iconoclasm in the Netherlands. The music affects them so dramatically precisely because of their religious fanaticism, which swings round from being fiercely Protestant to becoming fanatically Catholic. Their punishment seems out of all proportion to their offence, just as

---

[37] It seems unlikely that Kleist, in stressing this point, was making a veiled criticism of Hardenberg's secularisation of church property in the edict of 30 October 1810, as asserted by R. Steig, *Heinrich von Kleists Berliner Kämpfe*, 1901, though this cannot absolutely be ruled out.

that of the Marquis in *Das Bettelweib*. But then punishment, caused by chance or fate or an avenging deity, is not measured according to human standards, certainly not in the works of a writer who himself nearly came to a violent end because of the braying of an ass.[38] But should one speak of punishment, or not rather a leap of faith, a road to Damascus conversion? The brothers after their dramatic conversion show no signs of distress, and indeed display a certain serenity, albeit of a very serious and solemn kind, 'eine gewisse, obschon sehr ernste und feierliche Heiterkeit'. The world around them proclaims them to be mad, struck by God's lightning and living the life of puppets; but they treat this verdict with compassion and claim to have a deeper insight into the nature of Christ the Saviour than do their fellow-men. To onlookers they appear 'sinnverwirrt', 'distracted', and to suffer from the 'Ausschweifung einer religiösen Idee', 'the aberration of a religious idea'; the brothers claim to have been blessed with an insight into truth of such a shattering and absolute nature that nothing else is relevant to them but the adoration of the Cross and the singing of the *Gloria* in praise of God. Insanity and the revelation of higher truth – once again Kleist presents the reader with a paradox involving the baffling nature of truth and appearance, and the pendulum of human emotions.

The brothers are 'gottverdammt', 'gottlos', 'sinnverwirrt', possessed by the 'böse Geist', they are 'damned by God', 'godless', 'distracted' and possessed by the 'evil spirit'. Yet they live to a ripe old age and finally die – and it is on this note that Kleist, significantly enough, chooses to end the final version of the story – 'eines heitern und vergnügten Todes', 'a serene and contented death', after singing their last *Gloria in excelsis*. The word 'Heiterkeit', 'serenity', is used as a leitmotif throughout. It is used of the brother who is a preacher as he plans, with cheerful abandon, the attack on the church. It is used to describe the spiritual serenity of the Italian mass, a very different sort of 'Heiterkeit', and this serenity is

---

[38] Kleist and his step-sister Ulrike were sitting in a coach outside Frankfurt-am-Main when the braying of an ass made the horses bolt and the coach overturned. Kleist's reaction is characteristic: 'Und an einem Eselsgeschrei hing ein Menschenleben?' – 'And a human life depended on the braying of an ass?' Letter to Karoline von Schlieben, 18 July 1801.

transferred to the brothers after their experience in the church when they pursue their religious existence with 'ernste und feierliche Heiterkeit', a 'Heiterkeit' that remains with them up to the moment of their death.[39] Mad their conduct may be to the eyes of the outside world. Yet, for all the rigidity of their religious observances, the brothers lead a happy life and die a serene death.[40]

The power of music, as embodied in the saintly person of St. Cecilia, has wrought a miracle, attested by the Pope himself. This miracle is described by Kleist as 'dieses zu gleicher Zeit schreckliche und herrliche Wunder'. It preserves the convent, and it condemns the brothers. But the convent, for all its triumphant resurgence, cannot survive the Treaty of Westphalia; and the brothers, though apparently 'damned' and lost to the world of men, claim to enjoy religious insights granted only to the elect. Such is the power of music, the harmony of the spheres, the baffling mathematical formula that contains the riddle of truth.

---

[39] *Pace* Edmund Edel, 'Heinrich von Kleist *Die heilige Cäcilie oder die Gewalt der Musik. Eine Legende*', *Wirkendes Wort* 14 (1969), pp. 105-15, who thinks the brothers are 'heiter' because their hell on earth is finally coming to an end, a view that does scant justice to the text.

[40] The fact that the four brothers all die together, apparently at the same instant in time, after chanting their last *Gloria* is not without irony.

7
Michael Kohlhaas

Einer der rechtschaffensten zugleich und entsetzlichsten Menschen seiner Zeit.[1]

A

Michael Kohlhaas is the longest by far of Kleist's stories and arguably the greatest. It is unquestionably a masterpiece, but one that is by no means easy to come to terms with. It raises vast issues, to which in the very nature of things there can be no simple direct answer. Precisely what values are salvaged and upheld at the end of the story is something over which critics, as with other major works by Kleist, have been unable to agree.[2]

Michael Kohlhaas is a respected horse-dealer living in Brandenburg near the Saxon border. Setting out with a string of horses one day on a business trip to Dresden he is held up at the Saxon castle of the Tronkenburg just across the border, where he is told he needs an official pass if he wants to take his horses to Dresden. After some discussion Junker Wenzel, the lord of the castle, agrees to let him leave two horses behind as security and proceed with the rest to Dresden. In Dresden Kohlhaas, his business done, discovers that no pass was needed and the whole thing had been an illegal trick practised on him at the Tronkenburg. Returning there to claim his horses he finds that they have been reduced to a brokendown state through being overworked in the fields and that the stable-lad left behind to look after them has been thrown out of the Tronkenburg and sent home. Kohlhaas, who is

---

[1] 'One of the most upright and at the same time one of the most terrible men of his time.' This statement occurs in the opening sentence of the story.
[2] Well summarised by Ludwig Büttner, 'Michael Kohlhaas – eine paranoische oder heroische Gestalt?', *Seminar* 4, i, pp. 26–41.

grievously insulted to his face by Junker Wenzel when he complains of this, refuses to accept the horses in the condition they are in, and returns home to Kohlhaasenbrück to institute legal proceedings for the restitution of the horses in a proper condition and compensation for the damage done to the stable-lad Herse, who had been robbed and badly beaten up. His three attempts to obtain redress meet with failure, owing to the corruption of court officials, and the third attempt costs him his wife, who dies after making an unsuccessful attempt to present a petition to the Elector of Brandenburg. All legal means of satisfaction from Junker Wenzel in the matter of the horses seem barred to Kohlhaas and he determines to obtain justice by non-legal means. He attacks the Tronkenburg with a band of followers in an attempt to seize the Junker and, thwarted in this, pursues him throughout Saxony with an increasingly large army of followers, spreading fire and the sword in town and countryside alike, finally identifying himself with the Archangel Michael and setting up a provisional world government to visit terrible justice on all the supporters of Junker Wenzel. At this point of no return Martin Luther issues a public letter accusing Kohlhaas of godless injustice and revenge. Following upon a secret meeting between the two men, during which the social and religious aspects of Kohlhaas' conduct are subjected to particular scrutiny, an amnesty for Kohlhaas is arranged by Luther with the Saxon authorities and Kohlhaas, disbanding his forces, settles in Dresden to await, like any peaceable citizen, the outcome of his legal suit against Junker Wenzel in the Saxon courts. The bone of contention, the two horses, are with difficulty tracked down and brought, fearfully emaciated, into the market-place at Dresden by the knacker of Döbbeln. By ill chance disaster results from this, for a riot breaks out in the market-place, public opinion swings against Kohlhaas, the Saxon ministers feel strong enough to break Kohlhaas' amnesty and, following a frame-up involving a former member of his armed band now turned brigand on his own account, Kohlhaas is sentenced to death. At this point the Elector of Brandenburg steps in and claims Kohlhaas as a Brandenburg citizen, and the Saxon authorities have no alternative but to hand Kohlhaas over to stand trial in Berlin, though, by appealing to the Emperor in Vienna, they ensure that he will be tried according to Imperial and not Brandenburg laws. Further complications of a mysterious nature arise. The Elector of Saxony discovers that Kohlhaas is the possessor of a capsule containing a prophecy about the ruling house of Saxony made by a gypsy woman and given to him by her the day after his wife died. This capsule the Elector wants at all costs to acquire into his possession and he is prepared to arrange for Kohlhaas' escape from custody in order to get it. But Kohlhaas, anxious to avenge himself on the Elector of Saxony as head of the state where he has suffered injustice, refuses to part with the capsule. He is finally condemned to be beheaded in Berlin under Imperial law. Before he dies he discovers that the gypsy woman is the double or revenant of his dead wife Lisbeth. Junker Wenzel is punished by the courts. Kohlhaas gets full legal satisfaction, his horses are fattened up and restored to their previous gleaming condition, and his children taken under the protective care of the Elector of Brandenburg. Just before his execution Kohlhaas takes the slip of paper from the capsule, reads it, and, knowing that the Elector of Saxony is in the crowd watching him and planning to rob his corpse of the capsule, swallows it. Then, amidst the general lamentations of the crowd, but having achieved all he set out to do, he is beheaded.

Michael Kohlhaas was begun in Königsberg in 1804. The first quarter of it, up to the assault on the Tronkenburg, was published in 1808 in the sixth issue of *Phöbus* and taken over with only minor alterations in the completed version first published in 1810 in the first volume of the *Erzählungen*. The story is based on history. There was indeed a Hans Kohlhase, who for eighteen years, from 1522 to 1540, waged a campaign against Saxony as a result of an injustice done to him. He was finally executed in Berlin, along with his companion Georg Nagelschmidt. It is interesting to see how Kleist adapts his sources.[3] The real Kohlhase eluded Saxon justice and was

---

[3] The main source is the relevant section of Peter Hafftitz' *Märckische Chronik* contained in the *Diplomatische und curieuse Nachlese der Historie von Ober-Sachsen und angrenzenden Ländern* by Christian Schöttgen and G. Kreysig, Part III, 1731. A possible source is Nicolaus Leutinger's *De Marchia Brandenburgensi eiusque statu Commentarii*, Frankfurt, 1729.

only finally arrested when he attempted armed robbery on Brandenburg soil; Kleist, to point the difference between the rulers of Saxony and Brandenburg, has Kohlhaas rescued from Saxon injustice by the intervention of the wise and just Elector of Brandenburg. The real Kohlhase rarely had more than ten followers at any one time in his band; Kleist, eager to build up the stature of Kohlhaas, has him amass what amounts to a private army. The real Kohlhase is executed along with Nagelschmidt; Kleist, anxious to underline the difference between Kohlhaas' motives and those of a common brigand, however similar their actions may appear to be, casts Nagelschmidt as a murderous criminal partly responsible for the death sentence passed on Kohlhaas in Dresden. The real Kohlhase did indeed have a meeting with Luther, and received communion from him; in Kleist's story Luther refuses Kohlhaas communion, thus pinpointing the religious and moral aspects of his campaign. Margaretha, the wife of the real Kohlhase, outlived him by many years; Lisbeth, the wife of Kohlhaas, dies as a result of her unsuccessful attempt to help her husband's cause at the Brandenburg court, and her death is a crucial factor in the motivation of Kohlhaas' subsequent actions. The real Kohlhase was broken on the wheel and suffered a long and terrible death; Kleist's Kohlhaas is honourably beheaded, and his death is almost a triumph.

Michael Kohlhaas, as has already been said, raises vast issues of general importance, and they need to be outlined here, since they are easily lost sight of in the confusing welter of detail with which the story is packed. What is justice? Is it something tangible that can be tied down in a code of law, or an abstract ideal, an absolute value, belief in which prevents human life from degenerating into a naked fight for survival? What is the relation between the ideal of justice and the law as such? Is the law liable to become something impersonal and absolute, where the individual is lost sight of as the legal machinery takes over? Can the law be twisted, to permit legal injustice, and what happens when there is a discrepancy between the spirit and the letter of the law? These questions are raised in *Michael Kohlhaas*. What is the connection between what is legally and what is morally right and wrong? Where does man-made law stop and divine law take over? What is the role of an established church in society? How far should one go in turning the other cheek and forgiving one's neighbours, and how are the absolute demands of conscience to be reconciled with an awareness of the fragile nature of the world, the 'Gebrechlichkeit der Welt'? These too are problems with which *Michael Kohlhaas* is vitally concerned. What is the relationship of the individual to the state, and what obligations does the social contract impose on them both? What happens if the state is not democratic but totalitarian? Is it then permissible to resort to lawlessness in order to impose a rule of law? What of human motivation in all this, and the way in which idealism can degenerate into fanaticism, and a quest for justice become merged with an urge for revenge?

The ideal of justice, the workings of the law, the social contract between the state and the individual, the demands of religion and the claims of conscience, the pursuit of legal satisfaction and the desire for revenge, all this is presented and debated in *Michael Kohlhaas*. If Kohlhaas were merely a man wanting his horses back, driven to avenge a private grudge, refusing to listen to reason and indulging in violence and bloodshed for its own sake, then the story would lose all point and become, what to some people it may well be, a tale of revenge sought by a man incapable of moderation, an apt vehicle for the pathological excesses of a distraught genius. This is not the case. Not all the answers to the problems raised may be unambiguous or acceptable. But that is relatively unimportant in relation to the magnitude of the issues involved, and these have to be realised clearly from the outset if the full scope of the story is to be properly appreciated.

B

The essential flavour and atmosphere of the story become apparent when its form and structure are analysed, not surprisingly in a story by Kleist where form and content are so closely interrelated. It can be divided easily into three sections. The first section contains all the events from the confiscation of the horses up to the intervention of Luther; the second section deals with the intervention of Luther and the attempts of Kohlhaas to obtain legal satisfaction in Dresden; and the third section starts with the intervention of the Elector of Brandenburg and contains all the subsequent events leading up to Kohlhaas' eventual execution. In the first section it is Kohlhaas, once the initial wrong has been done, who is the aggressive party, and the action appears to be controlled by human beings exercising their will-power. The style is forceful and dramatic and the story moves at a great pace. In the second section Kohlhaas is far more of a passive figure, a great deal of the action is carried on above his head and it is the processes of the law that take over, the people in the story get caught up in it and submerged in the intrigues and tangles that are a feature of it. The third section resolves the conflict and provides the final solution to the story, and it is worth noting that this solution is not the work of Kohlhaas, but of outside intervention. A state of deadlock has been reached, human reason seems powerless to resolve the conflict, the almost arbitrary intervention of the Emperor and the Elector of Brandenburg is needed, together with the intrusion of the irrational in the figure of the mysterious gypsy woman. Violence and action, the deadlock reached in the operation of the law, and the intervention of higher forces from outside to resolve the conflict; such is the basic pattern of *Michael Kohlhaas*.

It is a pattern that gets enormously complicated. Each of the three main sections of the story can be split up into subsections. The first main section falls into three subsections, namely, the account of the injustice done to Kohlhaas, his attempts to gain legal redress, and his attempts to dispense his own justice. But each of these three subsections can be further subdivided into three subsections. The account of the offence done to him is told in three scenes, the first Tronkenburg scene, the second Tronkenburg scene, and the interrogation of Herse. The attempts to gain legal redress are split into three, namely, the letter Kohlhaas writes to Dresden, the 'Supplik' he addresses to the Elector of Brandenburg, and the journey of his wife to Berlin. The attempts to dispense his own justice by hunting down Wenzel von Tronka similarly fall into three sections, namely, the attack on the Tronkenburg, the scene in front of the convent at Erlabrunn, and the events leading up to the setting up of the 'Weltregierung', the 'world government', at Lützen. In just the same way the second main section can be subdivided into three subsections, namely, the intervention of Luther, the attempts to secure justice in Dresden, and the fresh breach of the law; and each of these subsections can be further subdivided into three. The intervention of Luther subdivides into the meeting of Kohlhaas and Luther, the meeting of the Saxon privy council, and the granting of the amnesty. The attempts to secure justice subdivide into the search for the horses, the scene with the knacker from Döbbeln, and the consequences arising from this episode. The fresh breach of the law subdivides into the intervention of Nagelschmidt, the breach of the amnesty, and the events leading up to sentence being passed on Kohlhaas. The third main section falls into two halves, namely, the story of the capsule, and the events in Berlin leading to the final solution. And these two subsections each subdivide further into three subsections, on the one hand the intervention of the Elector of Brandenburg, the story of the capsule as told by Kohlhaas, and the story of the capsule as told by the Elector of Saxony; and on the other hand the appearance of the gypsy woman, the efforts of the Elector of Saxony to divert the course of justice in Berlin, and the final vindication and execution of Kohlhaas.

In this way the story has been divided up into twenty-four sections, or scenes – and this is certainly alarming, so alarming in fact, that one may well question whether the story should be chopped up in this way. Surely, to do this merely creates confusion. Yet confusion is exactly an impression that Kleist wishes to create and the form of the story in part serves this end. The legal labyrinth in which Kohlhaas gets lost and the absurdities of the legal processes when conditioned solely by the letter of the law, all this is brought out by the bewildering kaleidoscope of scenes, with the action getting bogged down in a welter of muddling detail. On the other hand the story could be split up in another way. The subdividing into scenes points to its essentially dramatic nature, and with this dramatic element in mind it is possible to divide the story into five acts, together with a prologue. The prologue would consist of the offence of confiscating the horses, and the five acts would then follow; firstly, the attack on the Tronkenburg, secondly, the intervention of Luther, thirdly, the appearance of the knacker from Döbbeln, fourthly, the emergence of Nagelschmidt, and fifthly, the triumph of Kohlhaas. Such a division brings out the interesting fact that a central scene of the story features the knacker from Döbbeln, a scene in which all the issues of the story are concentrated together in tragicomical fashion.

If it is possible to play around with the structure of the story in this manner, bringing out its essentially dramatic nature together with its deliberate confusion of detail, it is also possible to look at the incidents in it in a different way and to extract from them another basic pattern. The theme of the story is the quest for justice. The pattern of a quest, a search, a tracking down of a person or pursuit of some kind of satisfaction underlies *Michael Kohlhaas*. Kohlhaas seeks justice, and the scene of his efforts to find this moves backwards and forwards from Dresden to Berlin, Berlin to Dresden, and finally Dresden to Berlin. The pursuit of justice is linked with the idea of a chase, as Kohlhaas attempts to track down his adversary Junker Wenzel von Tronka, pursuing his zigzag course from Kohlhaasenbrück to the Tronkenburg, and from there to Erlabrunn, to Wittenberg, to Mühlberg, to Leipzig, to Lützen and to Dresden. There are the unavailing efforts of Otto von Gorgas and the Prince of Meißen to catch Kohlhaas, a futile chase through a maze of false trails and dead ends. There is the search for the horses, once the order has gone out from Dresden that they are to be recovered, a search that involves chasing up one doubtful report after another, with names dropped liberally to increase the confusion, until finally they turn up in the square at Dresden, led in by the knacker of Döbbeln. There is the unravelling of a secret, in this case the secret of the capsule, which further complicates and muddles the pattern of events. Finally, the quest of Kohlhaas for justice is balanced in the third section of the story by the endeavours of the Elector of Saxony to prevent the due processes of the law, so that he can recover the capsule from Kohlhaas. This quest on the part of the elector is equally complicated, runs into absurd difficulties, acquires almost an air of grotesque comedy as it develops, and ends in ludicrous failure, just as Kohlhaas has reached the goal of his quest. First of all the Elector of Saxony sends the Jagdjunker von Stein to try and bribe Kohlhaas, in vain. Then he tries, too late, to prevent the departure of the lawyer Eibenmayer for Vienna. Then he addresses a personal letter to the Emperor asking for proceedings to be halted, only to be informed that the matter has already gone too far. Then he sends a personal letter to the Elector of Brandenburg, only to be referred back to the Emperor. Then his chancellor, Kunz von Tronka, tries to obtain the capsule by trickery in Berlin and fails in this. Then, in a desperate attempt to find out the contents of the capsule, the Elector ludicrously consults two astrologers Oldenholm and Olearius (the story is littered with names), and is ill rewarded for his pains. Finally, he even plans to disinter the corpse of Kohlhaas and rob it of the capsule, and in this too he is foiled. What irony! The Elector is now prepared to exhume the corpse of the man whom his courts in Dresden once described as a 'useless grumbler', an 'unnützer Querulant'. He had been unable, in the case of Kohlhaas, to administer justice; and now he is unable to stop the machinery of the law, once his corrupt ministers have set it in motion.

There is, then, with these interlocking pursuits and quests a constant sense of movement in the story. The confusion this causes is further heightened by the interrogations and meetings and discussions which are scattered throughout, as if to underline the legal tangles and the deadlock of human ratiocination, scenes such as Kohlhaas' interrogation of Herse, the meeting between Kohlhaas and Luther, and the meeting of the Saxon privy council. Kleist then deliberately increases the confusion still more by the muddling layer of legal terms and paraphernalia which is spread thickly over it all. Documents are needed, letters written, inquiries held, lawyers briefed, and resolutions passed. Words describing legal processes are thick on the ground. Kohlhaas needs a 'Paßschein', which is based on a 'landesherrliches Privilegium', he makes a 'Beschwerde', a 'Klage', hands in a 'Supplik', issues 'Mandaten', engages in a 'Prozess', is granted an 'Amnestie', hopes that the appropriate 'Rechtsinstanz' will pass favourable 'Rechtsschlüsse', his case is taken up by 'Advokaten', 'Rechtsgelehrte', 'Assessoren' and 'Hofassessoren'. In the end the machinery of the law takes over, like an instrument of fate, and nothing can stop it. Names are freely bandied about. The Saxon lawyer is Eibenmayer, the Brandenburg lawyer Anton Zäuner,[4] the Hofassessor of the Emperor is Franz Müller. Small wonder that eventually Kohlhaas grows tired of the whole business and plans to escape and settle down somewhere abroad.

The affair of the horse-dealer and his two horses gains progressively in momentum. At first it is a private matter between individuals. Then the state of Saxony becomes involved. Then it grows into an affair involving the two rival and contrasting electorates of Saxony and Brandenburg. This then broadens out on to the plane of European politics, because of the conflict between Saxony and Poland. Finally the whole German 'imperium' is involved and the Emperor himself descends like a 'deus ex machina' to resolve the business. Like the ripples in a pond the affair of Kohlhaas, the horse-dealer, spreads out in ever-widening circles, and its location reaches out from the home of Kohlhaas and the castle of the Tronkas to the chancelleries of Dresden, Berlin and Vienna. In the first third of the story much of the action is in the open air, against a background of the mounting use of imagery of tempest and fire. In the other two thirds the action is carried on indoors and settings featuring Kohlhaas become more and more confined – until the moment on the Monday after Palm Sunday when he leaves the four walls of his prison for the final reckoning in the execution square.

Two symbols are used in the story as linking devices. One symbol occurring throughout is that of the two horses, reflecting, in the way that they are 'wohlgenährt und glänzend', 'well-fed and gleaming', at the beginning, 'unehrlich', 'dishonourable', in the middle, and 'ehrlich' and 'wohlgenährt und glänzend' at the end the progress of Kohlhaas' fortunes, as well as holding up a mirror, through the adjective 'dürr', 'skinny', used of them in their wretched state, to the pitiful figure of Junker Wenzel von Tronka. The

---

[4] Dietmar Nedde, *Untersuchungen zur Struktur von Dichtung an Novellen Heinrich von Kleists*, Diss., Göttingen, 1955 hazards the odd suggestion that he is called Anton Zäuner because he knows the law from A to Z.

other symbol is that of the capsule. It is first mentioned in the final third of the story, when Kohlhaas says it was given to him as a lucky charm by the gypsy woman. But it is worth remembering that it was given to him the day after his wife died – so one is told in a flashback, the only occasion the normal time sequence is interrupted – and it means that there is a continuous link between Kohlhaas and his wife, although he will not realise who the gypsy woman is until the day of his death. The existence of the capsule means that the private side of Kohlhaas' life is not lost sight of in the vast issues of state which his conduct as a public figure involves him in.

It might be useful at this point to make mention of the characters who appear in *Michael Kohlhaas*, or at least some of them, since to list them all would only create further confusion, though a confusion that might be welcomed by Kleist who, affecting the guise of chronicler, drops names liberally in order to impart the impression of at least a surface realism to his work while at the same time further weaving the web of entangling detail.

The main character is Kohlhaas, a Brandenburg citizen who carries on much of his business in Saxony and owns a house in Dresden. His adversary in the first half of the story is Junker Wenzel von Tronka, in the second half of the story the Elector of Saxony. Around the main characters Kohlhaas, Junker Wenzel and the Electors of Saxony and Brandenburg are grouped constellations of minor characters. Standing rather apart, but having a decisive influence on the action, are the three characters of Martin Luther, the knacker from Döbbeln, and the mysterious gypsy woman.

The characters grouped around Kohlhaas consist of his wife and family, the men who work for him, his neighbours, and his business and legal associates. Kohlhaas is bound to them by ties of mutual affection, loyalty and respect. As the scope of his actions increases others become associated with his cause, including such dubious characters as Nagelschmidt.

The Tronka clan, the main members of which apart from Wenzel consist of Hinz and Kunz von Tronka, comical enough names for such sinister characters, is powerful at the Saxon court and becomes more powerful during the course of the story. It is also related through marriage to the Kallheims, who are influential not only at the court in Dresden but also in Berlin. Its influence on the Elector of Saxony is further increased by the fact that Kunz's wife Heloise is a former lady friend of the Elector's. One way and another the Tronkas exert a powerful influence on the governments of Saxony and Brandenburg. Junker Wenzel has gathered about him at the Tronkenburg various servants, two of whom in particular, the castellan and the bailiff, are responsible through him for the wrong done to Kohlhaas. Two other Tronkas are mentioned. Antonia von Tronka, Wenzel's aunt, is abbess of the convent of Erlabrunn and a highly admirable person. Also at the Tronkenburg is a certain Hans von Tronka, of whom all that is heard is that he is seized by Kohlhaas in the assault on the Tronkenburg and hurled across the room, his brains bespattering the stone flags – a nice example of Kleist disposing of a minor character almost absentmindedly in a subsidiary clause.

The Elector of Saxony is surrounded by the members of his Privy Council, some of whom are 'bad' and some of whom are 'good'. Graf Kallheim and the two Tronkas, Hinz and Kunz, are interested in promoting Tronka interests; but Graf Wrede, the chancellor, and Prince Christiern von Meißen are both good and fair men and provide a counterweight to the machinations of the Tronkas. The Elector is also surrounded by other nobles, by lawyers and by astrologers.

Few characters are mentioned in connection with the Elector of Brandenburg, firstly because most of the action takes place in Saxony, and secondly because his almost godlike status is thereby preserved. His chancellor, Graf Kallheim, indirectly related to the Tronkas by marriage, is replaced during the course of the story by Heinrich von Geusau, the commandant of Berlin, in other words a 'bad' man is replaced by a 'good' man. In the Saxon court, on the other hand, Graf Wrede is dismissed and replaced by another Graf Kallheim, whose place is in turn taken by Kunz von Tronka, in other words a good man goes and two members of the Tronka faction get promoted. The promotions and demotions mirror the shifting importance of good and bad influences at the respective courts.

C

'Einer der rechtschaffensten zugleich und entsetzlichsten Menschen seiner Zeit', this is how Kleist describes Kohlhaas in the opening sentence of the story. The sentence is closed with a full-stop and a dash – and given Kleist's meticulous use of punctuation this means a great deal. It means that this pronouncement is singled out for special consideration by the reader. It is a judgement delivered by Kleist, and not just a relative statement to be understood in the light of the situation of this or that character. The two epithets used of Kohlhaas are in the superlative, and they are carefully chosen, since they replace the tamer and less meaningful 'außerordentlich' and 'fürchterlich', 'extraordinary' and 'frightful', of the Phöbus version.[5] It is quite essential to note that the two adjectives finally chosen are linked by the word 'zugleich'. No interpretation of the character of Kohlhaas can afford to ignore this. He combines in his person both these qualities, and although their respective influence may vary during the course of the story they are always present. In a sense they are two sides of the same coin. The drive and suppressed violence that underlie his determination to see right done, also, seen from the negative side, give the impetus to his desire to exact revenge for wrong, real or imagined. Once a crisis comes to shake a man out of his usual calm acceptance of things, then the opposing aspects of his character, balanced and under control in a 'normal' world, gain greater autonomy and tend to extremes, and can be seen in terms of plus and minus.

'Normal' people would not have reacted as Kohlhaas does to the wrong done to him by Junker Wenzel. But revolutionary changes in society and social patterns are not brought about by 'normal' people. A man obsessed by a sense of a particular value and determined at all costs to uphold it is likely to be one-sided, a fanatic, unswayed by reasons of commonsense, holding fast to his goal and not allowing himself to be diverted from it by human considerations that

---

[5] *Phöbus* has 'einer der außerordentlichsten und fürchterlichsten Menschen seiner Zeit', 'one of the most extraordinary and frightful men of his time' – there is no 'zugleich'.

would move an ordinary man. How he is judged by succeeding generations, it may cynically be noted, depends on whether he reaches this goal or not. Kleist, interested as he is in the complementary extremes of human character, is concerned to show how an excess of virtue – and an inborn sense of justice is a virtue – can lead to a corresponding excess of a negative quality: 'Das Rechtgefühl aber machte ihn zum Räuber und Mörder'.[6]

If the crucial 'zugleich' is lost sight of, then interpretations of Kohlhaas may well tend to be onesided. He will appear on the one hand as a man fighting for what is right, triumphantly establishing the principle of justice in a fallible world, and as a 'loving husband and father'.[7] On the other hand he will appear to be a creature motivated by revenge, a 'bad husband, a bad son of the Church and a bad father'.[8] Wives of great men may well find them uncomfortable people to be married to; orthodoxy frequently condemns idealists who depart from its norms; the children of outstanding men and active fanatics may well have unsettled lives. Kohlhaas is not necessarily a 'nice' man and he would no doubt make a somewhat overwhelming companion. His very sense of justice is an unsettling business. His virtues cannot be separated from his defects.

Kleist depicts the character of Kohlhaas in different ways. He delivers, as narrator, judgments on him; he reports judgments made on him by other characters; his conduct is mirrored in the contacts and dealings he has with others; and the various aspects of his character are shown in the different roles he plays in life. It is easy to forget he is a young man in his thirtieth year. One rarely gets inside Kohlhaas, nor does Kleist bother to give a description of what he looks like. Details of character, limited as they are, are strictly related to the story and the issues it raises.

Kohlhaas is a man of the world. He is aware that the world is not a perfect place, and is prepared at first to be tolerant of

---

[6] 'His feeling for justice however made him into a robber and a murderer.'
[7] Described thus in almost identical terms by Büttner, op.cit., and Charles E. Passage, '*Michael Kohlhaas*: Form Analysis', *Germanic Review*, 30 (1955), pp. 181-97.
[8] R.S. Lucas, 'Studies in Kleist. *Michael Kohlhaas*', *DVLG*, 44 (1970), pp. 120-45.

Junker Wenzel's attempt to extract tolls and fees. To this extent he is a realist, as one might well expect a horse-dealer to be. He is most civil in his dealings with others, addresses them with the proper deference and courtesy, and bows when appropriate. There will be no lack of good manners in the Kohlhaas household. He has a keen sense of what is right and wrong – it is as finely balanced as a pair of gold scales – 'sein Rechtgefühl, das einer Goldwaage glich' – and he is almost pedantic in his determination not to judge Wenzel until he has elicited all the facts of the case from Herse. He is keenly aware of his worth as an individual and it is the insult to his own integrity made by the Junker that he is not prepared to tolerate. He gets indignant at injustice, and when he thinks the state is turning a blind eye to it the violence latent in him erupts to the surface. Once, however, he feels that the state is prepared to treat his case on its merits, instead of denying him his rights as a citizen, he is very quick to disband his army of irregulars and become once again the model law-abiding citizen patiently awaiting the outcome of his law-suit. When things go badly he tends to get discouraged, be it at Kohlhaasenbrück or Dresden; but then his spirits rise again when there is fresh hope of justice or revenge.

He is shown in various roles. As a trader in horses he is respected for his fairness and honesty. As a citizen and neighbour in Kohlhaasenbrück he is looked up to and liked. He appears as a godfearing Christian of the Protestant faith, to which his wife becomes converted. Whenever possible he likes to have his children around him, be it in Kohlhaasenbrück, Dresden or Berlin, and, unsettling though it may be for them to be shuttled backwards and forwards, his affection and concern for them cannot be doubted. He is a devoted husband. It is true that he announces decisions to his wife rather than consults her, but he lives in the sixteenth century and not the twentieth. One of the reasons for his campaign, he claims, is to provide a secure existence for his wife and children. When his wife dies it is the thought of justifying her death to himself, for whatever reason, that enables him to carry on his campaign. As husband, father, neighbour, Christian, citizen and businessman Kohlhaas is shown in a favourable light.

But once he embarks on his campaign to secure justice and takes on the role of avenging archangel he is no longer 'das Muster eines guten Staatsbürgers', 'the model of a good citizen', and becomes a different person, or rather the other side of him takes over. He seems to lose all sense of proportion as he proclaims war on society, ravages Saxony and establishes his world government at Lützen, and even after making allowances for the fact that Kleist is deliberately indulging his technique of overstating contrasting extremes of human behaviour, it may not be fanciful to suggest that Kohlhaas succumbs to a temporary attack of megalomania. The point is that it is temporary and lasts only as long as Kohlhaas considers himself to be outlawed by society. The moment he feels that his rights as a member of society are protected by the proper workings of the law the violence subsides and he becomes a 'guter Staatsbürger' again. The potential for violence and revenge remains as part of his character, and were he to feel again that justice and due satisfaction were not obtainable because of the inadequacy of the law, then it would flare up once more – and does indeed at the end of the story when he takes his revenge on the Elector of Saxony.

Kohlhaas' character thus poses a teasing paradox. He is certainly very 'rechtschaffen'; but there is no doubt that he can also be 'entsetzlich', and Kleist is not concerned to gloss over this fact, though he may imply reasons why this side of Kohlhaas' character on occasions comes to the fore. Kleist then further heightens the riddle of Kohlhaas' conduct in two different ways. One is his use of what one might call a mirror technique. In the crucial scene with the knacker from Döbbeln the character Meister Himboldt is used, as will be seen later, to throw Kohlhaas' behaviour into relief. And then, when affairs in Dresden are taking a turn for the worse, the character of Nagelschmidt is introduced. Nagelschmidt, a former member of Kohlhaas' band who narrowly escaped being hanged on the orders of Kohlhaas shortly before the granting of the amnesty, has set himself up as the leader of an armed band of robbers and apes Kohlhaas in every detail, even claiming to represent Kohlhaas, to be a 'Statthalter des Kohlhaas', while the latter is detained in Dresden. He is then a mirror-image of Kohlhaas, and one is forced through him to ponder on the morality of Kohlhaas' behaviour. Is Kohlhaas in fact no better than Nagelschmidt, a common brigand? And if he is, if, although for all practical purposes they indulge in the same acts, there is still a difference in kind between them because of their different motivation, then what does this different motivation consist of? Kohlhaas' violence in the role of archangel exacts a kind of retribution in the figure of Nagelschmidt. At the other end of the scale Kleist introduces another mirror-image in the person of the gypsy, the Zigeunerin double of his wife Lisbeth. By her existence she confronts Kohlhaas anew with the problem of the rightness of his conduct and the consequences it has for his life and for that of his children, and she plays a material role in helping him to die at one with his conscience.

The appearance of the gypsy at the end and the prospect she holds out to him of freedom in return for giving the capsule to the Elector of Saxony pinpoints another technique Kleist uses in depicting the character and motivation of Kohlhaas. He subjects him to a series of temptations, raises possibilities, sometimes hypothetical, that bring Kohlhaas face to face with what he is doing. Early on in the story, after the second attempt of Kohlhaas to gain justice by legal means has failed, the reader is told how completely at a loss he would be if Junker Wenzel returned his emaciated horses to Kohlhaasenbrück, perhaps even sending them back with an apology. He would have been at a loss and the whole basis of his actions undermined because his view of the Junker and the world of which he is a part would have been proved wrong. Happily or unhappily the Junker does not make this gesture, Kohlhaas' sombre view of the world is confirmed, he makes his plans accordingly and feels at one with himself. Another such 'temptation' occurs in the scene with Luther where Luther, although prepared to use his influence with the Saxon authorities to get Kohlhaas an amnesty, invites him to forgive the Junker and go back to Kohlhaasenbrück in a gesture of Christian forgiveness, indeed makes this a condition for giving Kohlhaas communion. In the face of this request from the man whom he respects most of all Kohlhaas has to be very sure of his motives if he is to continue along his chosen path.

In Dresden he is subjected to another 'temptation' when Nagelschmidt offers to help him escape from his confinement, and distaste for Nagelschmidt conflicts in his mind with hatred for the authorities who he is convinced have broken the amnesty. On the journey from Dresden to Berlin there is another 'temptation', for the Jagdjunker von Stein, acting on orders from the Elector of Saxony, offers him freedom in exchange for the capsule, and this Kohlhaas declines, preferring to keep the possibility of revenge on the Elector open by keeping the capsule. And in Berlin he is given a final chance of freedom through the encounter with the gypsy woman.

In this way Kleist makes Kohlhaas constantly review his actions and the reasons for them and the reader too is implicitly invited to do the same. In assessing Kohlhaas' reactions to these temptations the reader may put a favourable interpretation on them and ascribe them to Kohlhaas' desire for justice, cost what it may; or he may view them unfavourably, finding in them confirmation of the view that Kohlhaas is concerned solely with revenge, however speciously he may seek to justify it. The fact is that Kleist, far too clever a writer to commit himself absolutely, leaves both interpretations open, and that with good reason, for in a sense they are both right. The ambivalence of Kohlhaas' character is consistent throughout, he is both 'rechtschaffen' and 'entsetzlich' – and that 'zugleich'!

Kohlhaas' two main adversaries present a grotesque contrast to the powerful figure of the avenging horse-dealer. Junker Wenzel is almost a comic figure,[9] a wretched weedy creature as 'dürr' as the two emaciated horses, a character who is anything but heroic as he escapes by a back door from the Tronkenburg, a comic-opera figure disappearing as it were through a trap-door. No sooner does he hear Kohlhaas' voice in the courtyard 'als er den Herren schon, plötzlich leichenblaß: "Brüder, rettet euch!" zurief und verschwand'.[10] He also cuts a ridiculous figure in Wittenberg where he has one fainting fit after the other and is surrounded by doctors

---

[9] Cf. my article, 'Junker Wenzel von Tronka', *GLL*, 18 (1965), pp. 252-7.
[10] 'Then, turning pale as a corpse, he cried to the lords: "Brothers, save yourselves!" and disappeared.'

trying to revive him with 'Essenzen und Irritanzen'. His progress through the streets of Wittenberg from his house to a more secure dwelling is described in terms of high comedy. Some clothes are thrown over him, his collar is left open because he finds difficulty in breathing, and then supported by two noblemen he totters through the streets against a background of curses and maledictions from the large crowd assembled to witness the spectacle. The helmet stuck on his head keeps falling off without his noticing it and has to be put back on again by a knight bringing up the rear. On his final appearance in Dresden all he can do is bewail his fate, proclaim faintly that he is the most pitiable creature in the world and sit down while he says this, so weak is he.

What a master-stroke of Kleist to make the arch-enemy of Kohlhaas in the first half of the story a comical weakling, a man as wretched as the horses are once they have spent some time in the Tronkenburg. One could almost feel sorry for Wenzel and be glad that Kohlhaas never actually got his hands on him. Such sympathy would be misplaced. Wenzel's actions are no less culpable because he is weak and a prey to the sinister suggestions of his servants, and it is no excuse to plead that he was unaware of what they were doing. Responsibility cannot be evaded in this way. Moreover, in the one scene where he does not appear in a comic light at all he consciously insults Kohlhaas, and then stalks off to partake of wine with his noble friends. He disappears from the scene when the two horses reappear in the marketplace at Dresden, and Kohlhaas no longer directs his vengeance against him, for the good reason that the law is brought to bear on Wenzel and when last heard of he is serving a two-year prison sentence for his part in the Kohlhaas affair.

More problematic is Kohlhaas' other adversary, the Elector of Saxony. He too is not an impressive figure. He is anything but strong physically and all too prone to faint when faced with something unpleasant and to succumb to the 'Nervenfieber' which Kleist reserves for some of his characters. He is not strongwilled, would prefer to avoid awkward decisions, goes red in the face when faced with ticklish questions of principle, another Kleistian trademark, and altogether would be happier in the company of pretty ladies or indulging in the pleasures of the chase than trying to sort out the conflicting advice of his various ministers. Yet he is by no means a bad man nor an unjust one.[11] He has good advisers on the Saxon privy council in Graf Wrede and the Prince of Meißen and is prepared to listen to them. He does after all give Kohlhaas an amnesty, and if this is conditionally phrased then that may only be a mark of common prudence. He can claim to be ignorant of the Kohlhaas affair in the beginning, since knowledge of it was withheld from him by the Tronka faction, though he can hardly have remained ignorant of it for very long. All in all he may be a weak man, but hardly a bad one.

A certain sympathy for the Elector and an awareness that he is not basically evil cannot however absolve him of responsibility for what happens to Kohlhaas in Dresden. He is an absolute ruler with the aura of that divine right by which Luther set such store. He cannot in the last analysis hide behind the ministers whom he has appointed. The only time he is prompted to action is when in his own interests he tries to get the capsule from Kohlhaas; and the methods he then employs, even down to being prepared to disinter Kohlhaas' corpse, are an apt comment on him. One may well question the moral validity of Kohlhaas' revenge; but one does not have to be particularly sorry for its targets. The Elector's character may be illustrated in two ways. He can be contrasted with the Elector of Brandenburg. This Elector did nothing for Kohlhaas in the first third of the story and, although he could claim ignorance of the affair, this does not entirely exculpate him; but once he did get to hear of it he acted promptly and, whatever his motives, had Kohlhaas moved to Berlin very quickly and stopped further injustice being meted out to him. The Elector of Saxony, on the other hand, did not dismiss corrupt ministers and move energetically to eliminate the source of injustice. His character is also illustrated in the incident when a former flame of his, the lady Heloise, wishes to visit Kohlhaas at the place where he is stopping overnight when being conducted from Dresden to Berlin and persuades the Elector to accompany her since in his hunting costume he

[11] As Kohlhaas himself says of him, 'Der Herr selbst, weiß ich, ist gerecht'.

will not be recognised by Kohlhaas. He smilingly agrees, saying as he does so 'Torheit, du regierst die Welt, und dein Sitz ist ein schöner weiblicher Mund!'[12] A gallant utterance no doubt, and quite characteristic of a ruler who prefers to evade his responsibilities and peer disguised in the company of a pretty lady at the man he has wronged.

At the very end of the story the Elector sees Kohlhaas swallowing the contents of the capsule, collapses fainting and returns wretchedly to Dresden sick in mind and body, 'zerrissen an Leib und Seele'. His line soon dies out.[13] Kohlhaas on the other hand, though he is executed for breaking the peace of the Empire, finds triumph in death, and his descendants thrive and prosper. Kleist drives his point home. Kohlhaas may have his less endearing side, but his very defects are inseparable from his strength. His adversaries on the other hand, frail creatures though they may be, fail to live up to their responsibilities and merit their inglorious end.

D i

One of the central scenes in *Michael Kohlhaas* is the meeting between Kohlhaas and Martin Luther. It is a fascinating confrontation between two men, basically similar in type though with diverging views, dramatically conceived, so that it could be transferred to the stage almost word for word, and dealing with two crucial issues, the relationship of the individual to society and the role of religion.

The meeting comes at a vital stage in the story. Kohlhaas' campaign against Junker Wenzel and the Saxon government has grown alarmingly, parts of Wittenberg and Leipzig have been laid waste by fire, people are flocking to Kohlhaas' standard, and Kohlhaas, as if possessed by some delusion of grandeur, has identified himself with the archangel Michael and established a provisional world government at Lützen. A point of no return seems to have been reached as the conflict escalates and Saxony mobilises more forces to meet the threat.

---

[12] 'Folly, you rule the world, and your throne is a beautiful woman's mouth!'
[13] The historical elector of Saxony was Johann Friedrich I (1532-1547) and he bears no resemblance to Kleist's elector. He was defeated in battle at Mühlberg in 1547, and his successor Moritz belonged to a rival branch of the family.

Then Luther – Doctor Martin Luther as the chronicler Kleist calls him, not without a touch of pedantic irony – deems it time to address a public letter to Kohlhaas, hoping to bring him back within the framework of human society and persuade him to call off his campaign. It is a quite astonishing letter and merits quoting in full:

> Kohlhaas, der du dich gesandt zu sein vorgibst, das Schwert der Gerechtigkeit zu handhaben, was unterfängst du dich, Vermessener, im Wahnsinn stockblinder Leidenschaft, du, den Ungerechtigkeit selbst, vom Wirbel bis zur Sohle erfüllt? Weil der Landesherr dir, dem du untertan bist, dein Recht verweigert hat, dein Recht in dem Streit um ein nichtiges Gut, erhebst du dich, Heilloser, mit Feuer und Schwert, und brichst, wie der Wolf der Wüste, in die friedliche Gemeinheit, die er beschirmt. Du, der die Menschen mit dieser Angabe, voll Unwahrhaftigkeit und Arglist, verführt: meinst du, Sünder, vor Gott dereinst, an dem Tage, der in die Falten aller Herzen scheinen wird, damit auszukommen? Wie kannst du sagen, daß dir dein Recht verweigert worden ist, du, dessen grimmige Brust, vom Kitzel schnöder Selbstrache gereizt, nach den ersten, leichtfertigen Versuchen, die dir gescheitert, die Bemühung gänzlich aufgegeben hat, es dir zu verschaffen? Ist eine Bank voll Gerichtsdienern und Schergen, die einen Brief, der gebracht wird, unterschlagen, oder ein Erkenntnis, das sie abliefern sollen, zurückhalten, deine Obrigkeit? Und muß ich dir sagen, Gottvergessener, daß deine Obrigkeit von deiner Sache nichts weiß – was sag ich? daß der Landesherr, gegen den du dich auflehnst, auch deinen Namen nicht kennt, dergestalt, daß wenn dereinst du vor Gottes Thron trittst, in der Meinung, ihn anzuklagen, er, heiteren Antlitzes, wird sprechen können: diesem Mann, Herr, tat ich kein Unrecht, denn sein Dasein ist meiner Seele fremd? Das Schwert, wisse, das du führst, ist das Schwert des Raubes und der Mordlust, ein Rebell bist du und kein Krieger des gerechten Gottes, und dein Ziel auf Erden ist Rad und Galgen, und jenseits die Verdamnis, die über die Missetat und die Gottlosigkeit verhängt ist.
> Wittenberg, usw.   Martin Luther[14]

[14] 'Kohlhaas, you who allege that you have been sent to wield the sword of justice, what venture is this of yours, presumptuous man, in the madness of your blind passion, you who are filled with injustice itself from head to foot? Because the sovereign whose subject you are has denied you your rights, rights in a squabble over

The style of the letter is revealing. The suppressed violence in it, the almost hysterical invective, and the arbitrary colouring of facts come fittingly from the pen of the man who founded the Reformation, inveighed against the Pope as Antichrist, and hurled, at least in legend, his inkpot at the devil. The Luther of the early years of the Reformation had much in him of Kohlhaas. He too was 'rechtschaffen' and 'entsetzlich', prepared to stand firm on what he considered an article of faith, even if this meant disrupting the whole fabric of Christendom. But there is too in the letter something of the Luther of 1525, who recoiled in horror at the atrocities of the peasants' revolt and at the radical social upheavals that other protestants were initiating in German cities; the Luther who believed that secular authority was ordained by God and that obedience was due to the divinely appointed ruler of the state. What a contrast this violent letter is to the one actually written by Luther to Hans Kohlhase, which started 'Mein guter Freund!' Kleist's Luther doctors the facts in a remarkable way. It is a distortion to say that Kohlhaas only indulged in 'leichtfertige Versuche' to get justice done. The issue of the responsibility of a ruler, particularly one divinely appointed with absolute powers, for his servants is cavalierly passed over. And the reader will be astonished at Luther's assertion that the Elector of Saxony knows nothing of Kohlhaas' case when only half a page previous to this he has read that the Elector is mustering an army of two thousand men against Kohlhaas. In

---

some empty possession, you rise up, abandoned wretch, with fire and the sword, and like a wolf of the wilderness burst in on the peaceful community he protects. You who lead men astray with this declaration, full of falseness and cunning: do you imagine, sinner, that this will avail you before God on that day whose beam will light up the recesses of all hearts? How can you assert that your rights have been denied you, you whose savage breast, goaded on by the lust for base revenge, completely gave up all efforts to achieve them after the first wanton attempts? Is a bench of constables and beadles, who suppress a letter brought to them or withhold a verdict they are supposed to deliver, is this your sovereign authority? And do I have to tell you, godless wretch, that this authority knows nothing of your case – what am I saying? that the sovereign you are rebelling against does not even know your name, so that when one day you appear before God's throne to accuse him he will be able to declare with serene face: this man I have done no wrong, Lord, for my soul knows nothing of his existence? Know that the sword you wield is the sword of pillage and bloodthirstiness, you are a rebel and no warrior of the just God, and your goal on earth is the wheel and the gallows, and beyond the grave damnation that is visited on evil deeds and godlessness.'

view of the panic Kohlhaas has caused throughout Saxony the Elector certainly should know what is going on, and if he appears 'heiteren Antlitzes' before God and says he was ignorant of the affair, then God might well ask what His divinely appointed servant had been spending his time doing. Luther exaggerates grossly when he says Kohlhaas is full of injustice from head to foot, but his mention of revenge as a motive, though overstated, is more to the point. The letter is an interesting example of Kleist's technique of pushing things to extremes;[15] its violence and hysteria match that contained in the proclamations issued by Kohlhaas from Lützen.

Kohlhaas reads the letter in Lützen, indeed he reads it three times, taking off his helmet as he does so out of respect for Luther, and he goes red as he digests its contents. Why does he go red? Out of shame at the 'ganze Verderblichkeit', the 'complete perniciousness', of his conduct, to use the phrase insinuated at this point by the narrator, or out of indignation at the accusation of injustice made against him? He wastes no time in setting off in disguise for Wittenberg, and knocks on Luther's door at night.

When Kohlhaas, hat in hand respectfully, says who he is Luther's reaction is immediate. 'Keep far away!' he exclaims, reaching for the bell to summon help, 'Your breath is pestilence and your presence destruction!' It is almost too good to be true, this overwrought reply of the choleric Reformer. It sets the mood for the first half of the interview. Kohlhaas, far from being a megalomaniac, is quiet and measured in his utterances; Luther indulges in exclamations – the verb 'rufen' is used constantly of him – and replies emotionally to Kohlhaas' reasonings, shuffling irritably around in the papers on his desk all the time. But at the end of the first half of the interview the verb used of him is no longer 'rufen' but 'sagen', and despite his own conviction of authority as being divinely imposed he has made far-reaching concessions to Kohlhaas' point of view.

Kohlhaas defends himself by saying that the war he wages against society is justified because he has been cast out and

[15] Cf. the useful article by Clifford A. Bernd, 'Der Lutherbrief in Kleists *Michael Kohlhaas*', *Zeitschrift für deutsche Philologie* 86, 1967.

'outlawed' from it. The word he uses is 'verstoßen'.[16] This word occurs five times in five lines, a good example of Kleist's leitmotif technique of repeating a key word or phrase. In this word is embodied the whole idea of the social contract by which Kohlhaas sets such store. Like Luther he acknowledges authority and clearly has deep respect for the concept of a ruler, a 'Landesherr'. He is quite prepared to render obedience to the state as his part of the bargain, but in return for this he expects the protection of its laws. If this protection is denied him the contract is broken, he is effectively cast out of society into the wilderness and forced to fend for himself by taking the law into his own hands. As he graphically puts it: 'Wer mir ihn versagt (i.e. den Schutz des Gesetzes), der stößt mich zu den Wilden der Einöde hinaus; er gibt mir, wie wollt Ihr das leugnen, die Keule, die mich selbst schützt, in die Hand'.[17] And if he has to revert to the laws of the jungle then he can hardly be blamed if things get violent. The words of Kohlhaas are echoed in the meeting of the Saxon privy council when the 'good' Prince of Meißen remarks that the cause of Kohlhaas is generally acknowledged to be just and he has been obliged by circumstances to take the sword into his own hands. This, from one point of view, justifies Kohlhaas' resort to force. Furthermore, if, as Luther suggests, the Elector of Saxony is accountable to no-one but God for his choice of servants, then the implication must be that the only way he can be brought to book in this world is through the illegal initiative of a private individual.

Luther reacts indignantly at first to these arguments of Kohlhaas, exclaiming in outraged tones and fiddling ill-humouredly with the papers on his desk. But in the end he concedes that Kohlhaas' cause may be just, 'gerecht', and offers to mediate with the Elector in order to secure Kohlhaas some sort of amnesty. But when Kohlhaas enumerates the reparation he seeks, pathetically modest when compared with the damage already caused to the state, Luther flares up again

---

[16] Cf. Siegfried Streller, 'Heinrich von Kleist und Jean-Jacques Rousseau', *Weimarer Beiträge* 8 (1962), p.551.

[17] 'Whoever denies me the protection of the law casts me out amongst the wild beasts of the wilderness; he puts into my hand, how can you deny this, the club with which I defend myself.'

as he catalogues the havoc Kohlhaas has wreaked. There follows another key sentence. While a tear rolls down his cheek ('indem ihm eine Träne über die Wangen rollte') Kohlhaas says: 'Hochwürdiger Herr! Es hat mich meine Frau gekostet; Kohlhaas will der Welt zeigen, daß sie in keinem ungerechten Handel umgekommen ist'.[18] Kohlhaas can satisfy himself rationally that as an outlaw he is justified in resorting to illegality in order to obtain justice. But his quest for justice has cost him his wife, and he has to satisfy his conscience that his wife's blood is not on his own hands. This issue of conscience will only be settled finally with the appearance of the gypsy woman towards the end of the story. Luther then asks another probing question, yet another example of the way Kleist examines the whole business from every possible angle. He asks Kohlhaas whether, in view of the personal cost to him and in view of his duty as a Christian, it would not really have been better to give up the whole affair, collect the horses and feed them up himself at Kohlhaasenbrück. A pertinent question: has the game really been worth the candle? Yet it shows that Luther is on a different wavelength from Kohlhaas and cannot understand his motivation. Kohlhaas concedes that it might have been better if he had given up – and saying this he walks to the window, a Kleistian trademark for characters faced with a personal decision[19] – but then again it might not have been, and anyway the price has been paid and he will carry on. His quest for justice goes beyond a mere balance-sheet of profit and loss. Furthermore, human beings are not blessed with hindsight, and the clock cannot be turned back. A man has to act in character, and if the same set of circumstances were to recur Kohlhaas would not react differently.

So far Kohlhaas has come out of the interview well. Luther, however grudgingly, has conceded that Kohlhaas' cause is just and has agreed to mediate with the Elector of Saxony – and this indeed he subsequently does, criticising the behaviour of the Saxon authorities in no uncertain fashion. But now Kleist

---

[18] 'Reverend Sir! It had cost me my wife; Kohlhaas wants to show the world that it was in no unjust cause she died.'

[19] Cf. supra p.43 f. Also Hans-Wilhelm Dechert, *'Indem er ans Fenster trat ... Zur Funktion einer Gebärde in Kleists Michael Kohlhaas'*, Euphorion, 62, pp. 77-84.

gives another twist to this fascinating confrontation. Kohlhaas has missed receiving communion at Whitsun because of his campaign, and he asks permission to confess and receive communion from Luther now. Luther says that Christ forgave His enemies and makes it a condition of Kohlhaas receiving communion that he forgive his enemies, notably Junker Wenzel. This indeed puts Kohlhaas on the spot. If he does not forgive Wenzel he will not receive the communion which, as a good Christian, he devoutly wants. But if he does forgive the Junker, then the justice he is fighting for goes by the board and his wife has died in vain. Two attitudes clash as Luther practises this religious blackmail on Kohlhaas and they are embodied in the two figures of the archangel Michael and the forgiving Christ. Kohlhaas replies to Luther that Christ too did not forgive all His enemies, another master-stroke on the part of Kleist. For while Kohlhaas may be right and while his remark, accompanied by a blush as he makes it, may cast a critical light on Luther's behaviour, there is as well the disturbing 'too', the 'auch' with which he mentions Christ, as if he is equating himself with the founder of the Christian religion. Kohlhaas has to leave without receiving communion. But that is not the end of the matter, for at the end of the story Luther sends the theologian Jakob Freising to administer communion to Kohlhaas in his cell.

So the scene between these extraordinary men is played out in the stealth of night at Wittenberg. Kohlhaas has gained one point, Luther's undertaking to try for an amnesty with a view to reopening his case, and lost another, for he is not prepared to pay the price of communion and forgive his enemy Junker Wenzel. He came, hat in hand. He leaves, his hands crossed on his breast, a look of pain and sorrow on his face.

ii

Pain and sorrow are not exactly the emotions that predominate in the scene where the two horses are brought into the market-place in Dresden by the knacker from Döbbeln. This splendid scene,[20] a central scene, perhaps *the*

---

[20] Cf. Clifford A. Bernd, 'The "Abdeckerszene" in Kleist's *Michael Kohlhaas*', *Studia Neophilologica* 39, 1967.

central scene, is basically comic, or would be were it not for the nature of the issues raised by it. The quality of the story, and the way Kleist disposes of his subject-matter, can be seen if one says that in his way the Döbbeln knacker is as important as Doctor Martin Luther.

The horses, it seems, have been found at last, and they are brought into the market-place by the knacker. Junker Wenzel, accompanied by the chamberlain Kunz von Tronka, comes to identify them. They are greeted by an extraordinary spectacle. A crowd of people, growing every minute, surrounds the cart to which the broken-down hacks are bound and roars with laughter to think that because of these two beasts the very existence of the state is threatened – 'unter unendlichem Gelächter einander zurufend, daß die Pferde schon, um derenthalben der Staat wanke, an den Schinder gekommen wären!'[21] By means of this grotesque contrast Kleist pinpoints the paradox of the story: the vast issues raised and the laughable pretext of the conflict. Junker Wenzel, whose condition is all but as sorry as that of the horses, is unable to identify them and his cousin Kunz takes it upon himself to settle the affair. Throwing his cloak back, so that his decorations and chain of office are exposed to view, he advances on the knacker.

He meets his match. The knacker busies himself with his own horse, a handsome beast, and hardly casts a glance at chamberlain Kunz. While the chamberlain fast loses his temper and is well aware that the crowd is laughing at him the knacker stolidly goes about his business, grooms his horse, then calmly leans against his cart and urinates in full view of everybody, the decorations and chain of office of Kunz notwithstanding. Then, ignoring the horses, he puts his whip across his broad back and walks across to a tavern to get some food, leaving the chamberlain fuming with rage and frustration.

The scene is splendidly told, actions and gestures embroidering the narrative, with the crowd laughing and grinning all the while. Yet again comedy breaks into the story.

---

[21] 'Amidst endless laughter calling to one another that the horses, on whose account the state was tottering at its foundations, had already fallen into the hands of the knacker!'

Just as Junker Wenzel had been depicted as a comic character, just as the horses had been described comically as they peered like geese out of the pigsty at the Tronkenburg, so their re-appearance in the market-place at Dresden is a matter for comedy, the 'unendliches Gelächter', the 'ceaseless laughter', of the knights when Kohlhaas first walked into the Tronkenburg is echoed in the 'unendliches Gelächter' of the crowd gathered around the two horses. Yet the horses, wretched and comical though they may be, occupy a key role in the story of Kohlhaas. And it is a measure of Kleist's mastery of his material that in this central scene, when the success of Kohlhaas' campaign is in the balance, all hinges on the person of – a urinating knacker!

Kunz sends for Kohlhaas to identify the horses, and Kohlhaas, 'der ehrliche Kohlhaas', 'honest Kohlhaas', as he is called at the beginning of this section, does indeed come, though not before Kleist has further spun out the story with more entangling legal intricacies and a case of mistaken identity, thus building up the ridiculousness of it all. One may well imagine the thoughts that go through Kohlhaas' mind as, courteously doffing his hat to Kunz whom he does not know, he gives the horses a cursory glance and says they are his, these horses that have cost him his wife and might cost him his life. Then, doffing his hat once more to Kunz, he leaves. A strange confrontation! The emaciated horses, the gaping crowd, and Kohlhaas face to face with the most influential Tronka, potentially his worst enemy – and not knowing who he is he treats him with studied politeness. He will show the same politeness to the Elector of Saxony when, disguised as a huntsman, he comes with his former mistress to visit Kohlhaas.

With the departure of Kohlhaas things rapidly take a turn for the worse in the market-place. The horses have to be led away and this a lad is preparing to do at the bidding of Kunz, making his way round a big heap of dung at their feet as he does so, another piece of grotesque realism. But he is stopped from touching the horses by the forceful intervention of a cousin, Meister Himboldt. Horses that fall into the knacker's hands are 'unehrlich' and can only be handled by knacker's men. Anyone else touching them would lose face. Kunz reacts angrily, a row flares up, general uproar ensues, Meister Himboldt assaults the chamberlain ('throw the murderous tyrant straight to the ground!'), the crowd joins in on Himboldt's side, and only the chance ('zufällig') intervention of a passing group of soldiers saves the badly injured minister from an even worse fate. Meister Himboldt is arrested, Kunz von Tronka assisted home, and the horses tied to a lamp-post.

Important issues are raised in this scene. Meister Himboldt is to some extent a mirror-image of Kohlhaas. He fights for the honour of his cousin and represents the people against autocratic authority. But his actions bring out the implications of Kohlhaas' campaign. If, fired by the example of Kohlhaas, citizens attack authority in the market-place and for whatever specious reason bring about a breakdown in law and order, then a serious threat to the stability of the state is posed that no government, good or bad, can afford to ignore. Perhaps it is better to punish an innocent man and reassert the image of authority. In Meister Himboldt Kleist also shows, as he does in the case of Piachi and Meister Pedrillo, how tenuous is the dividing-line between order and violence.

Some sympathy is due to Kunz von Tronka. However arrogant his display of authority may have been, he did make a genuine attempt to settle matters by taking over the horses, and it was scant reward for his pains that he should be led off home covered in blood. One is almost inclined to take his side in the matter. And this is to some extent what Kleist is aiming at in this scene. He is not concerned now with the issues of religion and conscience that were a feature of the scene with Luther. Here things are seen from a point of view far less favourable to Kohlhaas as the implications of his actions are considered as they affect the life of the state. His attack on authority, however justified, could encourage others. At the end of the story it will be his breach of the peace of the Empire that will bring about his execution.

This scene is a central one in the story. From now on things go steadily worse for Kohlhaas, now referred to as 'der arme Kohlhaas', 'poor Kohlhaas'. He himself is a passive figure in this and he has to await the outcome of events, powerless to influence them. His plight after the incidents in the market-place is almost as wretched as that of his 'unehrlich' horses as they are led off to the knacker's yard by the knacker of Dresden, specially summoned for this purpose.

E

It is now time to consider in rather more detail the main themes in *Michael Kohlhaas* already outlined in the opening section. The story is of course concerned with the character of Kohlhaas and the way in which excess of one quality in a person can lead to a corresponding excess of an opposing quality. This is clearly stressed in the opening paragraph, and to this extent the story is a study of character. But this character is depicted selectively in relation to particular themes and problems, some of which are stated in the opening paragraph and some of which emerge later, and these themes assume greater importance as Kohlhaas gets engulfed in events and becomes a passive figure awaiting the outcome of a sequence of events he has triggered off. What these themes are will have become apparent from what has already been written and they may be listed here, always with the proviso that there is something artificial about detaching themes from the body of a story, particularly when as in *Michael Kohlhaas* they so frequently overlap. These main themes are: the theme of justice, the problem of the law, the social contract, the role of religion, the problem of conscience, the theme of revenge, and the importance of chance and the miraculous.

'Das Rechtgefühl aber machte ihn zum Räuber und Mörder' – Kohlhaas' sense of justice, which 'made him into a robber and a murderer', is continually stressed, though it may be noted parenthetically that he does not have a monopoly of it, for the 'Gerechtigkeitsliebe' of the Saxon chancellor Graf Wrede is also underlined. A faith in justice as something absolute, an ideal that goes beyond purely factual issues of what is right or wrong according to the law, is a central feature of Kohlhaas. It is something subjective, this being stressed in Kleist's word 'Rechtgefühl', but in the case of Kohlhaas it is all the more finely balanced through being based on an awareness of the 'Gebrechlichkeit der Welt' and the 'allgemeine Not der Welt', 'the fragile nature of the world' and the 'general distress of the world'. This sense of justice is genuine, and any interpretation of the story that pretends it is not is perverse and wrong-headed. As far as Kohlhaas is concerned it is the principle that is important and not the particular bone of contention, a pair of horses. His commitment to justice is continually stressed. It is well illustrated when, in the company of the Berlin commandant Heinrich von Geusau, he receives the reply to his letter seeking justice from the Saxon authorities, a negative reply sent by a lawyer who, although apparently his friend, now wants nothing more to do with the affair. In a typically Kleistian touch the reader is told that 'Kohlhaas eine Träne auf den Brief fallen ließ'. This 'tear that falls on the letter' is not feigned. It is the sorrow of someone who senses the perversion of justice in the world. It is because of his sense of justice that he is outraged by the 'abscheuliche Ungerechtigkeit', the 'abominable injustice', he experiences at the Tronkenburg (the narrator's phrase, not Kohlhaas'), and feels himself attacked at his most vulnerable point when accused of 'Ungerechtigkeit' by Luther.

It is a 'vortreffliches Gefühl', an 'admirable feeling', according to the narrator, that makes him seek justice for what happened to him at the Tronkenburg, not only to protect himself but also his neighbours, and his wife backs him up in this 'from the bottom of her heart', saying that it is 'a work of God'. Indeed it is, for justice is an absolute, something, one might say, divine, and the man who sets out to establish justice is accountable ultimately to something absolute, be it God or his own conscience. But justice, absolute though it may be, needs to be tempered with wisdom and mercy and this is where Kohlhaas is vulnerable, for his all-or-nothing desire for justice tends to make him implacable and inflexible, however well acquainted with the fallibility of the world he may be. Moreover, however idealistic the sense of justice may be, the person imbued with it is subject to ordinary human weaknesses; the subjective nature of the ideal gets tangled up in human feelings and emotions and may be deluded or blinded by them. In the case of Kohlhaas the feeling for justice goes hand in hand with a desire to gain satisfaction, 'Genugtuung', for what he has suffered, and there is a danger at times that this 'Genugtuung' can degenerate into a pedantic catalogue of items lost and damage sustained. Furthermore, a sense of justice is not easily preserved in the wearisome business of everyday life, and Kohlhaas' 'Rechtgefühl' tends to wilt in the endless tedium of the legal processes in Dresden, when sheer fatigue and something approaching despair all but gain the upper hand. In this Kohlhaas is only human; but for a human being he is remarkably 'rechtschaffen'.

In a letter to Wilhelmine von Zenge at the beginning of 1800 Kleist discusses what course of study he should follow to prepare himself for a career, and considers the study of law, only to reject it: 'Nein, nein, Wilhelmine, nicht die Rechte will ich studieren, nicht die schwankenden, ungewissen, zweideutigen Rechte der Vernunft will ich studieren, an die Rechte meines Herzens will ich mich halten ... Ach, Wilhelmine, ich erkenne nur ein höchstes Gesetz an, die *Rechtschaffenheit*'.[22] It could almost be Kohlhaas speaking. Contrasted to the subjective emotion of 'Rechtschaffenheit', which comes from the heart, are the laws of reason, mutable, uncertain and ambiguous. *Michael Kohlhaas* is a story that shows the limitations of the law, the product of human reason, and the way individuals get caught up in its impersonal machinery.

As stated earlier Kleist deliberately wraps up the legal processes in a cocoon of jargon, legal paraphernalia and opposing practitioners, all remote and impersonal. To confuse the matter further there is more than one law, namely, that of Saxony, of Brandenburg, and the law of the Empire, centred on Vienna, presided over by the almost divine figure of the Emperor. It is eventually this law that Kohlhaas is deemed to have offended, for which he pays the penalty of being executed.

Kohlhaas' first attempts to gain legal redress in Dresden and Berlin meet with no success because his letters and submissions are stopped at source by venal officials and interested ministers; the law, then, depends on its servants and can be perverted. Later in Dresden, when it is generally agreed that right is on his side, delays occur because

---

[22] 'No, Wilhelmine, I do not want to study law, the precarious, uncertain, ambiguous laws of reason – that is not what I want to study; I want to abide by the dictates of my heart ... Ah, Wilhelmine, I only recognise one supreme law, that of integrity.'

procedures exist to block the operation of the law. When things go worse for him after the knacker of Döbbeln scene the Tronkas are quick to burrow around in ancient edicts to find obsolete laws to further their cause, a demonstration of the way the letter of the law can be used to pervert justice. The machinery of the law can be blocked by corrupt officials, and nothing of this may come to the ears of the lord of the land. But once the machinery is set in motion, then it seems that no power on earth can stop it, it is like some juggernaut careering along its pre-ordained way. At least this is what the Elector of Saxony must feel, for having invoked the law of the empire against Kohlhaas he is unable, for all his frantic efforts, to stop the processes of the law taking their appropriate course. Once the law is brought face to face with a situation that defies human reason, then its limitations are apparent. This is well brought out in the meeting of the Saxon privy council, where arguments and counter-arguments are advanced, and reason is unable to cope with the case of Kohlhaas the horse-dealer, and far less with his two horses which, although apparently alive, are in every legal sense dead. The ministers see no way of escaping from the magic circle, the 'Zauberkreis', in which they are trapped, and it seems that only a sign from heaven can resolve the impasse. A sign does eventually appear, though it is doubtful if the knacker of Döbbeln is sent by heaven.

In an ideal world law and justice would coincide, the 'Rechte der Vernunft' would harmonise with the 'Rechte des Herzens', to quote again from Kleist's letter. This is the solution eventually reached in *Prinz Friedrich von Homburg*, where the laws of the state are upheld as too are the claims of human feelings. And a solution is reached at the end of *Michael Kohlhaas*, where in a good state ruled by a just and wise ruler, namely in Brandenburg, the principle of justice is upheld and the rule of law is confirmed.

In Brandenburg, at least by the end of the story, the individual is protected by the law and is for his part expected to obey it. In Saxony the law is manipulated by people in power and the individual is forced to seek justice outside the law. The two states are contrasted in their attitude to the rule of law and the rights of the citizen, and the fact that this contrast is stressed at the end may well mirror the roles played by Prussia and Saxony in Kleist's own day in the struggle against Napoleon, a person symbolising for him tyranny and despotism. In its relevance to the actual political situation of 1810 the story is a practical demonstration of Kleist's intention of writing 'lauter Werke, die in die Mitte der Zeit hineinfallen',[23] just as his play *Die Hermannsschlacht* was at the end of 1808. In the last resort, however, this contemporary relevance is incidental to the basic theme of the relationship of the individual to the state. It is convenient for Kleist to show how this relationship can in practice work out in two contrasting ways. The rule of law operates in Brandenburg and Kohlhaas is happy to conform to it; the rule of law does not operate in Saxony and Kohlhaas, 'verstoßen' as he is, has to take the law into his own hands.

Not every individual would be prepared to do this. A model 'Staatsbürger' such as Kohlhaas would need to scrutinise his motives very carefully before embarking on such a course, always assuming that he was not impelled merely by greed or revenge. The cost, both personal and material, is after all very high. Kohlhaas has first of all to come to terms with himself and satisfy his own conscience, or as Kleist puts it 'die Schranke seiner eignen Brust', that what he is doing is right. Quite apart from considerations of law and religion he has to feel justified as an individual in what he is doing.

Kohlhaas has a firm belief in the worth and integrity of the individual. His existence centres around this belief. He is insulted as an individual by Junker Wenzel and it is this, rather than just the loss of a couple of horses, that constitutes the real offence against him. This clarity of conscience is continually put to the test. The final test comes in the scene at the end when the gypsy woman offers him freedom and the love and well-being of his children if he gives the capsule to the Elector of Saxony and is enabled to escape from prison – a temptation rightly rejected, for in so doing he would be false to himself and all that he stood for, as well as being very gullible in trusting to the promises of an elector whom previous experience had shown to be anything but reliable. But the

[23] Cf. letter to Karl Freiherr von Stein zu Altenstein, 1 January 1809, where he states his intention of writing only 'contemporary works'.

temptation is a very real one for the father who sees his
children in front of him, and it is little wonder that he is
confused, 'verwirrt', when he adduces reasons for its rejection.

Kohlhaas' consciousness of the worth of the individual
brings him into conflict with everything he holds dear, the love
of those nearest to him, the religion he devoutly believes in, the
social order of which he is a member. The strain this subjects
him to may be expressed in the odd tear he sheds, a clenching
of his hands or a fleeting look of pain on his face. At the end he
will feel that events have justified his stand. And this is shown
in the magnificent gesture with which he meets death. When
called upon to pay the supreme penalty he takes off his hat
and flings it on the ground, before advancing to the block – the
taking off of the hat and flinging it on the ground being the
final triumphant expression of individuality on his part.

But Kohlhaas is not just an individual, he is also a Christian
and this – the story takes place in the sixteenth century not
many years after Luther nailed his theses on the church door
at Wittenberg – is an important fact. He is a religious man, his
wife has adopted his faith, his children have been brought up
'in the fear of God', his own conscience has been conditioned
by his Christian beliefs. Yet the course of conduct to which he
commits himself brings him into conflict with Christian
doctrines of forgiveness and humility and he has to face the
fact that his actions run counter to the cherished beliefs of
those he loves and respects.

On her death-bed his wife Lisbeth, who had initially
commended his public-spirited actions as 'ein Werk Gottes'
but now senses the extremes to which he is prepared to go,
points to a verse in the Bible 'Forgive your enemies; do good to
them that hate you', gives him one last look, and dies. In the
confrontation at the convent of Erlabrunn, against a
background of storm and fire, the abbess holds a silver
crucifix in front of her and admonishes Kohlhaas 'Fürchte
Gott und tue kein Unrecht!', 'Fear God and do no wrong!'. A
condition of Kohlhaas receiving communion from Luther is
that he imitate his Redeemer and forgive his enemy Junker
Wenzel. He is continually being made aware of the Christian
doctrine of forgiveness and of turning the other cheek, and it
requires a very profound belief in the rightness of what he is

doing – or then a monomanic urge for revenge – to enable him to pursue his quest for justice.

But then Kohlhaas feels that God is on his side. Cast out, as he sees himself, from the society of men, 'out-lawed' as it were, he feels as if God has selected him from the ranks of men to defend the divine ideal of justice. Not for nothing has Kleist altered the name Hans of the historical Kohlhase to that of Michael. Kohlhaas assumes some of the characteristics of his namesake, the formidable archangel, and the 'Quis ut deus' denoted by the name Michael indicates the divine role he finds thrust upon him. Believing in the rightness of his cause and the divine ideal of justice to which he is committed he cannot acquiesce in the compromise implied in Christian forgiveness and turning the other cheek. It is clear from the scene between Luther and Kohlhaas that the two men are speaking a different language. Luther can only denounce Kohlhaas' sinful arrogance in purporting to dispense justice in the name of God; Kohlhaas feels that by a strange concatenation of circumstances he has been called upon to do just that. Not for the first or last time has the leader of a church found it impossible to talk with an idealist claiming to act in the name of God.

Thus Kleist poses the problem of how a Christian should act when basic principles are put to the test. At first he encourages the reader to think that Kohlhaas is a victim of religious megalomania, embellishing his desire for revenge with the aura of divine sanction. But the reader would be wise not to jump to hasty conclusions. For at the end of the story something remarkable happens. When Kohlhaas is confined in Berlin under sentence of death he is visited by Jakob Freising, sent by Martin Luther with a letter for Kohlhaas – alas, says Kleist, this doubtless remarkable letter has been lost, thereby in his usual masterly way opening the door to speculation only immediately to slam it shut – and also given authority to administer holy communion to Kohlhaas. What can this mean? Has Luther realised the good Kohlhaas was trying to do and, relenting, given him the blessing of the Church? Or is it just that he feels that a man faced with death should be afforded the comforts of the Christian religion? Kleist leaves the question open. But the fact that he goes out of his way to introduce this episode and so make it possible for Kohlhaas to die with the blessing of the church must cast into question Luther's former adamant stand and must too suggest that Kohlhaas' actions were not at variance with the Christian faith.

But does Kohlhaas die a Christian death? It is not easy to maintain this when one remembers that just before his execution he takes revenge on the Elector of Saxony by reading the prophecy on the piece of paper in the capsule and then swallowing it. Religion, justice, the call of conscience and the sanctity of the individual personality – perhaps these are high-flown notions speciously cloaking the real motive of Kohlhaas, namely that of revenge. For all his 'rechtschaffen' qualities he is certainly 'entsetzlich', prepared to ignore the pleas of wife and religious mentor as he pursues his revenge, this man who, anything but an archangel, vents his fury in senseless and implacable attacks on his fellow men. He wields Michael's sword, but to pursue his selfish purposes, and ultimately it is no divine ideal of justice that he embodies but the law of the jungle.

This is the other side of the coin in Kleist's presentation of Michael Kohlhaas. The theme of revenge runs through the story, first revenge against Junker Wenzel, and then revenge against the Elector of Saxony. This cannot be overlooked. It is right to commend Kohlhaas' quest for justice; but it is necessary to remember as well the bodies of innocent women and children flying out of the windows of the Tronkenburg and the fate of Hans von Tronka, hurled across the room by Kohlhaas and his brains bespattering the floor. If justice is seen to be done in the final scene of the story an act of revenge is dwelt on too. Kleist makes this quite clear. Yet again he shows the complementary plus and minus sides of the human personality. One has to accept the entire Kohlhaas, warts and all.

The theme of revenge occurs frequently in Kleist's works. One remembers Meister Pedrillo in *Das Erdbeben in Chili*, Piachi in *Der Findling*, and Congo Hoango and the negress with yellow fever in *Die Verlobung in St. Domingo*. Terrible scenes of revenge also occur in the plays *Die Familie Schroffenstein*, *Penthesilea* and *Die Hermannsschlacht*. This is a disquieting side of Kleist's work and it is not always easy to account for it satisfactorily. It is however, given his technique of presenting a situation in contrasting extremes, a necessary element, counter-balancing the tendency to build up positive features of human conduct, for example the heroism of Don Fernando in *Das Erdbeben in Chili* or the essential purity of the Marquise von O., and investing them with a quasi-divine status. It is important to note that the incidents of vengeful violence in the stories occur when the civilised fabric of human society has broken down, when the forces of law and order are found wanting and human action reverts to the jungle. Kleist is continually at pains to show how thin the dividing line is between what is called civilised and what is called barbarous behaviour. The jungle, into which Kohlhaas claims he is thrust once the protection of the law is denied him, is never far away from the ordered calm of normally functioning civilised society, and once man reverts to the law of the jungle then normal standards of conduct do not apply and justice can well become synonymous with revenge. It may furthermore be remarked that when absolutes are invoked, for example the absolute of divine justice, then 'normal' standards again do not apply. No doubt if the Archangel Michael arrives on earth to wield his sword the 'good' will suffer with the 'bad'.

Kohlhaas is unwilling to forgive Junker Wenzel. Eventually, however, the Junker is punished according to the law and Kohlhaas has no need to wreak his vengeance on him. It is a different matter where the Elector of Saxony is concerned. A distinction has to be made between blind revenge, the sudden emotional outburst, and what could be called purposeful revenge, which is what Kohlhaas employs against the Elector of Saxony. He carries this out at the end of the story, even though by then he is assured that at least in Brandenburg the rule of law applies and justice is available to the citizens of that state. The Elector of Saxony has, through his ministers, broken faith with Kohlhaas and double-crossed him. A subject of a state can be brought to book under that state's laws. But the absolute ruler of the state, God's anointed ruler, cannot be punished by the law and, at any rate within the context of the state, can only be made to suffer by non-legal means. Divine rulers and modern dictators have this in common. The only way the Elector can be made to pay for his misdemeanours in this world is through the means so miraculously afforded Kohlhaas at the end, means which Kohlhaas, in this no good Christian, takes delight in using to the full.

Divine vengeance and human revenge, retribution and legal satisfaction, the law of the jungle that looms behind the normal fabric of law and order, the absolute of revenge opposed to the absolute of Christian forgiveness, all these issues are raised in this incredibly rich story and find expression in the theme of revenge.

If the theme of revenge is a disturbing element in the story, the appearance of the gypsy woman and the capsule theme is at first sight even more difficult to reconcile with the rest of the narrative. What place has the miraculous and the supernatural in a story like *Michael Kohlhaas*?

Kohlhaas' horses might never have been detained at the Tronkenburg had not a violent shower of rain and hail occurred at the very moment when he was discussing the matter with Junker Wenzel, driving the Junker indoors. Then there would have been no story.[24] The element of chance plays a considerable role in *Michael Kohlhaas*. The death of Lisbeth, Kohlhaas' wife, is due to an unhappy chance; it seems to be only good fortune that enables Junker Wenzel to escape from Kohlhaas' pursuit; bad luck conditions the course of events involving the knacker from Döbbeln and his appearance in the market square at Dresden; a chance conversation between the Elector of Brandenburg and Heinrich von Geusau prompts that ruler to take a fresh interest in the case of Kohlhaas; ill luck dogs the attempts of the Elector of Saxony to stop legal proceedings on the part of the Empire against Kohlhaas. The list of examples could be extended.

When Kohlhaas hastens to the convent of Erlabrunn, only to find that Junker Wenzel has foiled him by slipping away again, he is about to set fire to the convent when the heavens open and a tremendous cloudburst stops him and brings him to his senses. Is this chance, or a miracle? Whatever may be the case in this particular instance, the irrational finds

---

[24] Cf. J.M. Ellis, 'Der Herr lässt regnen über Gerechte und Ungerechte: Kleist's *Michael Kohlhaas*', *Monatshefte* 59, 1967.

expression on a higher plane in the story in the introduction through the gypsy woman of the 'miraculous. The purely rational world has achieved nothing but deadlock. To resolve this deadlock Kleist has to resort to something non-rational, namely, the Zigeunerin, the double of Kohlhaas' wife, a person gifted with second sight, able to pierce the veil of lies and see through the welter of baffling detail to the reality beyond. A character completely in keeping with the attitude of mind of the sixteenth century, she is introduced into the story in the third final section, in the same way as another godlike, though far more shadowy, figure is also introduced, the figure of the Emperor, a sort of deus ex machina who resolves the legal deadlock by bringing a higher order of law, that of the Empire, to bear on the case of the horse-dealer.

Kleist, either deliberately or because he is careless in his stories of the minutiae of factual motivation, allows an element of hocus-pocus and mystery to gather around the Zigeunerin, thereby opening up possibilities for endless speculation as to the exact relationship of this mysterious character to Kohlhaas' dead wife. It is pointless to chase these hares.[25] What is important is to assess the role played by the gypsy woman in the story itself.

On the purely motivational level she provides, in the capsule, the means whereby Kohlhaas can get his revenge on the Elector of Saxony. The revenge is a fitting one, since it exploits the weaknesses of that individual, his superstition and folly, his desire to find truth in a piece of paper instead of ensuring the survival of his line by action and constructive endeavour. She acts as an agent of nemesis, enabling retribution to be visited on the ruler who was unable to uphold the rule of law in his own state.

On a much more fundamental level the gypsy woman, as the Doppelgänger of Lisbeth, is the means whereby Kohlhaas' actions become justified in his own eyes and faith in himself as a person is confirmed in him. He tells Luther that by pursuing his quest for justice he hopes to show the world that his wife did not die in an unjust cause. Now, just before he goes to face

---

[25] The matter is discussed by H. Meyer-Benfey, 'Die innere Geschichte des *Michael Kohlhaas*', *Euphorion* 15 (1908), pp. 99-140, and Karl Schultze-Jahde, 'Kohlhaas und die Zigeunerin', *Jahrbuch der Kleist-Gesellschaft* 1933/37, pp. 108-35.

execution, a figure apparently from another world, his wife speaking as it were from beyond the grave, blesses his efforts and enables him to justify himself in the light of his own conscience. First of all she tests him, holding out the hope of freedom and life with the children to whom he is so deeply devoted. But then she gives him her blessing and makes his revenge possible, paradoxically, since as Lisbeth on her deathbed she had pointed to the bible text urging the forgiving of one's enemies. She first appeared to Kohlhaas the day after Lisbeth died and gave him the capsule as a lucky charm to keep him alive. It does not keep him alive, but it helps to heighten the triumph of his death. In terms of the story the archangel Michael is balanced by the Zigeunerin. The introduction of this character may strike an odd romantic note in this generally realistic tale. But insofar as it is concerned with absolutes of justice and the triumph of right over wrong, some irrational agency is needed that stands above the confusion of worldly appearances where solutions can in the nature of things only be relative. Kohlhaas at the end of the story is a passive figure and his fate is in other hands. It is in the hands of the Emperor, who ensures that justice is administered on earth through the rule of law, with the result that Kohlhaas expiates his breach of the peace through death; and it is in the hands of the supernatural figure of the Zigeunerin, with the result that, his faith in his individuality confirmed and his revenge made possible, his death becomes a triumph.

F

There is of course something artificial in isolating particular themes and subjecting them to scrutiny. Kleist tells his story in a way that carefully avoids oversimplification of key issues and brings out instead the chaos and confusion of real life. He is aware that factors affecting human motivation, principles of human conduct and human emotions alike are essentially many-sided and contradictory, and he shows this in *Michael Kohlhaas* by his emphasis on paradox and ambiguity.

The tone is set by the opening paragraph. Kohlhaas is both 'rechtschaffen' and 'entsetzlich', in pursuit of justice he commits murder, excess of virtue leads to excess of vice. To

protect his wife and home Kohlhaas is instrumental in
destroying his wife and home. The fate of the state of Saxony
depends on two emaciated horses; and who can be sure that
Kohlhaas has correctly identified them as his own? What of
Luther's ambiguous behaviour? He upholds secular authority
as the divinely appointed instrument of God; yet he agrees
that Kohlhaas' cause may be just and persuades the secular
authority to deal with him. He refuses Kohlhaas communion
at one moment and goes to elaborate lengths to provide him
with it the next. People generally agree that Kohlhaas' cause
is just; and no-one bothers much about the corpses at the
Tronkenburg. In the pursuit of justice, when legal institutions
break down, revenge becomes legitimate. Kohlhaas pursues
an absolute of justice, but is aware of the 'Gebrechlichkeit der
Welt', he is in the one instance an idealist and in the other a
realist. One could extend the catalogue. Tragedy jostles with
comedy, issues of state revolve around a urinating knacker,
justice and integrity are fought for by a horse-dealer. At the
end Kohlhaas is executed because of his 'allzu rascher
Versuch', his 'all too hasty attempt', to establish justice,
though one might think his attempts to find justice were
anything but hasty. And the final solution, brought about by
chance, fate or divine intervention, is ironically not much
different from that suggested by the 'bad' Hinz von Tronka at
the meeting of the Saxon privy council. There is no shortage of
examples of paradox and ambiguity, and if nothing else it
should make one beware of basing interpretations of the story
on preconceived notions of what it is all about.

    Kleist's mastery is shown in this story in the way he appears
to have thought of every conceivable variation on the basic
theme and to have packed them all into his text. And 'packed'
is the right word, for these variations are decked out with an
incredible wealth of dramatic gesture and incidental detail.
From a trivial beginning, an offence involving two horses, the
affair develops with remorseless logic until the Electors of two
states and the Emperor himself are caught up in it. As
Kohlhaas gropes his way through the legal maze the reader
too is drawn into the labyrinth, and it needs more than one
reading of the text before the outlines and the details of the
story become clear.

At the conclusion of the story all the ends are tied up. Kohlhaas makes his peace with his religion when Jakob Freising administers communion to him in his cell. The rule of law is upheld as restitution is made, down to the last penny and article of clothing, for the losses suffered by Kohlhaas and his employees as a result of the wrong done to him at the Tronkenburg. Kohlhaas' honour is restored, and so too have his horses been made 'ehrlich' again after being rescued from the hands of the knacker. Junker Wenzel von Tronka has at last been brought to book and is serving a two-year prison sentence. The principle of the rule of law is vindicated through the execution of Kohlhaas because of his violation of imperial law, a higher law to which all men have to conform. Kohlhaas gets his revenge on the Elector of Saxony as he peruses the piece of paper he takes out of the capsule and then swallows it. He dies at one with his conscience, for his wife appears from beyond the grave to bless his actions. And the principle of individuality and the integrity of the human personality is symbolised in the gesture with which Kohlhaas, in front of 'eine unermeßliche Menschenmenge', 'an immense throng of people', in other words before the eyes of the world, flings his hat on the ground and goes to meet his fate. A tragic end no doubt. Yet how can one speak of tragedy when everything at the close is geared to the building up of his triumph?

The Elector of Saxony finds his way back to Dresden, broken in mind and body. History records that he dies and his line dies with him. Kohlhaas, on the other hand, is mourned by the people of Berlin. His sons are knighted by the Elector of Brandenburg and become pages at court. And as if to underline the fact that Kohlhaas, for all his faults, stood for something living, the story ends with the remark that descendants of the man once dismissed by the Saxon authorities as an 'unnützer Querelant' lived in recent memory a happy and productive life and the name of Kohlhaas lives on.

8
Themes and Style

Das gemeine Gesetz des Widerspruchs ist jedermann, aus eigner Erfahrung, bekannt.[1]

It is time to take stock of Kleist's stories, to note the main outlines of the world presented in them, the way they are put together and the style in which they are written, summarising points made in preceding chapters. The remarks that follow are bound in the nature of things to be based on generalities abstracted from the stories and can have only limited validity, since each story has to be considered in the first instance as a separate entity, judged according to its inherent truth and artistic merit. There can be no question of producing a common formula and applying it to each one.

Kleist's *Erzählungen* take place in a world of upheaval and chaos. In every one of them the settled order of things, the normal routine, is disturbed by some disaster or unforeseen event that makes a mockery of conventional human responses and places men and women in situations alien to their normal range of experience. These situations are 'unerhört' in every sense of the word and amply bring out the novel element implied in the word Novelle. Blacks murder whites, an earthquake reduces a city to ruins, the plague infects the members of a Roman family, a citadel is stormed and a woman raped, a marquis sets fire to his castle, a horse-dealer sets himself up as the representative of the Archangel Michael, and in a single moment of time four men are condemned to an

---

[1] 'The general law of contradiction is known to everyone, from his own experience'; this sentence occurs in *Allerneuester Erziehungsplan, Werke*, II, 330.

existence of grotesque insanity for the rest of their lives. Characters are caught up in situations over which they have no control, things happen to them and they must face the impact of unexpected events as best they can. The motivating force behind all this is chance. Things happen out of the blue, an earthquake, a drenching shower of rain, the sudden return of a Negro leader, a midnight assault on a fortress, and it is impossible to plan ahead to meet possible contingencies. It is impossible, because there is a complete breakdown in the rational world. Characters may deliberate, meetings may be held and courses of action debated, but all is subject to the unpredictable see-saw of events. This is brought out in what might be called Kleist's 'aber wer ...' 'but who' technique, the astonishment of a person at an unexpected sudden turn of fortune following hard on what had appeared to be a settled state of affairs. What is certain, and here one can almost speak of a pattern, is that if events appear to be tending in a particular direction they will then suddenly veer in the opposite direction. All is subject to chance and fate is always waiting to strike down the unwary; indeed Kleist seems to revel in laconic descriptions of how they are struck down.

The breakdown in the rational world and the fortuitousness of events helps to undermine the reality of things and to ensure that, however solidly based they may appear to be, an element of nightmare and unreality surrounds them. The predominance of chance opens the door to an irrational world and this combines with Kleist's tendency to polarise problems and conflicts and to project them on to a higher plane, in which the forces of heaven and hell, however symbolically understood, are involved; chance is mirrored in the emergence of the miraculous. These irrational forces can be positive or negative as they affect human beings who find themselves caught up in situations that reflect the contradictory nature of the universe itself. One test Kleist imposes on his characters is how they react to such situations.

Under the impact of the extraordinary situations created by Kleist human institutions are frequently found wanting. Organised religion, the operation of the law, social values and family ties, all these are subjected to scrutiny and found deficient. If the upheaval and chaos in the stories to some extent mirrors the upheaval in Europe created by the French Revolution and the Napoleonic Wars, the critical view of human institutions taken in them may be a reflection of the post-Jena depression in Prussia after 1806. Time and time again Kleist shows how officialdom and the establishment, whether represented by venal officials or corrupt priests, defend a scale of values often either obtuse or callously hypocritical ('steinigt sie! steinigt sie! die ganze im Tempel Jesu versammelte Christenheit!' *Erdbeben*). As the stories gather momentum accepted values may be unmasked as false, whether through the idyllic picture of one big human family that has survived the earthquake or in the words of an otherwise conforming mother ('ich will keine andre Ehre mehr, als deine Schande' *Marquise*). A second test Kleist imposes on his characters is how they react to conventional codes of behaviour and the values represented by social institutions when they find themselves caught up in unexpected situations.

Kleist often starts his stories with a baffling situation, a problem to be solved, a secret to be uncovered. Throughout the *Erzählungen* there runs the theme of truth and knowledge, the deceptive nature of appearances and the reality that may underlie them. His stories are constant variations on this theme, his characters have continually to grope their way through a confusing tangle of misleading appearances, finding out in the process that they are unable to trust the evidence of their senses and unable to rely on the operation of their rational faculties to provide answers to the riddles with which they are so unexpectedly faced. A third test imposed by Kleist on his characters is how they stand up to the conflicting nature of appearances and the contrast between what things appear to be ('Schein') and what they may eventually turn out to be ('Sein').

Not only appearances deceive; characters too deceive one another and themselves. Kleist weaves a web of misunderstanding, error and deceit in all his stories and his characters are enmeshed in it, consciously and unconsciously. Noticeable in this network of deception and self-deception is the breakdown in communication between human beings and the growing isolation of the individual. No speech passes between Toni and Gustav, as he awakes to find himself apparently betrayed and reacting blindly kills her; the 'Wer da?' of the Marquis echoes unanswered in the haunted room in the castle near Locarno before he sets fire to it and despairingly puts an end to his existence; the four brothers sit in silent adoration of the Cross, isolated from the community of men, and only break their silence at midnight to break out in fearful discordant chanting of the *Gloria*; in isolated seclusion a married woman adores the portrait of a dead lover; a prosperous Roman merchant is strung up in a deserted public square, refusing to surrender his soul to the protective ministrations of Mother Church; characters sit in solitary confinement and are trapped in the prison walls of their windowless individual lives. A fourth test imposed on Kleist's characters is how they react to the web of deceit and self-deceit, and the encompassing isolation in which they are entrapped.

These characters may turn out to be very different from what at first they appeared to be. Kleist delights in showing how apparently normal characters tend to extremes of conduct when jolted out of their routine existence by the intrusion of something alien – an earthquake, a Russian storming a fortress at night, a Swiss seeking sanctuary on an island where blacks are murdering whites, an old crone haunting a castle, the shattering impact of ethereal music. Against a background of chaos and a crumbling social framework the behaviour of characters is polarised and they become angelic knights in armour or satanic monsters of revenge. Initially 'neutral', to use the terminology of the *Allerneuester Erziehungsplan*, they then become charged with positive or negative qualities as they struggle to adjust to unexpectedly changed circumstances. The tensions in them erupt like the gases in a 'Kleistische Flasche'.[2] Once normality is re-established and a valid social framework reasserts itself again, they then revert to their former 'neutrality'. In the course of depicting such characters Kleist is able to indulge in psychological portrayal of a high order. But essentially he is

---

[2] A condenser invented in 1745 by Ewald Georg von Kleist, now more commonly known as a Leiden flask, and mentioned by Kleist in the essay *Über die allmähliche Verfertigung der Gedanken beim Reden* to illustrate an outburst of emotion.

not concerned with characters as total human beings, but rather his business is with how they react to particular situations, the circumstances of which he has carefully engineered to pinpoint this or that problematic aspect of human existence. Yet another test imposed by Kleist on his characters is to what extent they preserve their individuality and integrity when suddenly pitchforked into the jungle of human emotions and made for the first time aware of the contradictory plus and minus of the human personality.

Kleist's world would appear to be a tragic one, and certainly the first three *Erzählungen* considered in this study offer a picture of the world almost unrelievedly bleak and cheerless. Other stories, however, have non-tragic endings. It is essential to realise that Kleist is always at pains to show that there are two sides to everything. An old crone can exert a baleful (*Bettelweib*) or a benevolent (*Kohlhaas*) influence; organised religion can be repressive and hypocritical (*Erdbeben*) or comforting and protective (*Cäcilie*); a child may be a vindication of human love (*Erdbeben*) or carry within it the seeds of the plague (*Findling*). For all that, Kleist does indicate some ways in which human beings can rise superior to the circumstances in which they find themselves and reach a non-tragic solution to the problems with which they are faced. One is through the integrity of human feelings, be it love or selfless concern for others, faith in oneself and complete trust in dealings with others. It is of course true that every positive presupposes a negative: love can degenerate into lust, trust into mistrust, a belief in justice into a thirst for revenge. But the positive aspect of human emotions is stressed by Kleist and they provide something on which characters can fall back when the world around them is baffling and hostile. Another complementary way in which tragedy can be averted is through self-knowledge and an acceptance of human behaviour and the fallible nature of the world. The Marquise von O. acquires self-knowledge ('mit sich selbst bekannt'), and she accepts the 'Gebrechlichkeit der Welt'. Such self-knowledge and an acceptance of the world, so different from what once it appeared to be, is not easily gained. Kleist exposes his characters to cruel, almost sadistic, tests, bringing them to the abyss of despair, making them, to use the imagery of *Über das*

Marionettentheater, undertake a journey round the world before enabling them to find a way back into paradise[3] and to become properly integrated, undivided human beings. Nor is there any guarantee that a solution, once reached, will be permanent. The external world is ruled by chance, and who knows what situations characters may find themselves caught up in after the curtain comes down on the particular drama in which they have made their appearance. For all that, the validity of love, trust, self-sacrifice and justice remains unimpaired, however they may be put to the test in the ever-changing world of phenomena.

In his stories Kleist is like some kind of scientific experimenter as he puts different problems of life under the microscope. The ingredients are varied in the different experiments, the organisms in the test tube subjected to different procedures, the terms of the equation re-arranged. It can be a cruel and heartless business, this searching inquiry into the human condition, and the results obtained are rarely clear and unambiguous. What makes the experiments so fascinating to the onlooker is not only the compelling nature of their contents, but also the masterful way in which they are presented.

The opening sentences set the tone of the stories. Time, place, and the name of a main character are stated in them, with an insistence on factual detail that appears to guarantee the realism and accuracy of the story. And in this there is a paradox. For as the plot embarks on its outlandish twists and turns it gradually becomes clear, despite the chronicle approach, that the story is anything but realistic and historical. A background of chaos and upheaval is indicated in the opening sentences in a terse relative clause: blacks are murdering whites, an earthquake is about to break out, iconoclasm is rife in the Netherlands. And an extraordinary situation or remarkable paradox is adumbrated at times

---

[3] In this essay Kleist, using the imagery of the Garden of Eden, discusses the effect of consciousness on human actions, and says: 'Doch das Paradies ist verriegelt und der Cherub hinter uns; wir müssen die Reise um die Welt machen, und sehen, ob es vielleicht von hinten irgendwo wieder offen ist' – 'But Paradise is bolted and barred and the cherub is behind us; we have to make a journey round the world and see if perhaps it's open somewhere round the back', *Werke*, II, 342.

almost casually: a man is about to commit suicide when thousands are being killed off like flies; a respectable titled lady advertises for the father of the child she is expecting; a horse-dealer and son of a schoolmaster is both 'rechtschaffen' and 'entsetzlich'. The cool detonation of the opening bombshell, the laconic announcement of an extraordinary paradox, triggers off a story primarily concerned with the exploitation of a baffling situation, a riddle to be solved, a secret to be unmasked. The surprise technique rivets the attention of the reader from the opening lines onwards, as the story plunges *in medias res*. The baffling situation is caused by the unexpected arrival of a stranger or a chance event shattering the calm of an apparently normal state of affairs, and more often than not it happens during the night, thus producing a mood of eerie tension heightening the general bewilderment. The opening situation may appear to be exploited for its purely sensational impact; but it soon becomes clear that it is being used as a springboard for an investigation of issues of far-reaching metaphysical import. As the investigation proceeds Kleist gradually discloses relevant detail, so that the situation is endowed with different layers of meaning, various facets of the problem are revealed, and the whole issue developed with a mounting complexity and intricacy that appears eventually to defy rational analysis, until at last the riddle is solved, the secret revealed and the solution proposed, a solution which is not arrived at by rational means and which is sometimes deliberately incomplete and teasingly ambiguous.

The basic situation may be heightened and diversified in various ways. A flashback technique is used, retracing the steps leading up to the point of time indicated in the opening sentence, filling in details and adding to the general interest, while at the same time varying the treatment of time as the narrator explains the present in terms of the past, and by delving back into the past prepares the ground for future events. The situation is further exploited by a technique of shifting perspectives, being seen from various angles through the eyes of different characters. In addition, by stating a theme and developing it in subsequent variations, as for example in the treatment of the earthquake in *Das Erdbeben* or the description of the hauntings in *Das Bettelweib*, Kleist heightens the mystery and adds to the possible layers of meaning while himself standing aloof as impersonal narrator, only occasionally by means of a loaded phrase indicating his own standpoint in the matter. The situation is still further complicated by the facets of character revealed as the narrative progresses, with positive or negative qualities being manifested by hitherto 'neutral' persons. Flashbacks and interpolated incidents show the complex personality behind the apparently straightforward facade: Marianne Congreve and a Negress with yellow fever represent attitudes of love and betrayal focussed on the character of Toni, Elvire's midnight rescue from fire and water foreshadows the fixation of her worship of a portrait, a count throws mud at a swan (*Die Marquise*), and Trota saves Littegarde from a wild boar (*Der Zweikampf*). A mirror technique further diversifies the portrayal of character. The actions of Kohlhaas are mirrored in those of Meister Himboldt and Nagelschmidt; Marianne Congreve dies as a result of Gustav's actions and so does Toni; the shooting of five Russian soldiers who intended to rape the Marquise implicitly condemns the man who actually did rape her; Nicolo is a grotesque distortion of his mirror-image Colino. As if all this were not enough, the basic situation is additionally complicated by the reversals of fortune that overtake characters caught on the see-saw of chance.

A particular device employed by Kleist to bring out the contradictions and contrasts of people and events is that of the double, the Doppelgänger. The Doppelgänger is a useful means of indicating the opposing poles of the human personality and exploiting the angel-devil antithesis, such as in the figures of Colino and Nicolo. It adds to the mystery of a situation, since it defies rational explanation, and it contributes added dimensions of meaning through its evocation of supernatural forces. The inter-relation of appearance and reality, and the coexistence of rational and irrational interpretations and aspects of a given situation is brought out by Kleist through his use of the Doppelgänger motif.

The opening sentences give the time and place of the story, together with the name of a leading character, just as the first page of a drama sets the time and location and lists the dramatis personae of the piece that is to be played. Kleist's stories are indeed highly dramatic. Where possible they observe the unities, thereby achieving a concentration and compression that heightens the tension and helps to increase the isolation of the main characters. The action of some stories is spread over months and years; but by concentrating on central scenes in the progress of the narrative Kleist blurs the sense of time and focusses the reader's attention on particular pregnant incidents. Dramatic tension is further developed by the 'Flötenton im Orkan' technique, the device sometimes employed of having an interlude of lyrical sweetness and calm in between two moments of savagery and violence. The basic situation in each story has by virtue of its extraordinary and sensational nature a dramatic quality about it. And this situation is then decked out and embellished with an astonishing variety of scenic detail as Kleist fills out his canvas with parallel scenes, significant gestures, and interpolated incidents.[4] The reader is concerned in the main with the bizarre and paradoxical situations that form the backbone of the stories. But after they have been read there linger in the memory isolated, interpolated details, as for example Graf F. rolling away bombs and barrels of gunpowder from the blazing fortress, Nicolo cracking nuts indifferently while Piachi weeps for his lost son, eager boys perched hat in hand on the walls of the Dominican church in *Das Erdbeben* waiting for the Te Deum to begin, and the tear that rolls down Kohlhaas' cheek as he receives the letter from his Dresden lawyer telling him of the failure of his attempt to secure justice. Kleist offers little in the way of scenic description. Landscapes when they occur tend to be bleak, emphasising the isolation of the individuals silhouetted against them. But sometimes, at climactic moments, the stage is filled by a great crowd of spectators like a Greek chorus, the 'unermeßliche

---

[4] Friedrich Hebbel remarks of this: 'In one single situation there is more life packed in by him (Kleist) than you find in three volumes of our modern purveyors of novels. He always depicts the *inner* and the *outer* ('das *Innere* und das *Äussere*') *at one and the same time, one* by means of the *other*, and this is the only proper way to do it', letter to Elise Lensing, 23 May 1837, quoted in *Nachruhm*, p.258. Silz, op.cit., lists much of the detail in his invaluable chapter 'Repetitions and Recoveries'.

Menschenmenge' summoned by Kleist to witness key points in the action.

Kleist constructs his stories carefully, and their formal precision often contrasts sharply with the violence and brutality of the events portrayed. It is not possible, however, to construct an overall blueprint for the *Erzählungen*, and different ones are characterised by a particular mood or atmosphere. The interplay of black and white is the dominant feature of *Die Verlobung*; the symbolism of the plague runs like a dark thread through *Der Findling*; the pattern of the quest underlies *Michael Kohlhaas*; and the interaction of 'Scherz' and 'Ernst' sets the mood for *Die Marquise von O*. The savagery of the lynch mob in *Das Erdbeben* contrasts with the singing of the nuns in *Die heilige Cäcilie*, the desolation at the end of *Der Findling* stands in sharp contrast to the string of young Russians born to Count F. and his wife the Marquise von O. There is no lack of variety in the *Erzählungen*.

These stories are, then, narrated in a prose style staggering in its originality and quite unique in German literature. Long sentences, with the subject separated from the verb and the verb separated from the object by incapsulated clauses, themselves interrupted in turn by participial and adverbial phrases inserted generously, go on from line to line as the various incidents in the plot and stages in the argument are chronicled with meticulous care by a narrator apparently uninvolved subjectively in what he is recounting. The sentences have a forward dramatic impetus, the frequent use of phrases such as 'dergestalt, daß ...' and 'so daß ...', 'in such a way, that ... ' and 'so that ... ', urging the reader on to the final punchline or dramatic twist. The main elements in the sentences, the subject, main verb and direct object, by virtue of being isolated by all the incapsulations, stand out in greater relief, put under the spotlight as it were amidst the accompanying detail. But the forward impetus of the sentences, reinforced by the paratactic narrative method, is then all but brought to a halt by the plethora of attendant detail packed into them, so that a most curious combination of stationary and non-stationary elements is achieved. The sentences give the overall impression of speed, yet can only be read maddeningly slowly, and frequently have to be re-read if the various parts are to be seen in relation to the whole. Kleist designs his sentences as if they were mathematical equations; the main terms of the equation are stated, and then the various pluses and minuses, bracketed formulae and appended fractions are woven into the main body of the statement. They might equally be compared to the different pieces of a jigsaw puzzle, apparently haphazardly assembled and then fitting each into its allotted place to produce the finished puzzle. There is no padding in these infinitely complex structures, and every phrase has its allotted role within the overall pattern.

These sentences then grow enormously in length because of Kleist's use of what might be called his 'indem' technique, (conjunction = 'whilst', 'while'), whereby gestures accompany speech, subordinate actions fill out the main narrative, a whole wealth of attendant detail is brought in like so many stage directions to swell the basic statement, so that an effect of simultaneity is produced and characters' emotions are expressed through external gesture without any additional comment on the part of the narrator being necessary. Two examples may stand for many. When Kohlhaas returns home after discovering how his horses have been treated at the Tronkenburg he finds out from his wife what has happened to Herse, and as he asks her questions he takes off his coat, loosens his collar, and sits down in his chair (chairs and stools are Kleist's stock stage property), and these accompanying gestures give a good impression of the tension building up in him as he struggles to go through the normal routine of relaxing at home. When he arranges the sale of his house to a neighbour his wife's gestures are carefully noted as she kisses her child, busies herself with increasing urgency about the room, and generally strives to suppress her inner agitation at what her husband is doing. In doing this she does not say a word; her actions express her state of mind and make speech superfluous. There are countless examples of Kleist's 'indem' technique, and the result is to put flesh on the bare bones of the narrative and to add layers of meaning to the bald recital of facts laconically reported by the apparently detached chronicler. Since the narrator does not comment directly on these interpolated clauses it is up to the reader to speculate on their implied significance, and the open-ended nature of some of the interpolations adds to the depth and tension of the sentences. Through its introduction of significant detail and symbolic imagery, as for example that of fire, storms or battle, the 'indem' technique also means that occasionally a gleam of poetry illumines the dry factual prose.

Kleist's sentences, their parts carefully arranged to form an intricate whole, proceed on their way remorselessly and the argument develops with an almost icy logic, as if the inevitable nature of the fate governing the stories were expressed through the pre-ordained sequence of the syntax.[5] And yet this cool and carefully elaborated prose, the intellectual tour-de-force of an apparently detached reporter, is used to describe scenes of savagery and horror and to portray the anguish of soul of characters brought to the brink of despair. Violence and sadism is conveyed tersely in subordinate clauses; Meister Pedrillo clubs down Josephe, Hans von Tronka is hurled across the floor of the Tronkenburg, the brains of Gustav bespatter the walls, and all this is narrated almost *en passant*. Tricks of style reinforce the overall effect. Verbs are generally active and, because of the German characteristic of throwing verbs to the end of dependent clauses, they are stored up by Kleist and then released in batches, like so many bullets out of a machine-gun. One wonders if Kleist's exploitation of the peculiarities of German word-order may not be an unconscious projection of his own nervous stammer. Another trick of his is to repeat a conjunction or adverb many times with cumulative effect, leading up to some telling point, as for example in the passage from *Das Erdbeben* quoted earlier.[6] Direct speech may be inserted, often without warning, into the narrative with telling effect, an effect frequently heightened by the deliberate omission of inverted commas. On the other hand indirect speech is often used, partly to report a situation or incident with the greatest possible terseness and compression, partly to achieve on occasion a mood almost of

---

[5] Thomas Mann's description of Kleist as being 'Dionysian ... god-possessed, ecstatically excessive right down to every turn and nuance of his language, overloaded with expressions as it is', 'Heinrich von Kleist und seine Erzählungen', *Reden und Aufsätze, Werke* IX, 1960, cannot be accepted without reservation. There is a great deal of calculation in Kleist's effects.

[6] See above p.26, footnote 25.

unreality or detached irony. A famous example is the scene in *Die Marquise von O.* where the count turns up unexpectedly and asks the Marquise to marry him. There are no fewer than thirty-three clauses beginning with 'daß', and far from being a stylistic blemish this insistence on indirect reporting, with its use of conditional tenses and its evocation of another time sequence, creates an effect of something akin to unreality – the scene is in all conscience fantastic enough – and produces an impression of irony well in accord with the prevailing atmosphere in the story. Kleist's leitmotif use of words and phrases, repeated several times within a few lines to hammer home a point and to reinforce an irony, has already been noticed.[7] Two further examples may be given: there is the repetition of the word 'Schweinekoben' as Herse tells Kohlhaas how his horses were cooped up in a pigsty at the Tronkenburg, the ludicrousness of the situation contrasting with the mounting anger of Kohlhaas at what has happened and anticipating, in the grotesqueness of the contrast, the scene with the knacker from Döbbeln; and there is the repeated use of the word 'Hebamme' as the Marquise von O. protests her innocence to her mother, all this leading up to the glorious paradox of 'eine Hebamme und ein reines Bewußtsein'. Another feature of the style is Kleist's treatment of time. On occasions time is drastically compressed, as in the opening sentences of *Das Erdbeben*, and this increases the dramatic effect. Switching of tenses from past to present further heightens the drama of a situation. And flashbacks, reverting to the past to explain the present and anticipate the future, introduce different layers of time simultaneously and add to the density of the narrative. A final point to be noted about Kleist's style is the ambiguous impression deliberately produced by the variation in mood. Incidents are recounted directly and factually in a way that creates an overall impression of clarity. But this clarity is then brought into question by the studied use of conditional tenses and qualifying phrases, particularly in the loaded sentences with which the stories open and close.[8]

[7] See above p.99.
[8] Kleist's method is well defined as 'the dialectic interlacing through language of words that disclose and veil the truth' by Hans Heinz Holz, *Macht und Ohnmacht der Sprache*, 1962, p.11. This is the best study of Kleist's language.

No consideration of Kleist's prose style, however brief, would be complete without mention of his highly individual use of punctuation. Punctuation marks are used by Kleist as a composer uses musical notation. In the first place they are liberally employed to separate out the different component parts of a sentence, so that all the pieces in the jigsaw, large and small, stand out clearly and their logical relationship to one another is underlined. The dialectical nature of the prose, with one part balanced against another and its various subdivisions appropriately arranged, is brought out by the punctuation. In the second place the punctuation is used to indicate pauses or caesuras in the sentence, and the length of the pauses is precisely calculated, so that what follows is given added emphasis. This becomes clearer if the sentences are read aloud, as ideally Kleist wished them to be. There is all the difference, as far as Kleist is concerned, between a semi-colon and a colon, between a full-stop and a full-stop followed by a dash, or two dashes, or three dashes. In this way punctuation is used to underline the meaning of what is being said to a far greater extent than is usual, and the interpreter of Kleist's stories has to take careful note of this. Some examples may illustrate the point. The paradox of the opening sentence of *Michael Kohlhaas* is followed by a full-stop and a dash, so that in this way the combination of 'rechtschaffen' and 'entsetzlich' qualities and the force of the word 'zugleich' is emphasised. The second paragraph describes how Kohlhaas was riding to Saxony with a string of horses, musing on how to invest the profit he would make, when he comes to the toll barrier Junker Wenzel has illegally erected to bar the way. A colon precedes his musings on what he will do, thus slowing down the pace, and another colon then follows, before the barrier is mentioned, so that the reader has to pause before then finding out about the illegality that triggers off the whole affair. The opening sentence of *Die Marquise von O.* states that the Marquise is a lady of spotless reputation with several well brought-up children, and then after a colon gives the contents of the newspaper advertisement. The reader has to pause before the startling piece of information is sprung on him, and the colon also neatly plays off the respectability of the first half of the sentence against the outrageous nature of the second half. The story Babekan tells in *Die Verlobung in St. Domingo* of her betrayal by Herr Bertrand and the sixty lashes she received on the orders of Herr Villeneuve is marked off by a full-stop followed by two dashes, doubly emphasising the betrayal and cruelty practised by whites on blacks in a story whose opening sentence states that blacks are murdering whites. When in *Die Marquise von O.* Count F. presents himself at eleven o'clock on the morning of the fateful third of the month, the reaction of the Marquise is unexpectedly violent: 'Auf einen Lasterhaften war ich gefaßt', she says, 'aber auf keinen – – – Teufel!', 'I was prepared to meet someone depraved, but not a – – – devil!' The three dashes, together with the exclamation mark, amply underline the angel-devil theme taken up in the final sentence of the story. It is entirely fitting that in *Die Marquise von O.* the business of the rape, as has been seen,[9] should be conveyed by a punctuation mark.

For all its unique character Kleist's style does not lack variety. It can be dry and factual, like some legal protocol. It can acquire an unreal, almost nightmarish and grotesque flavour, when the speed of the narrative accelerates, as in the lynching scene in *Das Erdbeben* and the assault on the Tronkenburg in *Michael Kohlhaas*. It can be coarsely comic, as in the scene with the knacker from Döbbeln, or loaded with subtle irony, as in *Die Marquise von O*. It can emphasise auditory elements, as in *Das Bettelweib*, or under the influence of painting be full of plastic touches, as in *Die Verlobung*. A good example of his style, and one which may help to illustrate some of the points made, is the opening sentence of the passage describing the assault on the Tronkenburg made by Kohlhaas and his small band of followers. It goes as follows:

> Er fiel auch, mit diesem kleinen Haufen, schon, beim Einbruch der dritten Nacht, den Zollwärter und Torwächter, die im Gespräch unter dem Tor standen, niederreitend, in die Burg, und während, unter plötzlicher Aufprasselung aller Baracken im Schloßraum, die sie mit Feuer bewarfen, Herse, über die Windeltreppe, in den Turm der Vogtei eilte, und den

[9] See above p.77.

Schloßvogt und Verwalter, die, halb entkleidet, beim Spiel
saßen, mit Hieben und Stichen überfiel, stürzte Kohlhaas
zum Junker Wenzel ins Schloß.[10]

What a sentence! It gives an impression of speed and violent
action, but it is so packed with detail that it has to be read
more than once before it can be properly understood. Twenty
different parts, meticulously marked off with commas, go to
form the whole. The backbone of the sentence is the statement
'Er (Kohlhaas) fiel auch in die Burg und stürzte zum Junker
Wenzel ins Schloß', dramatic enough in all conscience as
Kohlhaas erupts into the castle. But this basic statement is
then filled out with subsidiary detail. Kohlhaas and his small
band ride down the tollkeeper and gatekeeper, though
apparently without premeditated intent. The two men just
happen to be standing in the way and are bowled over, almost
by oversight, in a subsidiary clause, a drastic example of the
operation of chance. While Kohlhaas plunges into the castle
Herse's activities are mentioned as he sets fire to the huts and
attacks the castellan and the steward, and the backbone of this
subsidiary statement, namely, 'während ... Herse ... den
Schloßvogt und Verwalter ... mit Hieben und Stichen
überfiel', is similarly broken up and filled out with detail, so
that the pattern of the whole sentence is mirrored in its
dependent parts. Details, like stage directions, are added both
to bring the scene to life and to show how unprepared for the
attack the inhabitants of the castle were. The tollkeeper and
gatekeeper are chatting together by the main gate, and the
castellan and steward are sitting down playing cards in their
shirt-sleeves, a splendid realistic touch. The verbs used of
these two groups of minor characters – 'standen' and 'saßen' –
are the only non-active ones in the sentence. Time and place
are recorded, carefully marked off by commas. Flames leap up

---

[10] 'With this small band, then, as night of the third day was falling, he stormed into
the castle, riding down the tollkeeper and the porter, who stood chatting by the gate,
and while, as all the castle outbuildings, into which they had tossed lighted brands,
suddenly crackled into flames, Herse went hurrying up the winding staircase into the
bailiff's tower and with stabs and blows set about the castellan and the steward, who,
in their shirtsleeves, were sitting over a game of cards, Kohlhaas hurtled into the
castle after Junker Wenzel.' I have translated literally, even to the point of
unintelligibility, in order to bring out the flavour of the German.

suddenly, a suitable introduction of the fire imagery as the Archangel Michael goes about his business. And the impression of actions simultaneously breaking out all over the place is brought out by the use of the present particle ('niederreitend'), the preposition 'unter' combined with the '-ung' terminal ('unter plötzlicher Aufprasselung'), and the use of the conjunction 'während', its force being emphasised by the fact that it is separated by interpolated clauses from the verb it governs. The sentence shows how Kleist can combine violence of subject matter with a rationally designed framework of form. The whole unit is a brilliant blending of spontaneous actions simultaneously breaking out with a backcloth of vivid detail, the forward impetus of the verbs being checked by the scenic elaboration interspersed between them, the different terms of the equation clearly marked off by commas, and all of it plunging irresistibly on to the punch line 'stürzte Kohlhaas zum Junker Wenzel ins Schloß'. If the Archangel Michael were to appear on earth his actions could hardly be more sudden or dramatic, or catch his victims more unprepared. In this way Kleist launches the attack on the Tronkenburg, and he manages to sustain the same pace and to load his sentences with the same significant detail for pages to come.

The opening sentence of *Michael Kohlhaas* starts with a paradox: Kohlhaas is both 'rechtschaffen' and 'entsetzlich'. The opening sentences of *Das Erdbeben* and *Die Marquise von O.* both in their different ways present highly paradoxical situations, and both stories end on a paradoxical or ambiguous note. The paradox is Kleist's basic means of expression, it is the form of statement most central to his way of thinking. He sees life, whether it be universal metaphysical problems or the riddle of the human personality, in terms of opposition, of plus and minus, of a 'Polarverhältnis'. These opposites coexist and are presented in the form of a paradox. The stories are riddled with paradoxes. Two emaciated horses almost bring the state of Saxony to its knees (*Michael Kohlhaas*); a mother finds honour in her daughter's shame and the sobs of an army colonel shake the foundations of the house (*Die Marquise von O.*); the anger of a lynch mob surpasses the fury of an earthquake (*Das Erdbeben in Chili*); a misguided lover shoots the girl who is saving his life and that of his friends (*Die Verlobung in St. Domingo*); the ethereal singing of nuns results in the discordant chanting of four deranged brothers for whom insanity is a form of bliss (*Die heilige Cäcilie*). This technique of using paradox to probe into the nature of truth is one that Kleist also uses in many of his critical writings. In *Von der Überlegung. Eine Paradoxe* he reverses the normal precept to think first and act afterwards and asserts that it is better to act first and think afterwards.[11] In *Betrachtungen über den Weltlauf* he inverts the usual way of looking at the progress of human civilisation by stating that man started in a state of perfection and then through the various stages of culture and civilisation gradually degenerated until finally reaching the stage where he is just plain rotten. In *Über das Marionettentheater* the limitations of human consciousness are demonstrated and the thesis, startling at first sight, advanced that the two highest forms of existence are embodied either in the puppet or in God. This playing with paradox, this constant demonstration of how one extreme produces its opposite, of how 'Zufall' operating in one direction inevitably results in a reversal of fortune in the other direction, and of how both extremes are immanent in any human situation, all this represents the central feature of Kleist's attitude to life. The element of paradox is present in almost everything he wrote, in his critical writings, in the situations in his stories and the behaviour of the characters in them, and in the majority of the anecdotes, which revolve around a central paradoxical point, and it is reflected as well in the dialectical nature of his sentence construction. Any interpretation of his works has to take this into account. If they are viewed from one standpoint only, and labelled as 'tragic' or 'existentialist' or whatever designation is currently in vogue, then this can only lead to over-simplification.

The essential nature of a paradox is that it combines two opposing points of view, and in the way it is formulated mirrors the problem of appearance and reality. Kleist is generally careful not to clear up his paradoxes and present a clear statement at the end of each story. Life is too complex for

[11] See below p.188.

this. This is the reason for the anonymity he preserves in the main as narrator, and it is the reason too for the highly conditional phrasing of some of his sentences. When he says that up to the age of thirty Michael Kohlhaas might have been held to be a model citizen the phrase he uses is 'würde haben gelten können'. When at the end of *Das Erdbeben* the reader is told that Don Fernando, comparing Philip with the son he had lost, was almost glad of the exchange, the phrase used is 'so war es ihm fast, als müßt er sich freuen', again highly conditional. Kleist deliberately allows an element of ambiguity to remain, and it is left to the reader to wrestle with the paradoxes that conclude the stories. Real life does not yield its secrets easily, any more than music reveals the mystery of its power through the signs on the printed page. Perhaps, when human reason has done its inadequate best, all that man can hope for is a revelation of truth from some irrational source, be it divine revelation through music, or the sibylline utterances of a gypsy woman, or then, and this is what is afforded in the last story to be examined, *Der Zweikampf*, truth as a sign of grace from on high.

9

Der Zweikampf

Wo liegt die Verpflichtung der höchsten göttlichen Weisheit, die Wahrheit im Augenblick der glaubensvollen Anrufung selbst, anzuzeigen und auszusprechen?

Gott ist wahrhaftig und untrüglich.[1]

'Duke Wilhelm von Breysach, who since his secret alliance with a countess Katharina von Heersbruck, a lady of the house of Alt-Hüningen who appeared to be beneath him in rank, had lived in a state of enmity with his half-brother, Graf Jakob der Rotbart, was making his way home, towards the end of the fourteenth century as the night of St. Remigius began to fall, from a meeting he had had in Worms with the German Emperor, a meeting at which he had obtained from the Emperor his consent to the legitimisation of a natural son of his born to his wife before their marriage, a Count Philipp of Hüningen, this by virtue of the fact that the children born to him in wedlock had since died.' With this characteristically involved, not entirely intelligible, and rather unlovely sentence Kleist embarks on his story *Der Zweikampf*. Time and place are mentioned, a secret marriage and the enmity of two brothers indicated, and the prospects of future happiness foreshadowed with the successful conclusion of a diplomatic mission. As usual Kleist raises hopes only to dash them to the ground. Duke Wilhelm is assassinated and brought home by his chamberlain, Friedrich von Trota, to die in the arms of his distraught wife. Circumstantial evidence points to Graf Jakob as the culprit. When called upon to answer the charge he

---

[1] 'What obligation is there for supreme divine wisdom to declare and pronounce the truth the very instant it is invoked by the believer?'
'God is truthful and cannot err.' The first sentence spoken by Trota, the second by Littegarde in their scene together in prison.

defends himself with a startling alibi, asserting that at the time of the crime he was in the arms of the virtuous Frau Littegarde von Auerstein, a beautiful widow of spotless reputation. Frau Littegarde's father dies of a stroke upon hearing of this allegation; and her indignant brothers turn her out of house and home. Destitute and despairing she throws herself on the mercy of Friedrich von Trota, who immediately espouses her cause and before the imperial court at Basle declares her innocence, calling Graf Jakob a liar and slanderer and challenging him to trial by combat, the victor to be declared innocent and the vanquished guilty according to the sure and inexorable judgement of God. The duel to decide the honour of the lady takes place. Trota draws first blood, grazing his opponent's wrist, but then, after a protracted conflict, stumbles by chance and gives Graf Jakob the opportunity to bury his broadsword three times in Trota's breast. Graf Jakob is declared the winner, and Trota and Littegarde are found guilty before God and man and sentenced to death by burning at the stake.

Miraculously Trota's apparently mortal wounds heal and he recovers; whereas Graf Jakob's surface wound turns gangrenous, the infection spreads, drastic attempts to stem the contagion prove ineffectual, and it gradually becomes clear that he is doomed to die a wretched death. Still he continues to swear, even on the holy sacrament, that on the night when Duke Wilhelm was assassinated he was lying in the arms of Littegarde, and on this point his conscience is clear. The mystery is finally cleared up. Far from being in bed with Littegarde Jakob was in fact in the arms of her maid Rosalie, an old flame of his, who managed to masquerade as her mistress and inveigle the count by night into the castle under the impression that he was enjoying a rendezvous with Littegarde, an impression she was able subsequently to maintain. News of this is brought to Jakob as he lies on his deathbed in Basle, on the very day that Trota and Littegarde are to be consigned to the flames. Realising now that in fact, though apparently victorious, he lost the duel, Graf Jakob confesses to the murder of his half-brother Duke Wilhelm, having employed a man to shoot him with an arrow. He dies and his body is consigned to the flames intended for Trota and

Littegarde. They are released, proclaimed innocent, and showered with honours. They marry and live happily ever after. The Emperor hangs a chain of honour around Trota's neck. And the wording of the statutes governing ordeal by combat is amended, whereby after the statement that guilt is straightway brought to the light of day through the result of the duel the phrase is inserted 'If it be God's will'.

Der Zweikampf was published in the second volume of the *Erzählungen* in 1811. The main source[2] is a story in Froissart's *Chroniques de France* telling of a duel between Jacquet le Gris and Jehan de Carouge over the honour of a lady. Kleist was probably familiar with the original version in Froissart; but he will also have been familiar with the adaptation of it by C. Baechler in the Hamburg *Gemeinnützige Unterhaltungsblätter* of 21 April 1810, which forms the basis of his own *Geschichte eines merkwürdigen Zweikampfes* published in the *Berliner Abendblätter* on 20/21 February, 1811. In addition to this Kleist may well have been influenced by Cervantes' story *Los Trabajos de Persiles y de Segismunda*, where there is a similar deceptive result of an ordeal by combat. The motif of a man being shot by an arrow in the dark occurs in Kleist's anecdote *Sonderbarer Rechtsfall in England* (*Berliner Abendblätter*, 9 February 1811), where the paradoxical limitations of the law are also demonstrated. Various verbal echoes make it clear that Kleist used Baechler when writing his story, so that the final version must date from after April, 1810, and indeed there is no good reason why *Der Zweikampf* should not be considered the last story Kleist wrote. It does however contain echoes of earlier works by Kleist. The situation of fratricide and of characters being completely misled by appearances mirrors that of his first play *Die Familie Scroffenstein*; the duel scene has many similarities with the duel in the fifth act of *Das Käthchen von Heilbronn*; and the final outcome of the story has much in common with the atmosphere of the concluding scenes of *Prinz Friedrich von Homburg*. All this goes to show how tightly knit Kleist's works are and how difficult it is, where clear indications are lacking, to make meaningful guesses about when they were written.

---

[2] For sources see Sembdner, *Werke*, II, p.908 and p.919.

Der Zweikampf

The story revolves around two situations, both of them baffling and mysterious. In the first place there is the murder of Duke Wilhelm, a murder that occurs in the first paragraph during the course of which Graf Jakob and Trota are introduced, and which is only cleared up at the very end. The *corpus delicti* is an ornately fashioned arrow, and this is traced back to Jakob der Rotbart. The arrow appears to establish his guilt. But the alibi he produces leads on to the central situation, namely, the truth or otherwise of his assertion that he was in bed with Littegarde and the championing of her cause by Friedrich von Trota. As proof of his alibi Jakob produces a ring given to him, so he alleges, by Littegarde, and which she acknowledges to be hers. These are the two basic plots, and the concrete evidence consists of the arrow and the ring, both apparently equally conclusive, the one pointing to the guilt and the other to the innocence of Graf Jakob. The time sequence of the story is not entirely straightforward, since it has to delve back into the past in order to establish the facts concerning Jakob's alibi. Moreover, during the course of the narrative various incidents in the past concerning the relationship of Trota and Jakob to Littegarde are disclosed by Kleist. The action centres on various highly dramatic scenes. These are located either in the castles of the three principal characters, or then in Basle before the assembled populace, grouped according to rank and status from the emperor downwards. The central scene, however, where the most profound issues of the story are debated, takes place in the intimate surroundings of a prison cell, where Trota visits the distraught Littegarde. The story starts with murder at night at the hands of an assassin hiding in the bushes; it ends in the full light of day with the triumph of innocence and faith.

Der Zweikampf contains all the familiar ingredients of a Kleistian plot. There is the central situation, where factual evidence runs counter to an intuitive awareness of truth, and it concerns a woman who suddenly and unexpectedly finds herself torn out of her sheltered existence, her innocence and honour apparently condemned in the eyes of the world. There is a web of intrigue, deception and self-deception, centring on the character of Graf Jakob. There is the contrast between appearance and reality, and the problem of knowledge and revelation, paradoxically presented. The themes of love and trust, faith and conscience, are introduced through the characters of Trota and Littegarde. The limitations of legal institutions are ironically shown, and a contrast made between what is right in the eyes of the law and what is right in terms of individual conscience. The frailty of the institution of the family is dramatically, indeed melodramatically, demonstrated as Littegarde is thrown out of house and home by her brothers, eager in their righteous indignation to get their hands on her property. Chance, or chance operating on a higher plane as a miracle, conditions, or appears to condition, the motivation of the story. Irony is once again at the heart of the narrative technique. As in other stories there is a background of violence and the clash of weapons. And the symbol of the plague occurs again, conjuring up a picture of evil and corruption with the plague-like contagion that invades the body of Graf Jakob. The description of this deserves to be quoted as a magnificent example of Kleist's prose, with its involved sentence structure, drastic content, hint of irony, and the laconic finality of the concluding verdict:

> Ein ätzender der ganzen damaligen Heilkunst unbekannter Eiter, fraß auf eine krebsartige Weise, bis auf den Knochen herab im ganzen System seiner Hand um sich, dergestalt, daß man zum Entsetzen aller seiner Freunde genötigt gewesen war, ihm die ganze schadhafte Hand, und späterhin, da auch hierdurch dem Eiterfraß kein Ziel gesetzt ward, den Arm selbst abzunehmen. Aber auch dies, als eine Radikalkur gepriesene Heilmittel vergrößerte nur, wie man heutzutage leicht eingesehen haben würde, statt ihm abzuhelfen, das Übel; und die Ärzte, da sich sein ganzer Körper nach und nach in Eiterung und Fäulnis auflöste, erklärten, daß keine Rettung für ihn sei, und er noch, vor Abschluß der laufenden Woche, sterben müsse'.[3]

---

[3] 'A malignant pus of a kind unknown to the entire medical science of the day ate its way like a cancer through every part of his hand right down to the bone, to such an extent that, to the horror of all his friends, it was found necessary to amputate the whole of his infected hand and, when this did not put a stop to the consuming infection, to cut off his arm as well. But even this remedy, which was held in high esteem as a radical form of treatment, only increased the malignancy instead of diminishing it, as would easily have been realised today; and, as his body, consumed by rotting putrefaction, gradually began to disintegrate, the doctors proclaimed that there was no way of saving him, and that before the week was up he would have to die.'

One almost feels sorry for the man who murdered his half-brother and tried to seduce a virtuous widow.

In *Der Zweikampf* are gathered together the basic themes of Kleist's works. It is highly appropriate that these themes should be assembled for the last time in what is arguably one of the best and most profound of his stories. It is based, as has been stated, on one of Froissart's chronicles. It is interesting to compare the sources of Kleist's works with the final products as they issued from his pen. A picture of a judge, a pair of lovers and a woman with a broken jug becomes transformed into the broad comedy and metaphysical subtlety of *Der zerbrochne Krug*. A trivial enough tale of a *Sonderbare Geschichte, die sich, zu meiner Zeit, in Italien zutrug* emerges finally as the profound story of *Die Marquise von O*. Molière's polished comedy on the theme of Amphitryon is used as the basis for the conflict of soul and metaphysical exploration portrayed in Kleist's *Amphitryon*. A dry, succinct report in an old chronicle gets magnified into the daemonic story of Michael Kohlhaas, the horse-dealer. And a French account of two knights fighting a duel over the honour of an innocent lady is transformed into the metaphysical profundity and psychological perception of *Der Zweikampf*. The narrative is then told with a sweep and a strength characteristic of Kleist as the action, both external and internal, is conveyed in a panorama of colourful scenes and cliff-hanging incidents dramatically portrayed against a background of mediaeval chivalry and faith in the omnipotence and wisdom of God, with the fortunes of the main protagonists oscillating in typically Kleistian fashion between triumph and disaster.

The central incident is the duel that gives its name to the story. By way of prelude to an examination of this duel it might be appropriate to quote an anecdote that appeared in the *Berliner Abendblätter* on 22 November 1810 and which to some extent by its paradoxical ending anticipates the outcome of the duel in *Der Zweikampf*:

> Two famous English boxers, one born in Portsmouth, and the other in Plymouth, who for many years had heard of one another without their paths actually having crossed, decided, upon meeting in London, to hold a public contest to see which of them would end up champion. Accordingly both of them, in

the presence of a crowd of people, squared up to one another in
the garden of a public-house; and when, after a few minutes,
the man from Plymouth struck the man from Portsmouth such
a blow on the chest that he spat up blood, the latter, wiping his
mouth with his fist, cried out: well done! – Soon afterwards,
however, when they had faced up to one another again, the
man from Portsmouth struck the man from Plymouth such a
blow on his body with his clenched right fist that, rolling his
eyes, he fell to the ground, exclaiming: that's not bad either – !
Whereupon the crowd standing round in a circle broke out
into loud cheers and, while the man from Plymouth, whose
internal organs had been damaged, was carried away dead,
acknowledged the man from Portsmouth as the victor. – The
man from Portsmouth, however, is reported to have died the
following day of a violent haemorrhage.

The duel in *Der Zweikampf* is fought on different levels:
actual, metaphysical, and psychological. It is brilliantly told.
The two knights appear clad from head to foot in shimmering
armour in the lists to fight out their duel before almost all the
nobles of southern Germany and Switzerland, the emperor at
their head, and before an 'unermeßliche Menschenmenge'
crowded together on stands and scaffolding. The two
contestants take their place and light and shade is distributed
between them, according to established custom. Midway
between them, in the background, Frau Littegarde sits on a
dais covered over with red cloth. Her fate is in the balance. If
Trota wins the duel, then her honour is vindicated. If he loses
it, then both he and she have to face death in the flames. At a
sign from the emperor the herold blows a fanfare and battle
begins. Almost at once Trota wounds the arm of Graf Jakob,
who is not bothered by it and only renews the encounter with
increased intensity, raining blows on Trota from all sides.
Trota stands firmly on the spot he has chosen, not actively
attacking Jakob, but parrying all the blows and rendering
them fruitless. Kleist resorts to his favourite imagery of storms
to describe the contest: 'Jetzt wogte zwischen beiden
Kämpfern der Streit, wie zwei Sturmwinde einander
begegnen, wie zwei Gewitterwolken, ihre Blitze einander
zusendend, sich treffen und, ohne sich zu vermischen, unter
dem Gekrach häufiger Donner getürmt umeinander

Der Zweikampf 177

herumschweben'.[4] The fight goes on like this for almost an hour when a growing murmur from the crowd registers disapproval at Trota's defensive tactics, successful though they undoubtedly are. Trota's reaction is bold, but dogged by ill fortune and punished by the none too gentlemanly opportunism of his opponent:

> Er (Trota) trat mit einem mutigen Schritt aus dem, sich von Anfang herein gewählten Standpunkt ... hervor, über das Haupt seines Gegners, dessen Kräfte schon zu sinken anfingen, mehrere derbe und ungeschwächte Streiche, die derselbe jedoch unter geschickten Seitenbewegungen mit seinem Schild aufzufangen wußte, danieder schmetternd. Aber schon in den ersten Momenten dieses dergestalt veränderten Kampfes hatte Herr Friedrich ein Unglück, das die Anwesenheit höherer, über den Kampf waltender Mächte nicht eben anzudeuten schien; er stürzte, den Fußtritt in seinen Sporen verwickelnd, stolpernd abwärts, und während er unter der Last des Helms und Harnisches, die seine oberen Teile beschwerten, mit in dem Staub vorgestützter Hand, in die Kniee sank, stieß ihm Graf Jakob der Rotbart, nicht eben auf die edelmütigste und ritterlichste Weise, das Schwert in die dadurch bloßgegebene Seite'.[5]

Heaven hardly seems to be on the side of Littegarde's champion. Jakob is declared the victor, and the fainting Littegarde and the apparently mortally wounded Trota are carried off to their separate prison cells. The effect on the spectators is like that of a tragedy, as they all rise to their feet

[4] 'Now the battle between the two warriors surged backwards and forwards, their encounter was like two tempests colliding in the air, like two storm-clouds shooting bolts of lightning at each other as they crashed together, their massive bulks, not mingling, towering up into the sky and, circling each other, discharging salvo upon salvo of thunder.'

[5] 'Boldly he stepped forward from what from the very beginning of the contest had been his chosen spot, raining down a succession of doughty blows with undiminished strength upon the head of his adversary, whose resistance was already beginning to flag, but who nonetheless was able to feint and duck and parry the blows skilfully with his shield. But in the very first moments of this contest, which had become so transformed, Herr Friedrich suffered a misfortune that hardly seemed to indicate the presence of higher powers directing the battle; catching his foot in his spurs he tripped and stumbled, and as he sank to his knees under the weight of his helmet and armour, stretching out his hand in the dust to support him, Count Jakob der Rotbart, not in the most generous or chivalrous fashion, plunged his sword into Trota's exposed side.'

amidst cries of horror and pity ('unter dumpfen Ausrufungen des Schreckens und Mitleidens').

The duel is told in vivid colours by Kleist, and it is easy to imagine the clash of the two adversaries invoking the judgement of God on the honour of the lady seated in the background between them on a chair covered with red cloth. But the duel has other dimensions. Trota, for all that he is a real person, is as well an almost idealised figure, blood brother to Don Fernando in *Das Erdbeben in Chili* and Colino in *Der Findling*, a knight in armour battling for his lady; and Graf Jakob, with his 'schwarze Seele', his 'black soul', seems almost devilish as he darts in and out trying to pierce the guard of his opponent.[6] The duel comes to life on another plane as a struggle between good angel and bad angel for the possession of a human soul, and the mediaeval background is just the right setting against which to stage a supernatural conflict between good and evil. Trota is deliberately portrayed as a Christ figure when he visits Littegarde in her cell; and Jakob is caught up in a Cain and Abel situation with the murder of Duke Wilhelm. The use of language builds up the impression of a conflict surpassing merely human dimensions, not only in the uproar of the elements already noted, but also in the constant, often ambiguous, references to divine providence and supernatural intervention, and the insistent dating of the action by religious feast days. Duke Wilhelm is slain on the night of St. Remigius (1 October), Graf Jakob faces his accusers on the 'Montag nach Trinitatis', and the duel itself is fought on St. Margaret's day (13 July). And this is appropriate when it is remembered that issues of divine truth and justice are involved going beyond the individual fate of the persons concerned. Yet again Kleist pursues his method of polarising human conflicts and using them as a mirror for the conflict of plus and minus forces in the universe.

But if the duel can be viewed on two planes, actual and metaphysical, it also exists on a third, on a psychological plane. Who are the characters affected by its outcome? Graf

---

[6] John M. Ellis, 'Kleist's *Der Zweikampf*', *Monatshefte* 65, 1973, finds Jakob 'thoroughly impressive' and Trota a 'weak and irresolute simpleton'. Jakob may be an agreeable villain, apart from the business of murder and fornication; but Ellis distorts the character of Trota.

Jakob der Rotbart is a rich widower living in the seclusion of his castle, holding parties there to which he invites the pretty women of the district. He enjoys a good reputation with the common folk, but is 'frei und ausschweifend', 'free and licentious', and a lover of wine, women and hunting. He is cunning and calculating, and his actions are based on a keen appreciation of the factors involved, be it the opinion of the populace, the impression to be made on his judges, or the best way to achieve his secret ambitions of power. In the matter of the murder of his half-brother his calculations go astray, for the legitimisation of the duke's bastard son deprives Jakob of his lawful right to the throne, and in this he could justifiably feel aggrieved. If the past-master of intrigue miscalculates in this respect, his intentions in respect of Littegarde prove to be even more the target of error and deception. Through the intrigues of the maid Rosalie, a sort of Doppelgänger of Littegarde, he is the victim of a 'zonderbares Mißverständnis', a 'strange misunderstanding' and the 'blinding of his senses', and the 'Verblendung seiner Sinne', characteristically Kleistian phrases. The deceiver is the victim of deception, ironically enough, and in this there is poetic justice. Jakob's piety is a pose and his chivalry, as shown in the way he takes advantage of Trota in the duel, is a sham. He professes love for Littegarde, yet cannot distinguish her charms from those of Rosalie. His one saving grace is that he fought the duel genuinely believing in the truth of his assertion that he had visited Littegarde at night. For the rest he is a fraud, false in every way, an example of perverted intellect and abused feeling. The contagion which invades his body is symbolic of him, and it is fitting that he should be consumed by flames, flames which are, a grimly humorous touch on Kleist's part, as 'rötlich' as his beard.

Friedrich von Trota is a very different sort of person, as 'white' as Jakob is 'black'. The first sight the reader has of Jakob is at his castle, drinking with his friends and entertaining ladies. How differently Trota is presented! He is first discovered at his desk in his castle, immersed in documents, a much more sober and responsible way of employing his time. His character will emerge when the main themes of the story are discussed. Suffice it to say here that he is in every respect the opposite of Jakob. He is a man universally looked up to, who respects human feelings and is incapable of intrigue and devious cunning. He is a fitting champion to defend the honour of Littegarde. What sort of person is she?

'Nun muß man wissen', writes Kleist as he brings the reader into his confidence, 'daß Frau Wittib Littegarde von Auerstein, so wie die schönste, so auch, bis auf den Augenblick dieser schmählichen Anklage, die unbescholtenste und makelloseste Frau des Landes war'.[7] The superlatives are characteristic of Kleist, never a writer to shrink from going to extremes, making all the more dramatic the sudden turn of fortune's wheel. Littegarde is another of those women in Kleist's works whose outward beauty mirrors a beauty of soul and a purity and integrity apparently unaffected by human conflicts and the ways of the world. She is the last in the line of women suddenly confronted with a dreadful situation not to be explained rationally, which threatens to dislocate and disrupt their entire personality. Elvire finds the image of her angelic rescuer transformed into the figure of evil incarnate. The Marquise von O. is torn between the consciousness of her purity and the very tangible evidence of her pregnancy. Eva, in *Der zerbrochne Krug*, is forced, though innocent, to make it appear that she had admitted a lover to her room. Alkmene, in *Amphitryon*, finds herself with two husbands, not one, and her personality is in danger of becoming split between her earthly and her supernatural longings. So too Littegarde finds herself in a situation where she is in danger of succumbing to madness and despair amidst the confusion of circumstances surrounding her. There is tangible evidence – the ring – to bear witness against her. The organs of justice pronounce her guilty. And worse still, the very God in whom she believes appears to proclaim her guilty.

Is she then blameless? And has not the duel being fought to decide her fate already been taking place within her? She lives 'still und eingezogen' at her father's castle, withdrawn from the world, though still young and beautiful, and she is

[7] 'Now the reader must know that the lady Littegarde von Auerstein was, up to the moment of this defamatory accusation, not only the most beautiful but also the most blameless and spotless lady in the land.'

planning to withdraw herself even more from the world by sacrificing 'den Reiz meiner aufblühenden Jugend', (lit: 'the charm of my blossoming youth'), as she puts it, and becoming the abbess of a nunnery on the banks of the Rhine. Yet another widowed lady, like the Marquise von O., tempting fate by leading an artificially sheltered existence, conforming passively to the conventions demanded of her station, repressing her natural instincts by withdrawing from the world. It appears that she is by no means indifferent to Trota. She knows that he loves her, and indeed he had proposed marriage to her, a marriage warmly supported by her father. But she hesitated, unable or unwilling to take the plunge, until out of consideration for her brothers she writes declining his offer, though the letter costs her much effort and many tears. The reader also learns, another example of the way Kleist releases significant detail at appropriate moments, that Trota once saved her life when she had been attacked while out hunting by a wild boar, a highly symbolic piece of information in view of her present situation. Yet she tearfully puts him out of mind and, bowing to her brothers' wishes, rejects marriage in favour of becoming an abbess. Can one speak here of a repression, conscious or unconscious, on her part? And if, as seems highly probable, Trota occupies half of her thoughts, there can be no doubt that Graf Jakob occupies the other half. She had, it appears, attended several balls given by this gentleman, out of deference to her father's wish for her to find a second husband. Indeed, Jakob put on special parties for her and conceived a passion for her, so much so, that on these occasions he singled her out for his special attentions in a way she found 'particularly repellent', 'auf eine schon damals sehr anstößige Weise'. She is well aware of his 'bad reputation', his 'schlechter Ruf', she treats his advances with 'coldness and contempt', with 'Kälte und Verachtung', and is finally outraged to find in the room in his castle set aside for her a formal declaration of love. She immediately leaves the castle of a man whom she 'hates in the innermost depths of her being', a man who, and Kleist chooses his words carefully, is 'ihr in der tiefsten Seele verhaßt'. There can be no doubt that Graf Jakob occupies, consciously or unconsciously, a large place in her thoughts, though she may strive to suppress his image in her mind. And it is therefore quite clear that the duel fought over her fate is at the same time a duel going on in her own mind between angel and devil, to use the terminology of *Die Marquise von O.*, as she sits on her dais halfway between Trota and Graf Jakob.

Doubts may be raised at this point about such a psychological approach to the story, and it might be thought that to view it in such a way is to make of Kleist a twentieth-century, post-Freudian writer. It should by now, however, have become clear that Kleist is keenly interested in the various facets of the human personality, the plus and minus sides of a person's character. And it should equally have become apparent that he knows perfectly well what he is doing when he carefully inserts into his text loaded phrases and interpolated incidents designed to bring out, implicitly or explicitly, different traits of character. Wilfully to ignore this aspect of his stories and to assert that he is concerned solely with metaphysical issues is to approach Kleist from an unnecessarily one-sided standpoint and to lose sight of the richness and variety of his narrative method. It is of course equally true that his interest in the wider issues of the human situation conditions his approach to this or that character, and the particular problem with which a story is concerned necessitates a highly selective treatment of character traits, especially in so condensed a literary form as the Novelle. Psychology and metaphysics go together in Kleist. It would, for instance, be very much in keeping with the attitude found elsewhere in his works to say that the accusation made against Littegarde, coming out of the blue as it does, is the result of ill chance, of 'Zufall'. It could, however, equally well be asserted that her particular situation in life and the contacts she has with Trota and Graf Jakob should make it peculiarly appropriate that the lightning, when it strikes, should pick on her. In order to appreciate the richness of a story like *Der Zweikampf* the reader has to make a conscious effort to experience the action from the standpoint of each individual character, be it Littegarde, Trota or Graf Jakob. In the case of Littegarde it gradually becomes apparent that there is nothing fortuitous in the way she has been cast in the role she has to play. In *Der Zweikampf* it is not only Trota who fights a duel.

Der Zweikampf 183

Littegarde has to fight one too, both with herself and with the world as it presents itself to her.

At first she gives way to despair. Her warrior knight has lost his duel and only proved her guilt in the eyes of the world. Her plight is even worse than that of the Marquise von O. Not only is there a conflict between her consciousness of innocence and the verdict pronounced by the outside world. In her case the God in whom she believes and whose judgement given in the duel cannot err has declared her to be guilty, and this fact she has to accept. Her individual conscience and her faith in God pull her in opposite directions, and it is little wonder that she is on the verge of madness. To accentuate the desperate and cruel nature of her situation Kleist progressively isolates her from all human help and support. Her father dies when he hears of the accusation against her; her brothers turn savagely against her; the mother and sisters of Trota heap recriminations on her after the duel, because of what will happen to Trota. She is separated from Trota, for she can only see in him the proof of her guilt, he now appears to her as an accusing judge and not an angel of deliverance; his unswerving devotion to her becomes more unbearable than any insults heaped on her by her enemies. And perhaps worst of all, she believes herself to be deserted by her God, who pronounces against her in the duel. Like Gretchen in Goethe's *Faust* she lies in her dungeon cell on a heap of straw, distraught and half-crazed. She plumbs the depths of despair. It is Trota who leads her back to inner harmony.

Recovered from his wounds he insists on seeing her in her cell, despite her wishes to the contrary. She recoils at the sight of him, like a sinner annihilated by the loving figure of Christ, and at this point Kleist implicitly compares Trota to Christ. An extraordinary dialogue ensues between them, with the overwrought language mirroring Littegarde's distraught state of mind. She says the sight of him is unbearable to her: 'Die Hölle, mit allen Schauern und Schrecknissen, ist süßer mir und anzuschauen lieblicher, als der Frühling deines mir in Huld und Liebe zugekehrten Angesichts!'.[8] These outbursts,

---

[8] 'Hell, with all its terrors and horrors, is more sweet for me to gaze upon and more pleasant than the springtime of your face and the love and kindness it shows to me.'

with their religious colouring, then culminate in her reply to Trota's question as to whether she was in fact guilty: 'Schuldig, überwiesen, verworfen, in Zeitlichkeit und Ewigkeit verdammt und verurteilt ... Gott ist wahrhaftig und untrüglich; geh, meine Sinne reißen, und meine Kraft bricht. Laß mich mit meinem Jammer und meiner Verzweiflung allein!'.[9] Such is the depth of despair reached by one who, when comforting Trota's mother before the duel, said 'Keine Schuld befleckt mein Gewissen; und ginge er ohne Helm und Harnisch in den Kampf, Gott und all seine Engel beschirmen ihn!'[10] – ironic words to recall at this juncture, doubly ironic in view of the eventual outcome of the story. At this point Kleist's technique of making the pendulum swing from one extreme to the other comes into operation. Trota, recovering from the fainting fit which he has inevitably had, for with Kleist an attack of fainting is often a salutary excursion to the restoring springs of the unconscious self, questions Littegarde again. He finds out about the letter Graf Jakob sent her when she stayed at his castle. The memories awakened in her by his questioning bring back a sense of her innocence, crushed as it had been by the judgement of God, and the purity of her feeling reasserts itself. When Trota asks her again if she is innocent he receives a very different answer as Littegarde proclaims her innocence in the lyrically highly charged words 'Wie die Brust eines neugebornen Kindes, wie das Gewissen eines aus der Beichte kommenden Menschen, wie die Leiche einer, in der Sakristei, unter der Einkleidung, verschiedenen Nonne!'[11] This complete reversal is a remarkable example of Kleist's technique, and he has made it all the more effective by the half-religious, half-hysterical language he chooses to employ for the occasion. Littegarde's regaining of a belief in her innocence is not, be it noted, the result of any religious belief on her part, indeed she avows her innocence in spite of

---

[9] 'Guilty, condemned and cast out, damned and convicted for all time and all eternity ... God is truthful and cannot err; go, my senses are at breaking point, and my strength is failing me. Leave me alone with my misery and my despair.'

[10] 'No guilt stains my conscience; and if he were to enter the lists without helmet or armour God and all His angels will protect him!'

[11] 'Innocent as the breast of a new-born babe, as the conscience of a man coming from the confessional, as the corpse of a nun who has died in the vestry taking the veil!'

what her religion tells her she must believe. Trota, like a modern psycho-analyst, by probing into her past reawakens in her a consciousness of her own worth and rekindles a faith in human qualities that, contrary to all the evidence, enables her to triumph over despair and become again at one with herself. Yet another duel has been fought in the prison cell, and well might Trota return to his own cell feeling that he has brought comfort to the woman he loves.

The duel is the central feature of *Der Zweikampf*. How appropriate that the action in what is very probably the last work Kleist wrote should revolve around a duel. There could be no more fitting way of representing the background of conflict in his works than by means of a duel, and no better way of symbolising his whole life and attitude to the world. Kleist sees human life as a conflict, and the world as a place where opposing principles collide. Conflicts of one sort or another occur in all his works, whether it be the rival branches of a family conducting a vendetta in *Die Familie Schroffenstein*, Greeks fighting Amazons in *Penthesilea*, the battles and diplomatic tussles between Romans and Germans in *Die Hermannsschlacht*, or blacks massacring whites in *Die Verlobung in St. Domingo*. Dominant personalities clash with one another, Penthesilea fights Achilles, Hermann fights Varus, each character standing for opposing attitudes to the world. The dualism and opposing poles of man's make-up are ranged against one another and find expression in the disposition of characters. Alkmene is placed between Jupiter and Amphitryon, Eva, in *Der zerbrochne Krug*, is caught between Adam and Ruprecht, Graf Wetter vom Strahl, in *Das Käthchen von Heilbronn*, is torn between the opposing attractions of Käthchen and Kunigunde. The dualisms of human existence are further portrayed by Kleist in his use of the Doppelgänger motif, most drastically demonstrated in the anagrammatic pair of characters in *Der Findling*. His dialectical approach is also shown in the fact that he tends to write his plays in pairs, viewing a similar problem from different standpoints.[12] Everywhere in Kleist's works soul and body, feeling and intellect, appearance and reality, the pluses

[12] Cf. p.9.

and minuses of the human situation, caught in the intricate web of the world, are at odds with one another and fighting out their duels. And this sense of continual tension, of a duel being constantly fought, is carried over into his style and narrative technique, with its emphasis on paradox and its contrasting of epic and dramatic elements. It is significant that it is Kleist of all people who should write an essay *Über die allmähliche Verfertigung der Gedanken beim Reden*, for his language is a continuous dialectical process of phrase and sentence being played off one against the other, rushing on in a constant interplay of spontaneous expression and retarding reflection. Speaking is thinking aloud, developing ideas as one thought battles against the other.

It is tempting as well to see this pattern of a duel mirrored in Kleist's own life, his whole existence being as it were a 'Zweikampf' with the conflicts within him and the obstacles cast in his path by ill luck and the 'verderbliche Zeit'[13] in which he lived. The scholar-soldier and poet-civil servant was conscious of the way he moved from one extreme to the other in his efforts to find some escape from the insoluble conflict between his own creative ambitions and the demands imposed on him by the world in which he lived. One almost feels that with Kleist every external encounter of his life was a kind of duel, posing problems tackled dialectically and emotionally, offering human contacts rejected or accepted as he set out now on this course, now on that, until, with the failure of his battle with Hardenberg to keep the *Berliner Abendblätter* afloat and his final rejection at the hands of his family, he eventually gave up the fight and committed suicide.

Throughout his life Kleist was struggling for some kind of harmony. This inner peace he only found in death. In the letters he wrote before putting an end to his existence there is an extraordinary serenity, 'Heiterkeit', and sense of peace in the way he looked forward to quitting this life. Some of this exultancy may be ascribed to suicidal euphoria. But there is as well a feeling that death has been mastered by the man who some years before said that to pass from life to death was like going from one room to another.[14] A similar mastery of death

[13] The 'pernicious age' is mentioned in a letter to Ulrike von Kleist, August 1808.
[14] In a letter to Rühle von Lilienstern, 31 August 1806.

occurs in his last play and his last story. Prinz Friedrich von Homburg has to come to terms with death before he can be fully restored to life, and he welcomes death in some of the most wonderful lines of verse Kleist ever wrote. Nor is it a Romantic night of death to which he looks forward. Death and immortality shine towards him 'mit Glanz der tausendfachen Sonne', 'with the radiance of the thousandfold sun', death and the sunshine of triumph and fulfilment are inseparable. Similar words are used by Trota in *Der Zweikampf*. Reassured of Littegarde's innocence he too becomes once more completely certain of himself, and all qualms in the face of death vanish. 'Der Tod', he says, 'schreckt mich nicht mehr, und die Ewigkeit ... geht wieder, wie ein Reich voll tausend glänziger Sonnen, vor mir auf!'.[15] He has won his duel with himself, and the weapons he has used to achieve victory are 'Gefühl' and 'Vertrauen'.

It is 'Gefühl' that breaks through the doubts and uncertainties of the world, the deceits and deceptions to which men are necessarily prone, and the deadlock facing man in his quest for knowledge. The conventional bulwarks of human existence, social institutions, religion, law, the kind of love approved of by society, are examined by Kleist and found wanting. If the intellect seeks a key to the riddle of life it gets tangled up in the confusion of answers provided.

Faced then with this apparent impasse and bitterly aware since his encounter with Kant of the inadequacy of reason, Kleist erects the ideal of 'Gefühl' as the means of salvation, an essentially irrational evocation of the deepest and purest human emotion, unriven by human dualism, transcending with intuitive sureness the uncertainties and problems of life, an absolute with which to combat the relative values of human existence. On such a feeling love between human beings has to be based, and without this implicit trust, or 'Vertrauen', a love relationship may founder when faced with the fortuitous and tragic complexities of everyday life.

Trota possesses this quality of 'Vertrauen' to a high degree. In this respect he is very different from the unfortunate Gustav in *Die Verlobung*; but he very much resembles a friend who

---

[15] 'Death no longer has any terrors for me, and eternity rises before me again, shining like a realm of a thousand radiant suns!'

gave Kleist support at a critical time in his life and whose unerring 'Gefühlsblick' (lit: 'eye of feeling') and unselfish and unquestioning support are rapturously praised by Kleist in a letter to Wilhelmine.[16] Ludwig von Brockes could well have stood as model for Trota. Trota immediately takes up the defence of Littegarde's honour, even though all the signs point to her guilt. Such is his intuitive trust in her that, without listening to anything she might say, he offers himself in her service. Trota does not reflect. In this he is, so to speak, an exponent of the view put forward by Kleist in his short, though important, note *Von der Überlegung. Eine Paradoxe.* In this Kleist says that we should not think first and act afterwards, but act first and think afterwards, for reflection kills action, 'die zum Handeln nötige Kraft, die aus dem herrlichen Gefühl quillt'. A trained wrestler or athlete acts first, however helpful reflection on his fight may be once it has been fought; and so too with life, says Kleist, in language particularly appropriate in the light of the duel imagery under review: 'Das Leben selbst ist ein Kampf mit dem Schicksal; und es verhält sich auch mit dem Handeln wie mit dem Ringen'.[17] Trota has this quality of unreflecting trust and is prepared to risk everything for Littegarde. He has complete faith in her. Even the frightful wounds he receives in the duel he puts down as a judgement of God on his own sins, not on any of Littegarde's. In the duel itself Trota adopts a somewhat unusual 'Kampfstellung'. He stands firmly on the spot he has chosen and parries with complete sureness the quick darting thrusts of his opponent as they rain down on him. But this recalls exactly the position of the bear in the essay *Über das Marionettentheater*, where the bear is able with consummate ease to parry every blow aimed at it by a skilled swordsman trying to hit it with a rapier. Without reflection, unconsciously, it does much better what the man is consciously striving to do. For since eating of the tree of knowledge and being cursed with consciousness, human beings cannot act without reflection; unreflecting purity of

---

[16] Letter to Wilhelmine, 31 January 1801: 'He always followed his first impulse; he called this his "eye of feeling" ("Gefühlsblick"), and I myself have never found that he was deceived in this ... When I disclosed my situation to him in Pasewalk he didn't reflect for a single moment about following me to Vienna.'

[17] 'Life is a battle with fate; and action is like wrestling.'

emotion is no longer possible and the Garden of Eden is closed to man. But perhaps there is a back way into the Garden of Eden, and one such route suggested by Kleist is that of 'Gefühl', a return to the well-spring of pure feeling enabling man to regain the long-lost inner harmony. Not only does Trota possess this quality, but he is able to rekindle it in Littegarde, so that together they attain a harmony of soul against which death, or the threat of death, is powerless. And in doing this he utters lines which stand as a testament to the feeling which Kleist sought, and generally sought in vain, in himself and others: 'O meine teuerste Littegarde, bewahre deine Sinne vor Verzweiflung! türme das Gefühl, das in deiner Brust lebt, wie einen Felsen empor: halte dich daran und wanke nicht, und wenn Erd und Himmel unter dir und über dir zu Grunde gingen! .. Im Leben laß uns auf den Tod, und im Tode auf die Ewigkeit hinaus sehen, und des festen, unerschütterlichen Glaubens sein: deine Unschuld wird, und wird durch den Zweikampf, den ich für dich gefochten, zum heitern, hellen Licht der Sonne gebracht werden!'.[18] The imagery of height and depth that runs through the story reaches its climax in this passage, which could almost be Kleist's message to posterity. But if it is, then it is in essence remarkably similar to sentiments he expressed in a letter to Martini, before the Kant crisis: 'Wo kann der Blitz des Schicksals mich Glücklichen treffen, wenn ich es fest im Innersten meiner Seele bewahre?'.[19]

There is however a difference between the youthful sentiments, based on hope, expressed in the letter to Martini and the mature utterances of Trota. The ideal of feeling and faith in oneself put forward by Kleist has, if it is to be valid, first of all to be put to the test and subjected to the stresses and strains of human existence. It is for this reason that Kleist does

---

[18] 'My dearest Littegarde, guard your senses against despair! Build up the feeling that lives within you into a towering rock: cling to this and do not waver, even if the earth beneath and the sky above you were to crumble in ruins! ... in life let us gaze forward to death, and in death to eternity, and hold fast to our firm and unshakable belief: your innocence will stand revealed and through the duel that I fought for you will be revealed in the serene and shining light of the sun!'

[19] 'How can fate's lightning strike me in my happiness if I cling to it firmly in the innermost recesses of my soul?' Letter to Christian Ernst Martini, 18/19 March 1799. The 'it' is the goal in life he has set himself.

not make Trota the obvious winner of the duel straight away, but subjects both him and Littegarde to the cruel test brought about by the apparent verdict of God through the ordeal of combat. Kleist's characters have to be brought face to face with the tricks of fortune, the fallible nature of the world, and with the range of behaviour of which man is capable; they have, stripped of all human support, to taste the bitterness of despair and the loss of confidence in their own thoughts and feelings, before, bolstered by a hard-won self-knowledge and a regained faith in themselves, they are enabled to survive the test and reach a position of inner certainty all the more valid for the suffering they have had to endure. Littegarde's former sheltered purity pales to nothing compared with the inner certainty of feeling wrung with the help of Trota from the adversity she undergoes. Before the duel Trota was prone to over-confidence and a priggishness that tempted fate. Moreover, he made the mistake in the duel of changing his tactics in response to the critical murmurs of the crowd, instead of pursuing the method of fighting which his intuition had suggested to him. His qualities have to be put to the test, before he can in the full sense of the word be deemed to be the victor in the duel. In suggesting 'Gefühl' as an antidote to the confusion of existence Kleist is not putting forward an easy way out. Paradise is not re-entered before the resources of the human personality have been tested to the full.

Although Trota and Littegarde have won a victory over themselves they still have to face death by burning. This is what the law, based on the statutes relating to duels, decrees. Yet again Kleist wrestles with the problem of the law. As in *Michael Kohlhaas* it is an institution that can be tinkered with by human beings to suit their opportunistic ends. Thus it is that Graf Jakob is cheated of his lawful hopes of gaining the throne by Duke Wilhelm's secret legitimisation of his bastard son, and the brothers of Littegarde indulge in devious 'Rechtsdeduktionen' in order to get their hands on her money. In the main, however, the law is not depicted as a corrupt institution in *Der Zweikampf*. It is shown as the agent of justice, and everybody, including the emperor himself, is anxious to see that justice is done. Trota may pour scorn on the purely arbitrary laws of man. But, as his mother points out, they are the laws of the land and 'sie üben, verständig oder nicht, die Kraft göttlicher Satzungen aus', they have divine sanction and embody absolute values, based on divine revelation infallibly manifesting itself through the medium of the duel. And herein lies a fallacy, inherent in the law as such. The letter of the law, as expressed in the statutes of the duel, is the product of human reason, imperfect in itself, and absolute reliance on legal wording may lead to absurd situations satirised by Kleist in *Der verlegene Magistrat*.[20] Furthermore, there is no reason to suppose that divine revelation will be content to conform to human expectations and express itself unequivocally in accordance with man-made codes. Human perception is fallible and appearances deceive, and any system of law, whatever claims it may make to be the agent of justice, has to take cognizance of this fact.

Truth and knowledge are the central themes of Kleist's work. He rings the changes on them continually, and perhaps his ultimate attitude to the problem of knowledge is contained in *Der Zweikampf*. The usual ingredients of a Kleistian situation are there, the secrets, insoluble riddles and baffling situations in which characters so unexpectedly find themselves enmeshed. The treatment of the problem covers all the aspects of it in this story, from the diplomatic manoeuvring of the widow of Duke Wilhelm and the calculated intrigue of Graf Jakob to the reliance on absolute truth and the belief in divine revelation on the part of all the main characters. Appearances deceive, as the protagonists get caught up in the 'Spiel eines sonderbaren Mißverständnisses', and the intervention of heaven is questionable and ambiguous, hedged with the irony of which Kleist is a past-master. Well might Trota, faced with the impenetrability of a situation where intuitive feeling conflicts hopelessly with rational deduction, exclaim 'Wo ist der Sterbliche, und wäre die Weisheit aller Zeiten sein, der es wagen darf, den geheimnisvollen Spruch, den Gott in diesem Zweikampf getan hat, auszulegen?'.[21] The limit of human reason has been reached, and the quest for truth and

---

[20] See above, p.88.
[21] 'Where is the mortal, and be he blessed with the wisdom of all ages, who would venture to interpret the mysterious verdict God has pronounced in this duel?'

knowledge can make no further progress.

But then another force is brought into play, namely, that of human feeling and trust. Appearances deceive, Jakob acts 'in der Verblendung seiner Sinne', human senses react to outward appearances and cannot penetrate to the truth. Trota shows the way. 'In meiner Brust', he says to Littegarde, 'spricht eine Stimme für Euch'. It is this 'inner voice', this 'Stimme in der Brust' that can light the path to knowledge. Reason alone will not arrive at the truth, because reason is dependent on the evidence of appearances. Nor can human institutions, such as religion and law, that are based on the supposition that absolute knowledge is available if certain conditions are fulfilled, that God, to use the mediaeval language of *Der Zweikampf*, will infallibly reveal the truth when called upon, hope to satisfy man's yearning for truth, for they are based on a misapprehension of the nature of divine revelation. There is no 'Verpflichtung' on God's part, as the quotation at the beginning of this chapter makes clear, to reveal the truth at a moment convenient to man. If truth is to be perceived, it must be without reliance on such divine props. A faith in one's inner voice, a faith that has to be preserved heroically when everything argues against it, may lead man to an intuitive awareness of truth. Jakob does not have this faith. It is true that he fights the duel genuinely believing in the truth of his allegation against Littegarde, and to that extent he is the victim of deception. But he is using this alibi to divert suspicions that he murdered his half-brother, and he enters the duel with this crime on his conscience. Trota has this faith and, apart from momentary waverings, remains true to it. Great strength of character is needed to persist in such an attitude. But for those who have it a link is then forged between the absolute without, God and divine revelation, and the absolute within, human feeling; and the duel is resolved. Whether or not Trota and Littegarde are burned at the stake or whether they survive is immaterial. They have won their duel, and the contingencies of the world do not concern them. In fact the situation is resolved and they are restored to life. The mechanics of the plot whereby this is achieved may well be contrived, although there is no doubt poetic justice in the fact that the arch-deceiver Jakob is himself outwitted and deceived in the matter of Littegarde. What needs to be emphasised is that, although it may appear to be chance that has decided the issue at the end, this is in fact not so. It is Trota who makes a solution possible. The truth is apparently miraculously revealed; but a miracle is only possible because of Trota's faith in himself and in Littegarde, a faith that enables him to see through appearances to the real truth manifested in the outcome of the duel. Such a faith makes possible divine revelation, to use the religious language Kleist chooses to employ in this story. Human values form the basis for a miracle of transcendental grace.

At the end of the story the emperor has the wording of the statutes relating to ordeal by combat revised. Following on the statement that guilt is revealed directly by the result of the duel the words are inserted 'If it be God's will'. Seen from one point of view this might appear to make a nonsense of the law, for guilt and innocence are only revealed in God's good time, which is a very different thing from time in this world. But the absolute claims made by the law on duelling are thereby toned down and through the compromise implied in the inserted phrase the law becomes humanised. The faith and trust of the individual, namely Trota, has had its effect on society, and the harsh letter of the law has been modified. The guarantee of truth through revelation is made less absolute; but the scope afforded to human feeling and an awareness of the imperfect nature of human institutions is, however conditionally phrased, accordingly increased.

Das Erdbeben in Chili opens with a scene in prison, with Jeronimo trying to hang himself in his cell, only paradoxically to be foiled in this by the outbreak of the earthquake in Santiago. Innermost feelings, love and trust do not help him and Josephe, and they fall tragic victims to the ways of man and the inscrutable workings of the universe. A central scene in *Der Zweikampf* takes place in prison, but the outcome is very different, for Trota and Littegarde emerge to find a situation miraculously changed and enjoy their moment of triumph. The difference reveals a real development in Kleist's attitude to the problems of life which, essentially the same though differently presented, occur in all his works. It is not true to say that the problem, and not the answer, represents the true reason for Kleist writing *Der Zweikampf*[22]. Values gradually emerge and are gathered together in this work which, though they are subject to the haphazard nature of the world and the unpredictable extremes of human behaviour, nevertheless do tend to mitigate the harsh view of life presented in his earlier works. They may to some extent be the product of hopeful yearning on Kleist's part and they may have been of little help to him as he battled against the obstacles fate cast in his path. But they are real values asserted by him as his hopes and expectancies crumbled and he sought release from the 'verderbliche Zeit', the 'pernicious time', in which he lived by suicide on the shores of the Wannsee. These values, integrity, trust, love and self-knowledge, together with an acceptance of the fallible and fragile nature of the world, find their outward expression in a symbol which runs through Kleist's published works and letters, the symbol of the wreath, the symbol of the 'ringförmige Welt' and the immortality for which he strove.[23] It is fitting that two of his last works should end with the introduction of this symbol. Prinz Friedrich von Homburg has a tangible sign of grace to mark the triumphant victory over himself in the victor's wreath placed on his head and the chain, the 'Kette', placed round his neck. And in triumphant vindication of the human values he has upheld Friedrich von Trota has placed round his neck by the emperor a sign of grace, a 'Gnadenkette' to mark his victory in the duel.

---

[22] As does Geary, *Heinrich von Kleist. A Study in Tragedy and Anxiety*, 1968, p.49.

[23] References to the image of the wreath are too numerous to quote. The image of the 'ringförmige Welt', the 'ring-shaped world', linked with the idea of harmony and completion, occurs in *Über das Marionettentheater*.

Bibliography

The following is a select list of titles from the vast amount of work that has been published on Kleist. I have attempted to include a reasonably comprehensive coverage of work on the *Erzählungen*, with particular emphasis on work published since 1945 in German or English. Perceptive observations on the stories are frequently to be found in the general works on Kleist, only a few of which are included here.

I. TEXTS, SOURCE MATERIAL

Helmut Sembdner, *Heinrich von Kleist. Sämtliche Werke und Briefe*, 2 vols, 3rd. ed., München, 1964. Referred to as 'Werke' in footnotes.

Helmut Sembdner, *Heinrich von Kleists Lebensspuren. Dokumente und Berichte der Zeitgenossen*, Bremen, 1957; revised ed., München, 1969.

Helmut Sembdner, *Heinrich von Kleist, Geschichte meiner Seele – Ideenmagazin. Das Lebenszeugnis der Briefe*, Bremen, 1959.

Helmut Sembdner (ed.), *Berliner Abendblätter*, (Fotomechanischer Nachdruck mit Nachwort und Quellenregister), Darmstadt, 1970.

Helmut Sembdner (ed.), *Phöbus. Ein Journal für die Kunst*, (Fotomechan. Nachdruck m. Nachwort und Kommentar), Darmstadt/Stuttgart, 1961.

Helmut Sembdner (ed.), *Heinrich von Kleists Nachruhm. Eine Wirkungsgeschichte in Dokumenten*, Bremen, 1967.

Martin Greenberg, *The Marquise of O. and other stories*, New York, 1964; reissued, Ungar Paperbacks, 1974. A useful, if not always ideal, translation of the stories.

II. GENERAL

Günter Blöcker, *Heinrich von Kleist oder Das absolute Ich*, Berlin, 1960.
Peter Dettmering, *Heinrich von Kleist. Zur Psychodynamik in seiner Dichtung*, München, 1975.
D.G. Dyer, ' "Plus and Minus" in Kleist', *Oxford German Studies* 2, 1967.
Ernst Fischer, 'Heinrich von Kleist', *Sinn und Form* 13, 1961.
J.-U. Fechner, 'Cervantes und Kleist – ein Kapitel europäischer Novellistik', *Levende Talen*, 1964.
John Gearey, *Heinrich von Kleist. A Study in Tragedy and Anxiety*, Philadelphia, 1968.
Clifton D. Hall, 'Kleist, Catholicism, and the Catholic Church', *Monatshefte* 59, 1967.
Michael Hamburger, 'Kleist', in *Reason and Energy*, London, 1957.
Robert E. Helbling, *The Major Works of Heinrich von Kleist*, New York, 1975.
Elmar Hofmeister, *Täuschung und Wirklichkeit bei Heinrich von Kleist*, Bonn, 1968.
Hans Heinz Holz, *Macht und Ohnmacht der Sprache. Untersuchungen zum Sprachverständnis und Stil Heinrich von Kleists*, Bonn, 1962.
Max Kommerell, 'Die Sprache und das Unaussprechliche. Eine Betrachtung über Heinrich von Kleist', in *Geist und Buchstabe der Dichtung*, Frankfurt/M, 1940.
Hans Joachim Kreutzer, *Die dichterische Entwicklung Heinrich von Kleists*, Berlin, 1968.
Helmut Kreuzer, 'Kleist-Literatur 1955-1960', *Der Deutschunterricht* 13, 1961.
Manfred Lefèvre, 'Kleist-Forschung 1961-1967', *Colloquia Germanica* 3, 1969.
Georg Lukacs, 'Die Tragödie Heinrich von Kleists', in *Deutsche Realisten des 19. Jahrhunderts*, Berlin, 1956.
Richard March, *Heinrich von Kleist*, Cambridge, 1954.
Hans Mayer, *Heinrich von Kleist. Der geschichtliche Augenblick*, Pfullingen, 1962.
Michael Moering, *Witz und Ironie in der Prosa Heinrich von Kleists*, München, 1972.
Donald P. Morgan, *Heinrich von Kleists Verhältnis zur Musik*, Diss. Cologne, 1940.
W. Müller-Seidel, *Versehen und Erkennen*, Köln/Graz, 1961.
W. Müller-Seidel (ed.), *Kleist und die Gesellschaft*, Jahrbuch der Kleistgesellschaft 1964.
W. Müller-Seidel (ed.), *Heinrich von Kleist. Vier Reden zu seinem Gedächtnis*, Jahrbuch der Kleistgesellschaft 1962.
Ludwig Muth, *Kleist und Kant*, Köln, 1954.

M. Pasley (ed.), *Germany: a Companion to German Studies*, London, 1972.
F.G. Peters, 'Kafka and Kleist: a literary relationship', *Oxford German Studies* I, 1966.
H. Pongs, *Das Bild in der Dichtung*, II, Marburg, 1939.
Hermann Reske, *Traum und Wirklichkeit in der Welt Heinrich von Kleists*, Stuttgart, 1969.
Eva Rothe, 'Kleist-Bibliographie 1945-1960', in *Jahrbuch der Schiller-Gesellschaft* 5, 1961.
D.F.S. Scott, 'Heinrich von Kleist's Kant crisis', *Modern Language Review* 42, 1947.
Helmut Sembdner, *In Sachen Kleist*, München, 1974. Contains an important chapter on Kleist's use of punctuation.
Walter Silz, *Heinrich von Kleist*, Philadelphia, 1961.
Reinhold Steig, *Heinrich von Kleists Berliner-Kämpfe*, Berlin/Stuttgart, 1901.
Siegfried Streller, 'Heinrich von Kleist und Jean-Jacques Rousseau', *Weimarer Beiträge* 8, 1962.
Dietmar Strotski, *Die Gebärde des Errötens im Werk Heinrich von Kleists*, Marburg, 1971.
Ursula Thomas, 'Heinrich von Kleist and Gotthilf Heinrich Schubert', *Monatshefte* 51, 1959.

III. GENERAL ON THE STORIES

E.K. Bennett, *A History of the German Novelle from Goethe to Thomas Mann*, 2nd. ed. 1961.
Hellmuth Himmel, *Geschichte der deutschen Novelle*, Bern/München, 1963.
Johannes Klein, *Geschichte der deutschen Novelle.*, rev. ed., Wiesbaden, 1960.
E. Lämmert, *Bauformen des Erzählens*, Stuttgart, 1955.
Fritz Lockemann, *Gestalt und Wandlungen der deutschen Novelle*, München, 1957.
Merker-Stammler, *Reallexikon der deutschen Literaturgeschichte*, 2nd. ed., 1958 ff., articles 'Anekdote' and 'Novelle'.
K.K. Polheim (ed.), *Theorie und Kritik der deutschen Novelle von Wieland bis Musil*, Tübingen, 1970.
Benno von Wiese, *Die deutsche Novelle von Goethe bis Kafka. Interpretationen*, 2 vols., Düsseldorf, 1956-1962.

Johannes Bathe, *Die Bewegungen und Haltungen des menschlichen Körpers in Heinrich von Kleists Erzählungen*, Diss. Tübingen, 1917.

Ruth Baumann, *Studien zur Erzählkunst Heinrichs von Kleist*, Diss. Hamburg, 1928.
Raimund Belgardt, 'Kleists Weg zur Wahrheit', *Zeitschrift für deutsche Philologie* 92, 1973.
Francis J. Brooke, *The Male-Female Relationships in the Dramas and Novellen of Heinrich von Kleist*, Diss. North Carolina, 1954.
Karl Otto Conrady, 'Das Moralische in Kleists Erzählungen. Ein Kapitel vom Dichter ohne Gesellschaft', Festschrift von Wiese, Bonn, 1963.
Hermann Davidts, *Die novellistische Kunst Heinrich von Kleists*, Bonner Forschungen NF, 5, 1913.
Manfred Durzak, 'Zur utopischen Funktion des Kindsbildes in Kleists Erzählungen', *Colloquia Germanica* 3, 1969.
Kurt Gassen, *Die Chronologie der Novellen Heinrich von Kleists*, Weimar, 1920.
Kurt Günther, *Die Entwicklung der novellistischen Kompositionstechnik Kleists bis zur Meisterschaft*, Diss. Leipzig, 1911.
Hans-Peter Herrmann, 'Zufall und Ich: zum Begriff der Situation in den Novellen Heinrich von Kleists', *Germanisch-Romanische Monatsschrift* 42, 1961.
Elisabeth V. Hippel, *Die Zeitgestaltung in den Novellen von Heinrich von Kleist*, Diss. Bonn, 1948.
Wolfgang Kayser, 'Kleist als Erzähler', *German Life and Letters*, n.s. VIII, and in *Die Vortragsreise*, Bern, 1958.
Helmut Koopmann, 'Das "Rätselhafte Faktum" und seine Vorgeschichte. Zum analytischen Charakter der Novellen Heinrich von Kleists', *Zeitschrift für deutsche Philologie* 84, 1965.
Eveline Krause, 'Die Tradition der Weiskopfschen Anekdoten unter besonderer Berücksichtigung Heinrich von Kleists', *Weimarer Beiträge* 8, 1962.
Hans Lorenzen, *Typen deutscher Anekdotenerzählung (Kleist – Hebel – Schäfer)* Diss. Hamburg, 1935.
Thomas Mann, 'Heinrich von Kleist und seine Erzählungen', in *Reden und Aufsätze, Gesammelte Werke* IX, Frankfurt/M, 1960.
Klaus Müller-Salget, 'Das Prinzip der Doppeldeutigkeit in Kleists Erzählungen', *Zeitschrift für deutsche Philologie* 92, 1973.
Dietmar Nedde, *Untersuchungen zur Struktur von Dichtung an Novellen Heinrich von Kleists*, Diss. Göttingen, 1955.
Richard Samuel, 'Heinrich von Kleists Novellen', Festschrift Pfeffer, Tübingen, 1972.
Herbert Singer, 'Kleists "Verhöre" ', *Studi in onore di Lorenzo Bianchi*, Bologna, 1960.

IV. INDIVIDUAL STORIES

Das Bettelweib von Locarno

Hellmuth Himmel, 'Musikalische Fugentechnik in Kleists *Bettelweib von Locarno*', *Sprachkunst* 2, 1971.

Jürgen Schröder, '*Das Bettelweib von Locarno*: zum Gespenstischen in den Novellen Heinrich von Kleists', *Germanisch-Romanische Monatsschrift* 48, 1967.

Emil Staiger, 'Kleist: *Das Bettelweib von Locarno*', in *Meisterwerke deutscher Sprache*, Zürich, 1957.

Egon Werlich, 'Kleists *Bettelweib von Locarno*', *Wirkendes Wort* 15, 1965.

Die heilige Cäcilie

Jakob Baxa, 'Die Taufe der Cäcilie Müller', *Euphorion* 53, 1959.

Edmund Edel, 'Heinrich von Kleist *Die Heilige Cäcilie oder die Gewalt der Musik*', *Wirkendes Wort* 19, 1969.

Günter Graf, 'Der dramatische Aufbaustil der Legende Heinrich von Kleists *Die heilige Cäcilie oder die Gewalt der Musik*', *Etudes Germaniques* 24, 1969.

Günter Graf, 'Zum Vergleich der zwei Fassungen von Kleists Legende *Die heilige Cäcilie*', *Etudes Germaniques* 25, 1970. .

Werner Hoffmeister, 'Die Doppeldeutigkeit der Erzählweise in Heinrich von Kleists *Die heilige Cäcilie oder Die Gewalt der Musik*', Festschrift Neuse.

Ferdinand van Ingen, 'Heinrich von Kleists Erzählung *Die heilige Cäcilie*', *Jahrbuch des Wiener Goethe-Vereins* 66, 1962.

Robert Mühlher, 'Heinrich von Kleist und seine Legende *Die heilige Cäcilie*', *Jahrbuch des Wiener Goethe-Vereins* LXVI, 1962.

Michael Scherer, 'Die beiden Fassungen von Heinrich von Kleists Erzählung *Die heilige Cäcilie*', *Monatshefte* 56, 1964.

Wolfgang Wittkowski, '*Die heilige Cäcilie* und *Der Zweikampf*. Kleists Legenden und die romantische Ironie', *Colloquia Germanica* 6, 1972.

Das Erdbeben in Chili

A.O. Aldridge, 'The Background of Kleist's *Das Erdbeben in Chili*', *Arcadia* 4, 1969.

J.C. Blankenagel, 'Heinrich von Kleist: *Das Erdbeben in Chili*', *Germanic Review* 8, 1933.

K.O. Conrady, 'Kleists *Erdbeben in Chili*: ein Interpretationsversuch', *Germanisch-Romanische Monatsschrift* 35, 1954.

J.M. Ellis, 'Kleist: *Das Erdbeben in Chili*', in *Narration in the German Novelle*, Cambridge, 1974.
Walter Gausewitz, 'Kleists *Erdbeben*', *Monatshefte* 55, 1963.
Peter Horn, 'Anarchie und Mobherrschaft in Kleists *Erdbeben in Chili*', *Acta Germanica* 7, 1972.
Richard L. Johnson, 'Kleists *Erdbeben in Chili*', *Seminar* 11, 1975.
Johannes Klein, 'Kleists *Erdbeben in Chili*', *Der Deutschunterricht* 8, 1956.
Josef Kunz, 'Die Gestaltung des tragischen Geschehens in Kleists *Erdbeben in Chili*', Festschrift Wegner, 1963.
R.S. Lucas, 'Studies in Kleist. II. *Das Erdbeben in Chili*', *Deutsche Vierteljahrsschrift* 44, 1970.
A.E. Owen, 'The background of Kleist's *Das Erdbeben in Chili*', *Arcadia* 3, 1968.
Walter Silz, '*Das Erdbeben in Chili*', in *Heinrich von Kleist*, Philadelphia, 1961.
Benno von Wiese, 'Heinrich von Kleist: *Das Erdbeben in Chili*', in *Die deutsche Novelle* II, Düsseldorf, 1962.
W. Wittkowski, 'Skepsis, Noblesse, Ironie, Formen des Als-Ob in Kleists *Erdbeben*', *Euphorion* 63, 1969.

Der Findling

Kurt Günther, '*Der Findling* – die frühste der Kleistschen Erzählungen', *Euphorion* 8, Ergänzungsheft, 1909.
Alfred Heubi, *Heinrich von Kleists Novelle Der Findling*, Diss. Zürich, 1948.
Werner Hoffmeister, 'Heinrich von Kleists *Findling*', *Monatshefte* 58, 1966.
Josef Kunz, 'Heinrich von Kleists Novelle *Der Findling*. Eine Interpretation', Festschrift L. Wolff, 1962.
Hans M. Wolff, 'Heinrich von Kleists *Findling*', *Univ. of California Publ. in Modern Philology* 36, 1952.

Die Marquise von O.

J.C. Blankenagel, 'Heinrich von Kleists *Marquise von O.*', *Germanic Review* 6, 1931.
Siegfried Bokelmann, 'Betrachtungen zur Satzgestaltung in Kleists Novelle *Die Marquise von O.*', *Wirkendes Wort*, 8, 1957/58.
Gerhard Dünnhaupt, 'Kleist's *Marquise von O.* and its literary debt to Cervantes', *Arcadia* 10, 1975.
Jacques Hassoun, 'Variations psychoanalytiques sur un thème

généalogique de Heinrich von Kleist', *Romantisme*, 1974.
Alfred Klaar, *Heinrich von Kleist. Die Marquise von O. Die Dichtung und ihre Quellen*, Berlin, 1922.
Dorrit Kohn, 'Kleist's *Marquise von O.* The Problem of Knowledge', *Monatshefte* 67, 1975.
Michael Moering, 'Die Ironie in der *Marquise von O.*', in *Witz und Ironie in der Prosa Heinrich von Kleists*, München, 1972.
W. Müller-Seidel, 'Die Struktur des Widerspruchs in Kleists *Marquise von O.*', *Deutsche Vierteljahrsschrift* 28, 1954.

Michael Kohlhaas

J.-J. Anstett, 'A propos de *Michael Kohlhaas*', *Etudes Germaniques* 14, 1959.
Clifford A. Bernd, 'The "Abdeckerszene" in Kleist's *Michael Kohlhaas*', *Studia Neophilologica* 39, 1967.
Clifford A. Bernd, 'Der Lutherbrief in Kleists *Michael Kohlhaas*', *Zeitschrift für deutsche Philologie* 86, 1967.
Clifford A. Bernd, 'On the two divergent paths of Kleist's Michael Kohlhaas', Festschrift Rose.
O.F. Best, 'Schuld und Vergebung. Zur Rolle von Wahrsagerin und "Amulett" in Kleists *Michael Kohlhaas*', *Germanisch-Romanische Monatsschrift* 51, 1970.
Ludwig Büttner, 'Michael Kohlhaas – eine paranoische oder heroische Gestalt?' *Seminar* IV, 1968.
John R. Cary, 'A reading of Kleist's *Michael Kohlhaas*', *PMLA* 85, 1970.
H.-W. Dechert, ' "Indem er ans Fenster trat ..." Zur Funktion einer Gebärde in Kleists *Michael Kohlhaas*', *Euphorion* 62, 1968.
D.G. Dyer, 'Junker Wenzel von Tronka', *German Life and Letters* n.s. 18, 1965.
J.M. Ellis, 'Der Herr lässt regnen über Gerechte und Ungerechte: Kleist's *Michael Kohlhaas*', *Monatshefte* 59, 1967.
Gerhard Fricke, 'Kleists *Michael Kohlhaas*', in *Studien und Interpretationen*, Frankfurt/M, 1956.
Fritz Heber, '*Michael Kohlhaas*, Versuch einer Interpretation', *Wirkendes Wort* 1, 1950/51.
Peter Horwath, '*Michael Kohlhaas*: Kleists Absicht in der Überarbeitung des Phöbus-Fragments', *Monatshefte* 57, 1965.
Peter Horwath, 'The "Nicht-um-die-Welt" theme. A clue to the ultimate meaning of Kleist's *Michael Kohlhaas*', *Studia Neophilologica* 39, 1967.
R.S. Lucas, 'Studies in Kleist. I. Problems in *Michael Kohlhaas*', *Deutsche Vierteljahrsschrift* 44, 1970.

H. Meyer-Benfey, 'Die innere Geschichte des *Michael Kohlhaas*', *Euphorion* 15, 1908.
Richard M. Müller, 'Kleists *Michael Kohlhaas*', *Deutsche Vierteljahrsschrift* 44, 1970.
Roy Pascal, '*Michael Kohlhaas*', *Proceedings of the Australian Goethe Society*, 1966/67.
C.E. Passage, '*Michael Kohlhaas*: form analysis', *Germanic Review* 30, 1955.
Karl Schultze-Jahde, 'Kohlhaas und die Zigeunerin', *Jahrbuch der Kleist-Gesellschaft* 1933/37.
Walter Silz, 'Three themes in *Michael Kohlhaas*', op.cit., ch.6.
Hubert Tellenbach, 'Die Aporie der wahnhaften Querulanz ... ', *Colloquia Germanica* 7, 1973.
Benno von Wiese, 'Kleist: *Michael Kohlhaas*', in *Die deutsche Novelle* I, Düsseldorf, 1962.

Die Verlobung in St. Domingo

Otto Hahne, 'Die Entstehung von Kleists *Verlobung in St. Domingo*', *Euphorion* 23, 1921.
Peter Horn, 'Hatte Kleist Rassenvorurteile? Eine kritische Auseindandersetzung mit der Literatur zur *Verlobung in St. Domingo*', *Monatshefte* 67, 1975.
Josef Kunz, 'Kleist – *Die Verlobung in St. Domingo*', *Mitt. Univbund Marburg*, 1960.
Wolfgang Mieder, 'Triadische Grundstruktur in Heinrich von Kleists *Verlobung in St. Domingo*', *Neophilologus* 58, 1974.
Johannes Pfeiffer, 'Kleists *Verlobung in St. Domingo*', in *Wege zur Erzählkunst*, Hamburg, 1953.

Der Zweikampf

K.O. Conrady, '*Der Zweikampf*. Zur Aussageweise Heinrich von Kleists', *Der Deutschunterricht* II/III, 1950.
Donald H. Crosby, 'Heinrich von Kleist's *Der Zweikampf*', *Monatshefte* 56, 1964.
John M. Ellis, 'Kleist's *Der Zweikampf*', *Monatshefte* 65, 1973.
H. Meyer, 'Kleists Novelle *Der Zweikampf*', *Jahrbuch der Kleist-Gesellschaft* 1933.
Katharina Mommsen, 'Kleist's duel story as Erlebnisdichtung', *Carleton Germanic Papers*, 1974.
H. Oppel, 'Kleists Novelle *Der Zweikampf*', *Deutsche Vierteljahrsschrift* 22, 1944.
Wolfgang Wittkowski, '*Die heilige Cäcilie* und *der Zweikampf*', *Colloquia Germanica* 6, 1972.

Index

A. HEINRICH VON KLEIST

LIFE
family background, 1-2, 5, 94
historical background, 2, 90-1, 153
Ideenmagazin, 4, 7, 96, 98
Lebensplan, 4, 7
life, 1-8, 105, 186
prison, 19, 33
suicide, 1, 2, 5, 8, 41, 186, 194
Würzburg, 6, 17, 93, 94, 95, 104

WORKS   1. Stories
Das Bettelweib von Locarno, 9, 16, 19, 80-7, 99, 105, 155, 158, 165
Die heilige Cäcilie, 9, 19, 86, 92-106, 155, 160, 168
Das Erdbeben in Chili, 3, 9, 11, 12-30, 31, 47, 48, 68, 83, 85, 98, 99, 104, 144, 145, 153, 155, 157, 159, 160, 162, 163, 165, 167, 169, 178, 193
Der Findling, 9, 19, 24, 25, 48-59, 63, 69, 71, 73, 85, 144, 155, 160, 178, 185
Die Marquise von O., 3, 9, 11, 23, 24, 52, 55, 58, 59, 60-79, 153, 158, 160, 163, 164, 167, 175, 182
Michael Kohlhaas, 9, 19, 39, 58, 77, 86, 99, 107-50, 160, 164, 165, 167, 190

Die Verlobung in St. Domingo, 3, 9, 19, 31-47, 48, 52, 68, 86, 98, 144, 160, 165, 168, 185, 187
Der Zweikampf, 9, 14, 19, 24, 45, 50, 52, 66, 69, 71, 86, 101, 158, 169, 170-94

WORKS   2. Plays
Amphitryon, 8, 9, 23, 63, 71, 75, 175, 180
Die Familie Schroffenstein, 8, 9, 18, 25, 50, 144, 172, 185
Die Hermannsschlacht, 3, 8, 9, 63, 141, 144, 185
Das Käthchen von Heilbronn, 8, 9, 24, 172, 185
Penthesilea, 9, 52, 60, 63, 69, 71, 98, 99, 101, 144, 185
Prinz Friedrich von Homburg, 3, 8, 9, 23, 38, 69, 75, 98, 99, 140, 172
Robert Guiskard, 8, 52, 98
Der zerbrochne Krug, 5, 8, 9, 38, 63, 71, 99, 175, 180, 185

WORKS   3. Anecdotes
Anekdote aus dem letzten Kriege, 89
Anekdote aus dem letzten preussischen Kriege, 90

Capuchin Monk, 51-2
Charité-Vorfall, 89
Der Branntweinsäufer und die Berliner Glocken, 91-2
Der Griffel Gottes, 89
Der verlegene Magistrat, 58, 88, 191
Geschichte eines merkwürdigen Zweikampfes, 172
Korrespondenz-Nachricht, 90
Mutwille des Himmels, 89
Sonderbare Geschichte, die sich, zu meiner Zeit, in Italien zutrug, 63, 90, 175
Sonderbarer Rechtsfall in England, 172
Two Boxers, 89-90, 175-6

WORKS   4. Other works
Allerneuester Erziehungsplan, 70, 151, 154
Berliner Abendblätter, 8, 38, 51, 58, 63, 82, 87, 89, 90, 93, 103, 172, 175, 186
Betrachtungen über den Weltlauf, 168
Brief eines Malers an seinen Sohn, 80
Phöbus, 8, 60, 61, 109, 119
Über das Marionettentheater, 155-6, 168, 188, 194
Über die allmähliche Verfertigung der Gedanken beim Reden, 154, 186
Von der Überlegung. Eine Paradoxe, 168, 188

SYMBOLS AND MOTIFS
arch, 7, 17, 98
blushing, 74, 125, 130, 133
fire, 7, 54, 73, 76, 167
flute, 98, 101, 102, 159
Garden of Eden, 19, 21, 98, 156, 189
jungle, 39, 58, 131, 145
light and shade, 7, 31ff
nightingale, 28
plague, 40, 51, 52, 56, 72, 160, 174
prison, 19-20, 94, 116, 154, 173, 193
storm, 98, 101, 176
unermessliche Menschenmenge, 150, 159-60, 176
Virgin Mary, 21, 45, 67, 68, 79
walking to the window, 43, 132

water, 7, 54
wreath, 98, 194

TECHNIQUE
changing perspectives, 65, 99, 101, 157
flashbacks, 12, 15, 34, 64, 66, 117, 157, 158, 163
opening sentences, 13, 35, 64, 107, 156-7, 158, 167, 170
punctuation, 77, 84, 119, 164-5
secret, 54, 55, 57, 66, 76, 100, 114, 153, 157, 191
style, 17, 25-7, 38, 83-4, 99, 160-7
treatment of time, 27-8, 34, 36, 66, 83, 157, 163, 173
variations on a theme, 83, 99, 100-1, 131, 149, 153, 157

THEMES
appearance and reality, 66-8, 79, 89, 105, 153, 158, 168, 173, 185, 193
chance, 12, 17, 24, 51, 58, 85-6, 89, 136, 146-7, 152, 166, 174, 182, 193
deceit, deception, 40, 44, 54, 77, 153-4, 173, 179, 187, 192-3
Doppelgänger, 57, 73, 102, 147, 158, 179, 185
extremes of behaviour, 11, 27, 32, 52, 56, 57, 74, 78, 104, 120, 137, 145, 154, 194
family, 24-5, 174
Gebrechlichkeit der Welt, 73, 79, 111, 137, 149, 155
irony, 15, 21, 22, 29, 40, 46, 58, 66, 73, 75-9, 89, 103, 106, 115, 128, 174, 184, 191
law, 22, 58, 59, 110, 113, 115-16, 139-41, 190-1, 193
love, 23-4, 40, 45, 54, 55, 63, 64, 69-71, 73, 74-5, 155-6, 187, 194
music, 7, 31, 94-100, 102-3, 106, 169
painting, 24, 28, 31, 37-8
paradox, 12, 13, 22, 29, 51, 76, 89, 91, 105, 122, 134, 148-9, 156, 167-9, 186

plus and minus, 27, 70, 103, 119, 144, 154-5, 158, 161, 167, 178, 182, 185-6
religion, 12, 19, 20-2, 58, 94, 105, 111, 122, 132-3, 142-4
revenge, 39-40, 50, 56, 58, 85, 111, 126, 144-8, 155
self-knowledge, 11, 69, 74, 79, 155, 194
social institutions, 11-12, 18-22, 49, 58, 152-3, 187
trust, 42, 44, 46, 155-6, 187-8, 192, 194
truth, knowledge, 11, 65, 76, 153-4, 168, 191

B. NAMES

Altenstein, Karl Freiherr vom Stein zum, 1, 13, 141
Arnim, Achim von, 11, 95
Baechler, C., 50, 172
Brentano, Clemens, 11, 87, 95
Brockes, Ludwig von, 6, 188
Cervantes, 10, 63, 172
Fichte, 3, 7
Fouqué, Caroline de la Motte, 101
Froissart, 172, 175
Goethe, 3, 5, 11, 48, 53, 96, 103, 183
Hardy, Thomas, 55
Hardenberg, 103, 104, 186
Hebbel, 159
Kafka, 86, 87
Kant, 3, 7-8, 187, 189
Kleist, Ewald von, 1
Kleist, Marie von, 2, 3, 5, 37, 96
Kleist, Ulrike von, 4, 8, 33, 105, 186
Knebel, Henriette von, 60
Lessing, 3, 50
Lichnowsky, Prinz von, 87
Lilienstern, Rühle von, 186
Lohse, Heinrich, 38
Lous XIV, 51, 57
L'Ouverture, Toussaint, 33
Ludwig, Otto, 100

Luise, Königin von Preussen, 5
Mann, Thomas, 162
Martini, C.M., 2, 189
Molière, 50-1, 175
Montaigne, 63
Müller, Adam, 3, 5, 93, 103
Müller, Cecilia, 93, 103
Napoleon, 2, 4, 90, 141
Novalis, 97
Pfuel, Ernst von, 97
Pfuel, Friedrich von, 83
Poggio, 87
Rousseau, 18, 75, 131
Schiller, 3, 45
Schlieben, Karoline von, 98, 105
Schubert, G.H., 3, 85
Schubart, C.F., 96, 97
Stock, Dora, 60
Tartini, Giuseppe, 53
Vogel, Henriette, 1, 5
Wackenroder, 96
Werdeck, Adolfine von, 96
Wieland, 5
Zenge, Luise von, 37
Zenge, Wilhelmine von, 6, 8, 17, 18, 21, 37, 43, 44, 93, 94, 95, 98, 101, 139, 188
Zweig, Arnold, 30